An Introduction to Pastoral Care

An Introduction to Pastoral Care

Charles V. Gerkin

Abingdon Press
Nashville

AN INTRODUCTION TO PASTORAL CARE

Copyright © 1997 by Abingdon Press

This book is printed on recycled, acid-free, elemental-chlorine-free paper.

Library of Congress Cataloging-in-Publication Data

Gerkin, Charles V., 1922–
   An introduction to pastoral care/Charles V. Gerkin.
     p.   cm.
   Includes bibliographical references and index.
   ISBN 0-687-01674-6 (alk. paper)
   1. Pastoral theology.   2. Clergy—Office.   I. Title.
BV4011.G455   1997
253—dc21   97-6702
                                                                   CIP

Scripture quotations are from the New Revised Standard Version Bible. Copyright © 1989 by the Division of Christian Education of the National Council of the Churches of Christ in the United States of America.

Portions reproduced from *The Nature of Doctrine* by George A. Lindbeck. © 1984 George A. Lindbeck. Used by permission of Westminster John Knox Press.

98 99 00 01 02 03 04 05 06—10 9 8 7 6 5 4 3 2

MANUFACTURED IN THE UNITED STATES OF AMERICA

Written in honor of my grandchildren

Jennifer, Douglas, Stephen, Katherine Elizabeth,
Jeremy, Mary Grace,
and Christopher

CONTENTS

ACKNOWLEDGMENTS

Because most of this book was written since my retirement from Emory University, I have no acknowledgments to make to an academic institution. I do, however, owe a debt of gratitude to my colleagues Rodney Hunter and Pamela Couture for their encouragement to complete the work. I also need to say a word of special thanks to the Reverend Charles Rolen, who volunteered to act as my assistant during the writing of the book. He searched libraries for sources, procured books for me, and generally was most helpful.

PREFACE

On Beginning with What We Bring

The purpose of this book is to invite the reader into the world of pastoral care. It is an invitation to accompany the author on a tour of an arena of ministry that includes some of the most important and, at times, difficult work that the Christian pastor has to do. This arena of pastoral work is multifaceted and full of surprises, unexpected problems, and opportunities for profound insight into the human situation. It is the arena within which the pastor is privileged to be with people where they live and breathe, succeed and fail, relate intimately and experience alienation. It is the down-to-earth world of human living.

To tour the world of pastoral care means to consider the caring task of the pastor in relation to individuals and to communities. Those communities include not only families living together and groups of people who work and play together, but also, most significantly, communities of faith who live and worship together as they seek to be faithful disciples of Christ in the world. Touring that world will cause us to encounter the inevitable tensions involved in providing pastoral care for individuals and for congregations.

Conversation Between Writer and Reader

Writing or reading a book is in many ways not only like going on a tour, but also like participating in a conversation. As writer, I want to converse with the reader, even though she or he may be unknown to me. I want to share what I have come to know and the ways I have come to think about the art and science of the practice of pastoral care within the Christian community and its tradition. As reader, the person who begins this book wants to converse with the author, at least to the extent of entering into the world of the author's thought to learn more about pastoral care.

If we are to think of the writing and reading of a book as a conversation, it is important to recognize that neither author nor reader come to the dialogue empty-handed. Both bring certain pre-conceptions to the conversation. Both bring a history that is linked, albeit often in tacit or unacknowledged ways, to the subject matter of the book, and both bring unique ways of thinking about their history.

This is no doubt particularly the case with a book on a topic such as pastoral care. The experience of care is such a significant a part of living that all readers of pastoral care books have some preconceptions of what pastoral care is. So in reading a book about pastoral care, both the writer and the reader seek to form a link between their prior experiences of care, including pastoral care.

What You As Reader Bring

As we begin our tour of the world of pastoral care, I invite you first to pause and reflect on your prior experiences of receiving and giving care, particularly pastoral care. What were those experiences like, and what did they mean to you? Perhaps it may be useful to focus on a specific experience of pastoral care you have received from another. What was it about that experience that made it an experience of care for you? What, if anything, about the experience identified it as *pastoral* care? What associations does the word *pastoral* conjure in your memory and imagination? Is it significant to you that the care you recall was offered by a *Christian* pastor? If so, how and why was that significant?

Some readers, of course, have read other books or heard others speak about pastoral care. What these readers remember about those experiences will also play a part in what they bring to this author-reader conversation. You may find that what comes to mind is not at all well organized, but seems rather more like a collage of images, themes, half-formed ideas, and impressionistic notions.This collection of memories and ideas comprises the preconceptions you bring to the reading of this book. These preconceptions will enter into the imaginative conversation you have with me as author of the book and will influence considerably the interpretations you make of what you read. Allow these memories and ideas to interact freely with what you read so that your reading may evoke interplay between what you bring to the reading and what you find in the book. Thus, in your imaginative play, you as reader and I as author may converse.

What I As Author Bring

Because I have asked readers to begin the reading of this book by reflecting on their own past experiences of giving and receiving pastoral care, I want now to reciprocate by sharing something of the experience of pastoral care that I bring to the writing of the book. I begin with a brief autobiographical sketch of my involvement in the work of pastoral care, for all reflection about the meaning of human experience and of care for persons begins from where we are.

It is difficult for me to recall where and when I first experienced what I have since come to think of as care given by a pastor. I was born into a pastor's home in rural Kansas and grew up in a series of parsonages just prior to and during the Great Depression of the 1930s. I do not recall my father ever using the term *pastoral care*. He was trained to offer such care only by his own experience of living and working with the farmers and storekeepers, housewives and young people who were the members of his small congregations. He worked in the fields with them, sat and talked and drank coffee with them, married their children and buried their dead. I do remember going with my father on his visits to the homes of his congregation, where as a small boy I listened as they talked about their concerns and about the ordinary things of life. When people wanted to talk about something that deeply troubled them, though I have no recollection of it, I was probably sent outside to play so that they and my father could talk more privately, intimately, and openly.

I do not recall that my father ever met formally with any of his parishioners in one or a series of conversations that he might have spoken of as *pastoral counseling*. The term was not in his vocabulary. His pastoral relationships were more informal than that, and took place in the fields, after church on Sunday, in people's homes, and on their front porches. It was clear that he had a special relationship

13

to the members of his congregation as a community. He was their pastoral leader, who, as he would have put it, "tended the flock" as they gathered for worship and social interaction, carried on the business of the church, and planned for the religious education of their children.

I am sure now that in inchoate but profoundly formative ways it was through observing and participating with my father in his ministry that my first images of what it meant to be a pastor and to offer pastoral care took shape. When, after a difficult decision to enter seminary, I first encountered several of the leaders of the so-called modern pastoral care movement, these childhood memories of my father found a profound resonance. The world of pastoral care and the world of my childhood began to come together.

Another formative experience involved in my early attraction to the pastoral care movement occurred in my final year of college as a pretheological student. Majoring in sociology and psychology, I undertook, under the direction of a wise and supportive teacher, a study of the psychology of religion that flourished during the late–nineteenth and early–twentieth centuries. Thus I read from the writings of William James, Edwin D. Starbuck, James H. Leuba, and George Albert Coe, all of which whetted my interest in the connections between human developmental experience and the appropriation of religious meanings.[1]

I began my seminary studies at a time when pastoral care had not yet established itself as a practical discipline in the theological curriculum. At my seminary, Garrett Biblical Institute, there was not yet a full-time professor of pastoral care or pastoral theology. There were however, occasional adjunct courses offered by persons engaged in specialized pastoral care ministries in institutions for the sick or troubled persons within commuting distance of the school. Thus I met and studied under Fred Kuether, then chaplain at Cook County Hospital in Chicago, and Carroll A. Wise, a pastoral counselor on the staff of a large church in Minneapolis. Wise later became the first pastoral care professor at Garrett.

It was during an evening introductory course taught by Fred Kuether that I first met Anton Boisen, generally credited with being the principal founder of what came to be called the clinical pastoral training (later clinical pastoral education) movement. Boisen had initiated on-site teaching programs with theological students at Worcester State Hospital in Massachusetts, where he worked as chaplain and had begun research in the 1920s on the relationship between religious conversion experience and mental illness. There he began the writing of his classic book, *The Exploration of the Inner World*.[2] He later moved to Elgin State Hospital in Illinois to continue his ministry and research. At Elgin in 1946 I completed my first unit of clinical pastoral training. There, as a fledgling pastor, I became devoted to Boisen's notion that theological education during that period had become so captive to the study of biblical and other historical texts as to neglect the study of what Boisen spoke of as "living human documents." Concrete experiences of pastoral care of living persons, said Boisen, are sources of theological insight of equal importance to those of the historic texts of the Judeo-Christian tradition.

Upon completion of seminary, I returned to Kansas to accept my first pastoral appointment as associate pastor of a large Methodist congregation in Topeka. There I affirmed my deep interest in pastoral care as the primary thrust of my ministry. In Topeka I later reentered clinical pastoral training at institutions related to the Menninger Foundation, a major psychoanalytically oriented research and training center for mental health professionals during the post–World War II period. In 1951 I was certified by the Council for Clinical Training (one of the organizations that later formed the Association for Clinical Pastoral Education) as a supervisor of clinical pastoral training. It was during this period that Karl Menninger himself became a strong supporter of the training of clergy in psychoanalytically oriented pastoral care of troubled people; and through the work of Veterans Administration chaplain Robert Preston, the clinical psychologist Paul Pruyser, and others like Chaplain Thomas W. Klink and myself, Topeka became a center for both clinical training in pastoral care and interdisciplinary dialogue between psychiatry and theology. Seward Hiltner was a frequent consultant and visitor to the Topeka program, and several of his doctoral students at the University of Chicago came for pastoral care training and research.

The facts of my beginnings in pastoral care represent and are in certain ways prototypical of the ways in which the mid-twentieth-century renaissance of pastoral care developed. The new interest in the care of persons, sparked by the work of Boisen, the Boston physician Richard Cabot, Massachusetts General Hospital Chaplain Russell Dicks,[3] and others gathered momentum in the late 1930s and early 1940s. By the late 1940s and early 1950s a number of seminaries established departments of pastoral care, and several ground-breaking books began to appear as standard textbooks in the field.[4]

The period between 1950 and 1970 was a time of rapid growth in the field of pastoral care. Clinical pastoral education programs flourished and became established in a wide variety of health and welfare settings, correctional contexts, clinics for substance abuse, and in a few parish programs of pastoral ministry. During that time I ministered and participated in the supervision of clinical pastoral education programs in a psychiatric hospital for veterans, a state-operated school for delinquent youth, and a large public medical center serving the physical and mental health needs of the poor. I also served for a short time as pastor of a midsize congregation in whose community the major industries were a federal prison, a large Army base, and a hospital and domiciliary for military veterans.

Having begun my pastoral care ministry at the same time that the field of pastoral care was in process of establishing itself as a recognized discipline in the theological curriculum, in significant ways the development of my thinking and activity in the field parallels the development that has taken place in pastoral care as a field of ministry and inquiry. As will be evident frequently in the chapters to follow, my roots are deep in the modern pastoral care tradition that developed out of dialogue between pastoral care practice and the simultaneously growing fields of psychoanalytic and psychotherapeutic psychologies, family systems theory, crisis intervention theory, ego psychology, and object relations theory. All of these theories and their accompanying techniques of therapeutic practice contributed significantly to the formation of what can rightly be called the psychotherapeutic paradigm for the theory and practice of pastoral care.[5]

By designating this period of modern pastoral care's development as the period of the formation and coming to dominance of the psychotherapeutic paradigm, I do not mean to say that the growing literature of the field and the increasingly sophisticated work of pastoral care practitioners was entirely taken over by the desire to learn from psychologists and psychotherapists. That desire certainly asserted a dominant presence. Alongside it, however, was developing a renaissance of interest in pastoral theology and the possibilities of making a distinctive contribution to theological inquiry through the avenue of reflection on what Seward Hiltner in 1958 spoke of as "pastoral operations."[6]

In that project, Hiltner carried forward in important ways the aspiration he had inherited from Anton Boisen to do constructive theological work in relation to concrete human experience. Other pastoral care theorists made contributions to this developing body of literature in pastoral theology, among them Wayne E. Oates, Carroll A. Wise, and Edward E. Thornton.[7]

As a maturing clinical practitioner and teacher of pastoral care, I participated in these developing emphases: both that of learning from the psychologies and that of developing pastoral care as a theological discipline.

Thus during the 1960s I endeavored to develop my skills as a pastoral counselor through work with a cross-section of troubled persons ranging from alcoholics and their families to poor and middle-class individuals undergoing a variety of health-related crises and problems of living. As a supervisor of clinical pastoral education, I sought to teach my students to appropriate psychological insights and to develop their abilities to do careful theological reflection on the human problems they encountered.

By 1970 my interest in contributing to the inquiry into the theological grounding for pastoral care theory and practice led me to accept an invitation to move from the clinical institutional contexts in which I had worked for most of twenty years to the faculty of a theological seminary. Whereas in my earlier work I had rubbed shoulders daily with psychiatric and organic physicians, mental health practitioners and other healthcare professionals, now I found myself in daily dialogue with biblical scholars, theologians, and ethicists. Relating the insights and dilemmas of pastoral care to the classic theological disciplines became an increasingly central aspect of my work and thought. I found myself having to relate what I had learned about pastoral care more closely to the day-to-day work of the parish pastor in the care and leadership of a congregation.

This movement in my career in pastoral care toward closer and more rigorous dialogue with the traditional theological disciplines and toward involvement in congregational life parallels a similar movement within pastoral care itself. Having learned significantly from the psychologies and psychotherapies and having striven to develop more carefully constructed ways of doing pastoral theology, the field began in the 1970s and 1980s to become a strong partner in the reformulation of theology as a *practical* discipline. Practical theology began to take its proper place alongside historical theology and systematic theology among the modes of theological inquiry. Likewise, during that period the study of the congregation as a primary locus of religious life gained a prominent place in practical theological interest. Pastoral theology began to assert its right to speak. Concomitantly, participation in the recovery of practical theology began to force pastoral theologians to move beyond earlier preoccupation with the individualism inherent in the psychotherapeutic paradigm.

Many of the results of my own participation in that resurgence of practical theological discussion and inquiry are contained in my four books published between 1979 and 1991.[8] In those writings I sought to develop what I called a narrative, hermeneutical methodology for doing practical theology in pastoral care and counseling with individuals *(The Living Human Document)* and in pastoral leadership of a community of Christian people *(Widening the Horizons* and *Prophetic Pastoral Practice).*

This prefatory summary of my lifetime of involvement in pastoral care and its connections to the maturing process of the modern pastoral movement discloses the preconceptions that I bring to our introductory dialogical tour of the field of pastoral care. My desire is to retain and value much of what was gained in the appropriation of the psychotherapeutic paradigm. The care of the people of God will always involve the pastor in the care of individuals with as much psychological savvy as he or she can muster. Likewise, I hope to retain what we have learned from group and family psychologies about the care of persons as they participate in systems of relationships that shape their lives.

The tour upon which we embark will also evidence my understanding that the field of pastoral care is now in a time of transition that has taken us beyond the predominance of the psychotherapeutic paradigm. So our tour will be an introduction to the possibilities and problems that appear when pastoral care is considered to be not only the care of individuals and families, but also the care of the Christian community and the tradition that gives that community its identity. Indeed, the perspective with which I begin this book asserts that in fundamental ways, the primary basis of care which the Christian community and its pastors offer to persons is the care that comes about by participation in the Christian community and its world of interpreted meanings. Thus the chapters that follow will disclose a way of engaging issues of practical theology which, while they give theological grounding for the caring ministry of the pastor, likewise have application to the broadest range of pastoral and communal practices in the life of the church and world.

PART I

Continuity and Change:
A Revised History of Pastoral Care
Sets a New Direction

To tour the world of pastoral care is also to enter into a tradition. Though it was not always known by this name, pastoral care has been a part of the Christian story and its tradition over many centuries of Christian history. Before Christianity, pastoral care was a significant aspect of the Israelite community's life and its tradition, out of which the Old Testament or Jewish Scriptures emerged. Thus to tour the world of pastoral care means to trace some of the roots of pastoral practice in earlier times as we seek to understand the long story of pastoral tradition. It means to catch a glimpse of the different emphases in pastoral care that have emerged in response to the changing scenes of human experience over the long reaches of time.

The understanding that pastoral care always involves a response to human experience is central to the tradition of care, as we shall see. It means that as human sociocultural experience has changed, pastoral care practices have likewise been modified to respond to the changing needs of people. Like all human history, the history of pastoral care is always in process, continually emerging into an open-ended future. Yet, as is the case with all human experience, there are deep continuities that have shaped and continue to shape the pastoral tradition. Our tour will therefore take us down some well-worn paths that other pastoral practitioners before us have laid, as well as into previously unexplored territory into which the new experiences of contemporary life have drawn us, calling for new pastoral response.

Thinking about the history of pastoral care in terms of the interplay of the old and the new in an evolving process of pastoral response leads us to organize that history into a rough chronology of periods or epochs during which pastoral care was marked by differing emphases. Included in that way of organizing pastoral history is the notion that there were and continue to be times of transition when elements of former practice and emerging emphases mix as older ways of responding to human experience give way to new modes of pastoral practice and thought. The time in which we find ourselves near the end of the twentieth century is such a time of transition.

The task of part 1 of the book will accordingly be twofold. First, we will walk—albeit rather hastily, taking great strides across the centuries—through the earlier periods of pastoral care practice from biblical times to the recent past in search of modes of care that have become paradigmatic in our tradition. Second, I will present an argument for a new chapter in pastoral care's history that acknowledges the transition we are experiencing and opens new modes of devising appropriate responses to human experiences in the postmodern world of the end of the twentieth century.

As we undertake these two tasks, it is important to recognize that we shall be reviewing this history and proposing a new chapter in the story of pastoral care from a particular vantage point and perspective. We will be looking at history with the eyes of people living during the time approaching the year 2000. What we see of the past will be colored by our contemporary ways of seeing. Although we may attempt to recover the ways of experiencing life and responding pastorally of earlier times more or less remote from our own, our perceptions of history will always be influenced by our own time and its ways of seeing and speaking about human experience. It is likewise important to acknowledge that this book is being written by a white male pastor who has participated in the pastoral care tradition for nearly fifty years while teaching and ministering within the North American culture of the West. Both these realities impose limits on our vision, and yet they provide a certain vantage point that can be revealing in significant ways.

CHAPTER 1

Earlier Chapters in an Old Story

To begin a tour of the world of pastoral care requires that we first locate that world within the larger world of Christian faith and tradition. Pastoral care as we know it today did not spring forth out of the shallow soil of recent experience. Rather, it has a long history; thus we have many ancestors who have shaped for us the way we approach the care of persons. The history of that care, like a family genealogy, reaches back as far as the collective memories of the Christian community can be extended. To understand the world of pastoral care as it is today thus requires a preliminary tour into its archaeology.

Biblical Models for Pastoral Care

Our most reliable source regarding the beginnings of pastoral care is, of course, the Bible. Turning first to that source, we learn that the care of the community of people who worshiped the one God, Yahweh, required the assignment of leadership roles to certain individuals. Our earliest pastoral ancestors are to be found among the leaders of the ancient people of Israel. From very early in recorded biblical history the custom was established of designating three classes of such leaders: the priests, a hereditary class that had particular responsibility for worship and ceremonial life; the prophets, who spoke for Yahweh in relation to moral issues, sometimes rebuking the community and its stated political leaders; and the wise men and women, who offered counsel of all sorts concerning issues of the good life and personal conduct. From time to time in the early history of the people of Israel, competition among these three vocational classes became intense. The prophets, among them Amos,

Jeremiah, and the authors of the book of Isaiah, were in their times dominant voices in giving moral guidance to the community. In later times, prophecy declined and the scribes and rabbis emerged as vocational groups who carried on the functions of the wise men and women and priests. They became the dominant force in providing pastoral leadership to the Hebrew community.[1]

Just who among these Old Testament leaders of the community from which Christian history sprang are we to identify as our earliest ancestors in pastoral care? Each in his or her own way was vitally concerned with the care and discipline of Yahweh's people, both as a community and as individuals. For the prophets that meant confronting the people with their deviation from the will of Yahweh. For the priests it meant faithful and reverent observance of worship and cultic practice. For the wise men and women it meant practical moral guidance in the affairs of living together as a community.

In our own most recent times, particularly with the increasing specialization among the disciplines of ministry studies—disciplines such as biblical studies, church history, theology, ethics, homiletics, pastoral care, Christian education, and evangelism—an assumption has emerged that the principal Old Testament ancestors of pastoral care practice were the wise men and women: those who gave moral guidance to individuals. The prophets have more often been claimed by ethicists and, on occasion, the homileticians as their predecessors. Pastoral leaders who see themselves primarily as leaders of worship have identified the Israelite priests as their spiritual ancestors.

A more holistic understanding of ministry, grounded in a narrative, hermeneutical approach to pastoral care theory, requires that we lay a broader ancestral claim than simply that of the Wisdom tradition and its earliest practitioners. The long story of the care of God's people has been shaped not only by Wisdom, important as that has been. People have found the care of God and God's people communicated to them in the richness of ritual practice as well as in wise guidance. Likewise, God's care has from time to time been expressed in prophetic acts of leadership and confrontation with the implications of the will and purpose of God for the mutual care of the people, indeed for the care of all human affairs and for the earth itself. Thus our narrative approach points us toward a recognition that in the long story of the people of God the metaphor of care has multiple origins. Its meanings embrace many roles within the historic community and varying emphases, which from time to time have asserted themselves as primary for the care of God's people in particular situations.

Why, you may ask then, have pastoral care givers recently focused primarily on individual guidance, grounded in the Wisdom tradition, as the principal mode of pastoral care? Why have the ancestral claims of the priestly and prophetic roles been relegated to a secondary place or given over to other functions of ministry? Has the practice of pastoral care been impoverished by its appropriation of its history as predominantly the domain of wisdom and guidance?

The answers to this question are, to be sure, complex. Indeed, the question itself needs to be modified somewhat by the recognition that the term *guidance* has been supplemented by some pastoral care historians with the addition of other metaphorical terms such as *healing, reconciling,* and *sustaining.*[2]

More will need to be said later about this way of categorizing the forms of pastoral care. At this point we only need to recognize that each of these four modes of care as they have been interpreted in the recent past carry a primary connotation of wise care of the individual or, as appropriate, the family. The larger communal roles of caring leadership that sprang from the priestly and prophetic ancestral models have not, until very recently, received substantive attention in relation to the modes and methods of pastoral care.[3]

To reclaim the prophetic and priestly Hebrew ancestors as equally important to the wise men and women of early Israelite history as root models for pastoral care practice involves us in a reconfiguration of the primary images that shape our understanding of what is involved in pastoral care of God's people. It means placing alongside the image of the wise and caring pastor providing care and concern for individuals and families another image of the pastor as caring leader of a community of worship and nurture—a community of care. It also places alongside that image one of the pastor as prophetic leader who cares both for the people and for the tradition that gives the community its identity. Care for the people of God involves care that confronts issues of justice and moral integrity in the life of the people.

Reclaiming all three Old Testament role models as primary for the caring ministry of the Christian community and its leadership suggests an interpretive structure for examining the long history of pastoral care that brings three foci of concern into a dialogical or, more accurately, trialogical interactive tension. Schematized, that interpretive structure looks like this:

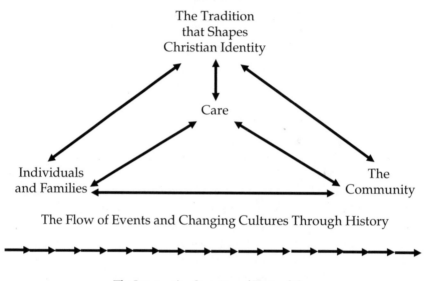

The Tradition
that Shapes
Christian Identity

Care

Individuals
and Families

The
Community

The Flow of Events and Changing Cultures Through History

The Interpretive Structure of Pastoral Care
Figure 1

Reading the history of pastoral care through the lens of this schema facilitates our reappropriating that history, giving significant attention to all three of the modes of care associated in Christian memory with the three primordial ancestral role models: the prophets who spoke for the tradition and its concern for response to the voice of God, the priests who led the community in its cultic worship, and the wise ones who offered guidance to the people in the daily affairs of individual and family life. The schema suggests that the care of the people of God always involves a trialogical tension and interaction among the three nexus points of the schema. It necessitates giving attention to ongoing care for the Christian tradition that grounds the faith and practice of the life of the people. It likewise involves attending to the life of the community of faith with care and discernment. And it involves giving careful attention to the needs and problems of individuals and families.

The prophetic, priestly, and wisdom models of caring ministry we inherit from the Israelite community are not, to be sure, the only biblical images with which we pastors have to identify. Another, in certain ways more significant, model is that of the caring leader as shepherd. Although the shepherding motif originated as a metaphor for the role of the king during the monarchical period of Israelite history, it was never institutionalized as a designated role within the religious community, as were the prophetic, priestly, and wisdom roles. It was first appropriated within the religious life of Israel as a metaphor with which to speak of the care of Yahweh for Yahweh's people. This motif is most clearly captured in the imagery of Psalm 23. Here the Lord God is depicted as the good shepherd who leads the people in paths of righteousness, restores the souls of the people, and walks with the people among their enemies, and even into the valley of the shadow of death. The carryover of that imagery from the care of God to the care to be provided by the human leaders of the community is not made explicit in the psalm; and evidence is lacking that the shepherd model ever attained a place of significance equal to those of the prophetic, the priestly, and the wise guide in later Old Testament literature, probably because it lacked an institutionalized role.

With the coming of Jesus, who, according to John's Gospel, identifies himself as "the good shepherd," the shepherding image takes its place as a primary grounding image for ministry. Applied to Jesus' ministry, the shepherding image incorporates not only the wisdom expressed in certain of the parables and the Sermon on the Mount, not only his priestly leadership in relationship to his followers, but also elements of prophecy such as are found in the story of Jesus' cleansing of the Temple and his confrontations with the Pharisees and Sadducees.

From early Christian times to the present the image of the pastoral leader as the "shepherd of the flock" has persisted as a prototypical image applied to both pastors and ecclesiastical leaders of the institutional church. The shepherding motif appears again and again in the writings of the early church fathers as the organizing metaphor par excellence for the work of the pastoral leader.[4] In more recent times the shepherd metaphor has been widely appropriated as a grounding metaphor for the care-giving pastor.[5]

The Epochs of Christian History and Pastoral Care

It is beyond the scope of this book to present a detailed history of twenty centuries of pastoral care practices in the Christian church. It is, however, important that we give some attention to the ways in which the history of pastoral care practice in the Christian churches has shaped the discipline of care in the contemporary Christian community. Many of the current issues and problems in the discipline of pastoral care have historical roots, the uncovering of which can assist us in understanding their present significance. Somewhat following the pattern established by the two classic pastoral care histories referenced earlier in this chapter, I will therefore turn now to the task of leading the reader on a brief reflective journey through several periods of Christian history, giving particular attention to the origins of various pastoral care practices and issues.[6]

The Primitive Church

During the earliest period of Christian history, the care of the nascent tradition by which Christians were identified was influenced by the anticipation of the immanent and cataclysmic *parousia*, the arrival of the risen Lord and the ushering in of God's kingdom. The care of the community of Christians involved concern for the purity of the congregation in a non-Christian, pagan culture. Individuals were to be assisted in sustaining their faith and right behavior in anticipation of that great event, which was expected to occur in their lifetime. Sustaining the faith at both communal and individual levels thus was the major mode of pastoral care practice by leaders of the faithful community.

Although the centuries have transformed the anticipation of the *parousia* into a more mystical and, for some, less concrete expectation of the second coming, we who exercise pastoral care in our time are still under the influence of a Christianity that lives in hopeful anticipation of the rule of God. That means our care for the tradition places upon us the commission that we are in important ways responsible for keeping the story of the faith alive and open to the future God is bringing about. It means caring enough for the Christian story to keep it vivid and lively in the consciousness of the people called Christians. Pastoral care thus has crucial communal dimensions having to do with initiating persons into the community that nurtures the faith and with sustaining individuals in their efforts to lead faithful lives while under the strain of everyday life in a predominantly secular world. Though today's world may not be overtly hostile to Christian belief and practice, as was the world of primitive Christians, it is a world that is increasingly shaped by secular lifestyles and values.

The Age of the Persecutions

By the second and third centuries of the Christian era, the immediacy of the expectation of the return of Christ to usher in the new Kingdom gradually diminished, and the community of Christians began to adapt to the necessity of sustaining its faith into an indefinite future. Meanwhile, the community's imperial Roman cultural context became more hostile. At first sporadic, and then more frequent persecution of Christian believers placed the Christian community under intense and terrifying pressure. Conformity to the state cultic practices was increasingly demanded and, by the faithful, refused. Many members of the community were inevitably compromised. Defections and temporary lapses into pagan allegiance to the emperors became common.

In that situation of cultural conflict and uncertainty, the care and protection of the community became a dominant concern of Christian pastoral leaders. Maintaining the boundaries of the community against the incursions of the Roman Empire and disciplining those Christians who failed to meet the expectations of the church became a dominant pastoral concern. Pastoral care within the community took on an air of reconciliation, as care for the community and care of individuals were combined in modes of disciplining members of the community who failed to follow the church's rules of worship and behavior. Reconciling those who had remained steadfast to the faith with those who failed to do so likewise became a preoccupying problem.[7]

Meanwhile, the care of the Christian tradition was also undergoing significant transformations, as the theological and ecclesiastical leaders of the community continued the process already begun in New Testament times of integrating the thought forms inherited from the Jewish tradition with other cultural traditions, most notably those originating in Greek thought. Two important aspects of that process that greatly affected pastoral practices during this period were the Greek concepts of *metanoia* (repentance) and *exomologesis* (confession). Both these terms appear in the New Testament, though *exomologesis* does so only in its verb forms.[8]

The earliest known Latin theological writer, Tertullian (160–220 C.E.), a native of Carthage in North Africa, strongly developed the concepts of repentance and confession as pastoral requirements of the Christian community that were designed to make reconciliation possible. Tertullian advised that an offending member be shunned by the faithful after having been rebuked publicly in the congregation. Privately, the offender was counseled to confess his or her sins in the presence of the congregation *(exomologesis).* By prescribed rules, the offender was barred from participation in the worship of the community, most particularly from the Eucharist, and only reinstated to full membership in the community after a stated period of penance. As pastoral care historians William Clebsch and Charles Jaekle write, "Confession thus became a kind of medicine of humiliation, possessing power to make better [persons] and better Christians, and as such demonstrating God's mercy."[9]

During this period, the church began to establish pastoral care practices that, on the one hand, emphasized discipline and the authority of the pastoral leader to set and enforce behavioral boundaries for members of the community, and on the other hand, emphasized the pastor's role as reconciler and healer of the wounds of the people. Much of the pastoral role became preoccupied with such matters as the appropriate administration of penance, which sins were subject to forgiveness after due repentance and which were not, the variety of penitential means by which the offender could become reconciled to the community, and the like. These practices were continued and elaborately developed over the course of history up until the time of the Protestant Reformation. Pastoral care focused on discipline, casuistry, and the exercise of penitential authority.

All this emphasis on discipline and casuistry notwithstanding, there is likewise to be found in the documents preserved from this period a record of consistent care for the individual. The pastoral leader was admonished to be a wise and vigilant shepherd of the flock. John Chrysostom in the fourth century thus speaks of the qualities required of the pastoral caregiver:

> So the shepherd needs great wisdom and a thousand eyes to examine the soul's condition from every angle. . . . The priest, therefore, must not overlook any of these considerations, but examine them all with care and apply all his remedies appropriately for fear his care should be in vain. . . . If a [person] wanders away from the right faith, the shepherd needs a lot of concentration, perseverance, and patience. He cannot drag by force or constrain by fear, but must by persuasion lead [the person] back to the true beginning from which he [or she] has fallen away.[10]

In this brief excerpt from Chrysostom's writings we can see evidence of the writer's allegiance to both the priestly and wisdom models of pastoral practice. Chrysostom clearly writes from the position of the priest who has liturgical and administrative responsibility for the care of the Christian flock. Yet he also appropriates the role of the wise leader who exercises "concentration, perseverance, and patience."

It is difficult for us who minister today to identify with the style of pastoral care that characterized Tertullian's or Chrysostom's time and place. The authority structure within which the pastor relates to those under her or his care has changed radically, particularly for pastors serving in Protestant polities that function as volunteer associations. However, reconciliation of individual church members to the community of Christians, whether that be the community of a denomination or a local congregational community, remains a significant aspect of pastoral care. The pastor must often stand in the gap between an individual parishioner and a community of faith, seeking to reconcile the one to the other. The caring tensions inherent in the schema depicted in figure 1 will, as they were in Chrysostom's time, be those of the interactions among concern for the faithful

31

preservation of the tradition of faith, the care of the community one represents, and the care of the individual. The authority to administer *exomologesis* and prescribe penance, so taken for granted in Tertullian's day, has, for most Protestant pastors, disappeared.

Nonetheless, John Chrysostom's admonition to pastors is still relevant to pastors in its emphasis on the need for concentration, perseverance, patience, and the desire not to overlook any consideration in bringing to bear those remedies that lead people back to the appropriation of the faith. As Chrysostom implies, it is the faith preserved in the Christian tradition that most fundamentally embodies the care of God for God's people.

Before moving on to the medieval period of pastoral practice, it is important to take note of the significance for later developments within the pastoral care tradition of a crucial precedent established during the earliest periods of Christian history, namely, that of borrowing from and accommodating non-Christian modes of thought present in the surrounding culture. Readers will recall that I mentioned earlier that the practices that developed with regard to *metanoia* and *exomologesis* were heavily influenced by Greek thought which, when adapted to the shepherding role of the priest in the Christian church, shaped in significant ways the modes of care as reconciliation that became dominant for centuries.

In our own time this traditional openness of the Christian churches to influences from outside its own language and tradition clearly legitimates the adaptation within pastoral care practice of secular, scientific modes of thought that have emerged from the human sciences of psychology, sociology, anthropology, and psychotherapy. As we shall see in later chapters, some of the most significant developments in pastoral care theory and practice during the twentieth century have come out of efforts to synthesize traditional Christian pastoral theory and practice with theories about human relationships and behavior that have origins outside the immediate purview of theology—efforts not different in kind from those made by pastoral thinkers during the patristic period. In meaningful ways, when we in our time work at the task of informing pastoral care practice with nontheological insights, we follow in the footsteps of Quintus Tertullian and John Chrysostom.

The Imperial Church After Constantine

The early fourth century brought a radical shift in the status of the Christian religion in its cultural context. The Roman Emperor Constantine became at first tolerant of the presence of Christians, ending the period of persecution. Later, particularly after the founding of Constantinople, the church gained the status of a favored religion under Constantine's rule.

Rather than being a persecuted minority group, the church suddenly was thrust into the role of providing a unifying set of meanings for the culture itself. The care of the Christian community and its tradition had to be expanded to include care of the whole society. The church that had been persecuted began to be transformed into the imperial church that not only set the behavioral and moral standards for the people of the society, but also dispensed state welfare funds and impressed upon the populace Christian interpretations of common troubles. Meanwhile, liturgical practices took on an air of pomp and circumstance adopted from official state ceremonies.[11]

John Chrysostom, one of the significant interpreters of pastoral care practice during the period of the persecutions, witnessed the church's transition into the period of the emergence of the imperial church. Chrysostom in fact became the Bishop of Constantinople. He was a powerful and persuasive preacher in the courts of Constantine, and consequently he significantly influenced the integration of broad cultural values and interpretations of human experience into Christian modes of interpretation and practice. He and other church leaders were influenced by Greek thought, most notably Greek Stoicism, not only in terms of their understanding of human behavior and the values to be cherished and cultivated within the religious life of the society, but also in terms of their techniques of pastoral practice.[12]

From the vantage provided by our historical distance from this period of Christianity's enculturation into the thought forms of imperial Rome, we can see how, though the pastoral leaders of this period remained true to the Wisdom tradition of pastoral practice, their wisdom, like that of the Old Testament book of Proverbs, embodied both religious insight and common sense. The pattern of appropriation of secular and other non-Christian modes of thought and practice into Christian pastoral and religious thought and practice became well established. Christian pastoral guidance was informed by contextual wisdom alongside or integrated into biblically based Christian wisdom.

Wise guidance was not the only form of pastoral care that was undergoing change and cultural influence during this epoch of Christian history. Priestly liturgical practice was also changing. The conduct of public worship became the chief clerical occupation and became increasingly formalized in the patterns of the imperial church. Likewise, during this period rituals of healing through anointing with holy oil became common and highly valued. Reconciliation became routinized into the administration of penance and the enforcement of standard church policies. Pastoral care of the sick, the bereaved, and the dying also were included in the routine practices of priests of the church.[13]

From our vantage point we can also see that during this time something of the unity of the Christian community as set apart from the rest of the world threatened to become muted or lost. The boundaries of the Christian community became indistinct. It is not surprising that during this time many deeply religious Christians fled to the Egyptian desert to live as hermits for the faith. It was also during this period that monasticism had its beginnings with its accompanying supposition that a truly religious vocation meant withdrawal from the society into a community that was set apart.[14]

Although its manifestations are very different in the radically altered circumstances of twentieth-century life, the problem of maintaining boundaries of the Christian community while remaining open to the surrounding society continues today. Like imperial Roman society, twentieth-century Western culture has been infused with Christian meanings and values alongside those that have emerged from secular processes. Likewise, the Christian community has widely appropriated ideas and values with non-Christian origins. As we shall see in later chapters of this book, these processes of cultural fusion and the problematic task of maintaining permeable boundaries for the Christian community have profound implications for the caring ministry of the church. One aspect of that problem can be seen when some pastors try to draw sharp boundaries around the community for whom they claim responsibility of care. They feel responsible only for the care of their own parishioners! Other pastors extend the boundaries of their care into the larger community, sometimes even to the pastoral neglect of their own flock.

We need to mark for further reflection the importance of liturgy and ritual practices for the care and healing of the people of God. As I have noted, these more priestly modes of care have tended to be neglected in recent times. Their significance is given less attention as pastoral care practitioners have been preoccupied with psychologically grounded modes of pastoral guidance. The recovery of liturgy and ritual as primary ways in which the Christian community cares for its own is, as we shall see, one of the creative growing edges of pastoral care practice in our time.

Much more could be said about this period of history when the Christian community moved from being a pariah community in imperial Rome to becoming the unifying force in that society. As we have seen, the effects of that radical shift remain active in the relationship between church and society in our own  cations of this altered situation impress the schema I presented earlier as the in care. Most important, that schema nee the cultural context that surrounds the both influences our understanding of th ministry *and* becomes itself an object o Thus what I presented earlier as a trial needs to become a quadrilateral schema. This revised interpretive structure for pastoral care may be schematized as in figure 2.

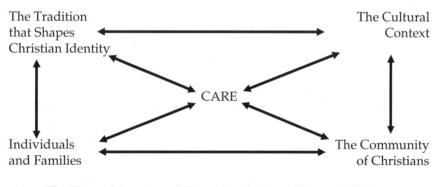

The Interpretive Structure of Pastoral Care: A Quadrilateral Schema
Figure 2

35

By introducing a fourth element (cultural context) into the schema of figure 1, figure 2 suggests that care as a primary metaphorical model for the ministry of the church not only involves care of the identifying Christian tradition, the contemporary community of Christians, and the particular needs of individuals within the community; care also always involves giving attention to the issues and concerns of the contemporary cultural context. Thus the schema suggests that there are four primary nexus points in constant interaction with one another that in significant ways shape any situation that evokes the need for care. Furthermore, the response of those who seek to offer care will also be shaped by influences and considerations emanating from each of the four nexus points.

The two-directional arrows that connect each of the four nexus points in the schema and that, in turn, connect each of them with the caring center of the schema are important in that they suggest the dialogical, interactive nature of the model. Taken together they form an ecology within which each arena of human activity influences and is influenced by the others. Likewise, care exercised toward any of the four nexus arenas will have its effect, great or small, on the quality of care received by the other three nexus arenas. For example, the manner in which care of the identifying Christian tradition is expressed will greatly influence the level and quality of care exercised toward individuals and families, the community of Christians, and the larger sociocultural context.

The schema of figure 2 also affirms that the extent and quality of care represented and expressed within each of the four nexus arenas will affect significantly the level of care given and received in other nexus arenas. For example, the level of care expressed within the Christian community will affect the level of care given and received by individuals and families. It will also influence the manner in which the identifying Christian tradition receives care from its members. And to a limited but significant degree, it will influence the level of care given and received by the surrounding cultural context.

It is important to note that the schema of figure 2 places at its center an image of care that is larger than the image of *pastoral* care conceived as simply involving the work of the ordained pastor. The pastor of the living Christian community is only one actor in the total enterprise of giving and receiving care, albeit an important actor.

The schema thus suggests that the pastor's primary contribution to the caring process is that of offering caring interpretive leadership within the community of Christians in relationship to its tradition, its individual members and families, and its sociocultural context. On occasion that means that the pastor may offer specific acts of care with and on behalf of individuals. Pastoral care in its larger meaning, however, involves the pastor in giving caring attention to concerns that reach beyond the individual to the community of Christians and the larger society.

Before hastening from the time of imperial Rome and the imperial church in our rapid tour of the history of pastoral care, we need to take note that, although we have found important similarities between that time in history and our own, there are also many great dissimilarities. The imperial period was the time when the church became established in ways that held the fragmenting elements of Roman society to its cultural center. Our time seems in many ways completely different, when the central religious values of Western society have become obscure and confused. Secularism seems more pervasive than it was in the recent past. In significant ways the church has been undergoing disestablishment. This means that the structures and meanings of care in our time are in many respects less clear and the leadership role of churches and their pastors less acknowledged than was the case in the time of the imperial church. Our models of care must be adapted to our changing situation. Nevertheless, our reflections on the situation of the church in the early stages of the medieval period have provided us with a useful interpretive structure to take with us on our journey.

The Fall of the Roman Empire and the Spread of Christianity Across Europe

No sooner had the Christian church established itself as the unifying cultural force for the Roman Empire than the Roman Empire itself began to crumble. The stability that the Empire had provided for the ancient Mediterranean world was broken up by the invasion of "hordes of rude peoples who swept over the territory we know as western Europe."[15]

Again it became the task of the church to provide some semblance of cultural unification. The fulfillment of that role moved in basically two directions: toward the establishment of an elite class that represented the continuation of classical Roman civilization, and toward the indoctrination of ordinary folk in Christian descriptions of life and prescriptions for their troubles in living. For both these tasks the rapidly growing order of Benedictine monks proved to be a key player in the Christianizing of Europe.

With the interpretive structure of figure 2 in mind, it is important to recognize that the fourth and fifth centuries were a time of considerable fomentation and controversy within the church regarding the proper care and interpretation of the Christian theological tradition. It was the time of the Arian and Nestorian controversies, the Council of Nicea, and numerous other events and struggles that established the shape of orthodoxy in regard to theology in the church. All these controversies and decisions had their effect on the ways in which pastoral and communal care developed. It was also the time when in the Western church the Trinitarian theology most fully expressed by Augustine of Hippo became the primary basis for what was to become orthodox medieval theology.

As Thomas Oden has argued in his brief but valuable study *Care of Souls in the Classic Tradition,* during this period of Europe's Christianization there was no one of greater stature than Gregory the Great (540–604 C.E.). If Augustine set the tone for medieval theology, Gregory established the basic patterns of pastoral practice in the postpatristic Christian community.[16]

Becoming a Benedictine monk at the age of thirty-four, Gregory established a number of monasteries in Sicily and Rome; and his followers were responsible for numerous missionary endeavors in Spain, the Lombards, Sardinia, and Britain. Thus his influence spread widely across medieval Europe. In the year 590 he became pope.

For our purpose here, two central themes of the pastoral care that flowed from the work of Gregory the Great are significant: his emphasis on individualized guidance of the souls of the faithful, and his stress on the regulation of ordinary life through the practices of prayer, meditation, and spiritual discipline. For Gregory each person and his or her particular situation in life demanded individual, contextually relevant attention. He wrote numerous guides for priestly use in the guidance of individual souls, culminating in the extensive dissemination of his *Pastoral Care*, which became the most widely read manual for pastoral practice of the Middle Ages.[17]

As Oden demonstrated, Gregory anticipated, both in his sophisticated understanding of human psychology and in his emphasis on the particularity of human individual needs, many of the emphases and issues that have marked the twentieth-century renaissance of pastoral care. The care of the poor and those in special situations of need was of particular concern to Gregory and his Benedictine followers. We who are the offspring of what has come to be called clinical pastoral care can claim Gregory the Great as one of our most important spiritual ancestors.

Important as was Gregory the Great in establishing the medieval model of pastoral care practice, from our historical distance we can also recognize at least two aspects of his methods that have over time proved to be flawed. First, virtually above all else, Gregory modeled the authoritarian role of the priest in his pastoral relationships. Pastoral authority for him meant authority over the people. Second, Gregory's pastoral methodology tended to be overly mechanical and prescriptive. It was not adequately flexible to meet the peculiar needs of individual supplicants. In those regards, as feminist patristic scholar Roberta Bondi, has reminded us, the desert fathers and mothers, with their far more sensitive grasp of communal relationships of support and mutual encouragement, provided a much more egalitarian and spiritually sensitive model of care than did Gregory. Theirs was a highly individualized care that made much greater use of nondirection in pastoral relationships.[18]

Two other interpretive connections between modern pastoral practice and the pastoral care developed in the early Middle Ages need to be noted. First, as has been the case in our time, there developed ways of thinking about human spiritual needs and disciplines that focused on analogies between the care of the soul and the care of the body. Such terms as *spiritual health* and *spiritual sickness* were common, as were analogies that compared spiritual roles and experiences with physical roles and experiences (e.g., the priest as physician of the soul). Second, during the early Middle Ages, healing of spiritual problems such as guilt and despondence through anointing with ritual oils and ointments was widely practiced. Indeed, healing became a primary mode of pastoral care practice.

Again with reference to the schema of figure 2, a somewhat less direct interpretive connection between the imperial period of Christian history and our immediate past may be found in the way in which the church of the early Middle Ages unquestioningly accepted a feudal society. For ordinary folk, acceptance of a disciplined, orderly life meant acceptance of their assigned place in the feudal scheme. Although Gregory gave significant attention to the physical needs of the poor and to their moral instruction, he and other pastoral leaders of his time generally did not dispute the social system that victimized the poor. The tendency to unquestioningly accept unjust social systems remains alive and well in the pastoral care movement of the twentieth century. Much work needs to be done before care of the poor and care of the society are congruous.

The Sacramentalism of the Middle Ages

If the analogy between the pastor as "physician of the spirit" and medical doctor as "physician of the body" began in the early Middle Ages, it flourished to the point of exaggeration in the high Middle Ages. Sacramental healing became the norm for pastoral practice. Included in the emphasis on various ritualistic practices was widespread pastoral issuance of indulgences of various types. Earlier manuals for priestly administration of penance were greatly elaborated, often with little attention to any theological grounding for the theory of care they embodied. Of these perhaps the most widely disbursed among the relatively poorly educated parish priests were the Celtic penitential manuals, described by John McNeill as "poorly written and often wretchedly copied, . . . with few exceptions almost the rags and tatters of Church Latin literature. Their lists of sins, and of penalties, mark them as products, no less than correctors, of a primitive society."[19]

It should be remembered that this was also the time of such figures as Francis of Assisi, the founder of the order of Franciscan monks. Far from being an exploiter of his priestly powers, Francis lived a life of humble service to the poor and dispossessed. Winning the loyalty of his followers as much by his deeds as by his words, Francis modeled a life of solidarity with the people. His administration of penance was as often as not designed to humble the proud and invite others into his lifestyle of selfless service rather than to punish wrongdoing. His pastoral care thus became a model of life among and on behalf of ordinary folk.

The heritage we in our time receive from this period of history is indeed a mixed one. Although the period of the high Middle Ages does not offer directly transferable models for contemporary pastoral care practice, our study of the period does raise two relevant questions. First, there is the question of how divine grace and forgiveness are to be received and appropriated by the people. In other words, How is the care of the Christian community for its people to express and embody the gracious care of God in ways that do not result in the aggrandizement of the church itself or the exploitation of the people's needs? How, in short, is the care of God and God's people best expressed in the ritual practices of the community? Second, there is the question of how the Christian community should care for the poor and the downtrodden. These are questions that we still try to answer faithfully.

The Era of the Reformation

If it is true that pastoral care includes care for the faith tradition, then it follows that there was no time in Christian history when pastoral care practice took a more radical turn than it did with the Protestant Reformation. Through the powerful leadership of Martin Luther and other Reformers, some factions of the church made a sharp turn away from the primacy of sacramentalism and priestly exercise of penitential discipline, and toward the care of souls in their individual search for salvation. Through the application of such doctrines as those of the priesthood of all believers and salvation by faith alone, care of the people by the newly reformed churches became more highly individualized than ever before.

Luther held that the sacramentalism of the medieval Catholic church was not only corrupt in its practice of issuing indulgences; it was likewise too mechanical and too easy. For him, the gospel required individual confession and complete personal involvement:

41

the search of the soul for its own direct relationship with God, its own personal salvation.[20]

Pastoral care of the people became a process of facilitating the individual's personal relationship with God. Reconciliation of the individual soul to God and guidance in the spiritual life of members of the community of faith became the central pastoral tasks.

Luther's pastoral care likewise concerned itself with the care and protection of those who were victims of the uncaring practices of their society. For example, at the beginning of a long letter of pastoral guidance to Prince Frederick of Saxony, Luther writes:

> Our Lord and Savior Jesus hath left us a commandment, which concerns all Christians alike,—that we should render the duties of humanity, or (as the Scriptures call them) the works of mercy, to such as are afflicted and under calamity; that we should visit the sick, endeavor to set free the prisoners, and perform other like acts of kindness to our neighbor, whereby the evils of this present time may in some measure be lightened.[21]

Here we see that Luther's conception of pastoral care involved a primary concern for those in special need, including the victims of "the evils of the present time." Furthermore, it is apparent that such pastoral concern was the responsibility of all Christians and not simply the clergy. Here again we see results of Luther's emphasis on the priesthood of all believers.

Thus far I have focused on the shifts toward individualism and toward the pastoral responsibility of all Christians that characterized Martin Luther's understanding of pastoral practice. Yet Luther was not, to be sure, totally individualistic, nor was he the only Reformer to advocate these changing emphases. With some variation they may be found in Martin Bucer and John Calvin as well, though Calvin tended to be somewhat more institutionally prescriptive and systematic in his efforts to provide avenues of reconciliation to God and neighbor for his followers.

Space does not allow for a full discussion of the varieties of individualized pastoral practice during the Protestant Reformation. The directions set by Luther may, however, be considered normative for this period of pastoral care history. As the contemporary theologian Theodore W. Jennings, Jr., has said, "Luther's famous dicta:

'that upon which your heart depends, that is your God' and 'faith alone creates both God and idol' may serve as the watchwords of modern theology in its turn to the experience of the individual as the new correlate of a doctrine of God."[22]

It should be remembered that the shift toward greater emphasis on the individual pursuit of salvation and direct relationship of the believer with God was not confined to Protestantism. This was also the time of Ignatius of Loyola, founder of the Society of Jesus and writer of the still widely followed *Spiritual Exercises*. Somewhat earlier, but in roughly the same historical period, Thomas à Kempis wrote his *Imitation of Christ*.

Both these Roman Catholic spiritual leaders attracted wide followings; both likewise placed primary emphasis on the quest of the individual soul for union with God, though they did so within a contemplative, communal structure. Thus, in contrast to the early Middle Ages, during the Reformation a spirit of humanism and individualism gained ascendance in both religious life generally and pastoral practice specifically.

It is important that we who practice pastoral care at the end of the twentieth century appropriate carefully the heritage we have received from the Protestant Reformation. Several issues being widely debated in contemporary pastoral care circles have their roots, or at least close parallels, in the Reformation period of pastoral care's history. For one, our own time, like the fifteenth and sixteenth centuries, is a time of conflict and tension between the priorities of individualism and the need for corporate or communal ordering of life. Although it would be unwise to locate all the roots of modern individualism in the Reformation, that period does seem to have played an important role in initiating the individualism that looms so large in Western culture. As I shall discuss more fully in the next chapter, pastoral care practices of the recent past have reflected an individualistic emphasis. We can easily recognize the need for greater attention to the Christian community and to the support of individual life by consensual, corporate models of values and purposes. Though it takes a different shape with changed conditions, the issue of pastoral care as authority of ecclesiastical, corporate structures versus pastoral care as a private relationship between a pastor and seeker remains for us a lively one indeed.

A second contemporary issue with roots in the Reformation is the question of where we place our focus. Should we concentrate on the salvation of individual souls, or on the care of those who suffer under the conditions of the times? Should the primary pastoral concern be with spiritual direction toward a salvific experience of close relationship with God, or should the primary pastoral concern be with what Luther called "the duties of humanity"—the care of the sick and the relief of the downtrodden?

A third contemporary issue with roots in the Reformation was the age-old issue of discipline. To a large degree pastoral practices prior to the Reformation had been built around the commonly held understanding that the priest as pastor is primarily an administrator of discipline by which individual believers either remain within the community of faith or are excluded from it. The Reformers strongly disputed the pastoral practices that had developed out of this paradigm of pastoral authority. With the Reformation, a pattern of mutual discipline by means of small-group interaction began to take shape in Protestant churches, particularly through the work of Martin Bucer. This pattern was later elaborated considerably by John Wesley, who created the unique system of class meetings for the mutual edification and discipline of his followers.

Over the centuries since Luther's time, the practice of pastoral care as discipline has dwindled until now in the practice of most Protestant and Catholic pastors it takes place only indirectly, certainly with less power to influence or exclude. Small groups within the churches are now seen more often as mutual support groups than as instruments of the administration of church discipline.

We who practice pastoral care are left with difficult questions as to how and to what extent our ministry is to assist people in the ordering of their lives and their relationship to the community of faith and its doctrines. Is pastoral care as discipline a lost art? Should discipline be restored to pastoral care practice?[23]

The Enlightenment

Our tour of the history of pastoral care comes now to the time that is most often associated with the beginnings of modernity—the Enlightenment. The Enlightenment was an age marked by the rise of secularism: the belief that human history as well as contemporary life can be understood without speaking of God or assuming divine activity in human affairs. The West's turn in this direction probably had its beginnings in the seventeenth century, though the origins of the Enlightenment, are more often associated with the rise of a European philosophical movement during the eighteenth century. The turn was marked by basic trust in human rationality, enthusiasm for the possibilities of human learning, and confidence in empirical methods of discerning truth.

As they were in earlier periods of history, practices of pastoral care were profoundly influenced by the spirit and assumptions of this time. The care of the tradition itself turned in rationalistic directions. Proofs for the existence of God were sought on rational, even empirical grounds. The contest between revealed theology and empirical science began.

In response to this new age of human thought and practice, pastoral care practices likewise opened a pathway toward a more scientific "practical" mode of operation. Among the writings that developed these new ways of understanding the work of the pastor, none was more influential than *The Reformed Pastor*, published in 1656 by Richard Baxter, an English Presbyterian pastor.

Like other pastoral literature of this period, such as John Bunyan's *Pilgrim's Progress* (1678), Baxter's book focuses on two primary concerns: sustaining people through the difficulties and pitfalls of earthly life in the quest for eternal salvation, and upholding personal morality. Diligent in his efforts to know and guide his people, Baxter made a practice of spending several hours with each family in his parish at least once a year. During his visits he vigorously pursued these two concerns. Writing of this pastoral activity, Baxter said:

> We must labour to be acquainted with the state of all our people as fully as we can; both to know the persons, and their inclinations and conversations; to know what are the sins that they are most in danger of, and what duties they neglect for the matter or the manner, and what temptations they are most liable to. For if we know not the temperament or disease, we are likely to prove but unsuccessful physicians.[24]

Baxter's ministry embodied three fundamental purposes: (1) to know the spiritual health of his people; (2) to reveal to persons the source of their true happiness, their chief good; and (3) to acquaint them with the proper means for attaining their true happiness and to prevent their pursuit of wrong ways of living. Baxter advocated and practiced faithfully giving special attention to the care of the physically sick and the dying. His intention was to offer the support of godly ministry in times of trouble and to prepare persons to face the ultimate transition into immortality.

In Baxter we can see the continuation of many of the primary themes of Reformation pastoral care. Like the Reformers, Baxter searched for new ways of resolving the problem of pastoral care as discipline. His care was directed toward the preservation of the faith among the people, countering the secularizing tendency of the times. Discipline, for him and other pastoral leaders of the time, sought to recover the morality deeply embedded in the Christian heritage from its Jewish origins. Pastoral care in fundamental ways meant care for the moral life of the people.

Though the work of Richard Baxter is prototypical for pastoral care practice during the time of transition toward modernity, other variations on his themes can be found in English-speaking Puritanism, classical Protestantism among Lutheran, Reformed, and Anglican communions, as well as German Pietism. German Pietists sought the same ends as Baxter by inducing a " 'religion of the heart' whereby the soul might find refuge from attacks upon traditional Christian dogma."[25]

We have much to learn from Richard Baxter. He modeled for us the fundamental importance of the pastor's intimate relationship with persons, and the necessity of knowing the details of people's struggle with living. From him we receive a strong admonition to treat our everyday relationships with great seriousness, shunning the temptation to allow those relationships to become simply casual and social.

Baxter also emphasized relationships within the family. His systematic, announced, and seriously undertaken annual pastoral "check-up" visit with each family in his parish is a model that might well be emulated by contemporary pastors who wish to keep in touch with the real life of their congregation. Many of the tools of family dynamics observation and family systems theory that we have readily available for our use were not available to Baxter. His profound concern for his people's spiritual welfare, however, is excellent motivation for contemporary pastors.

From Baxter and other pastoral leaders of this period we also receive an important model of moral and ethical concern. In many ways they combined the ancient priestly, prophetic, and wisdom roles of the pastor by being acutely sensitive to the issues of morality in the lives of those in their care. They certainly were not value-neutral in their pastoral work. Nondirection was not their method of relationship! As a matter of fact, they sought to become experts in giving advice as well as in directing the spiritual life of their parishioners. We who practice ministry today will find our modes of relationship tempered considerably by our more recent heritage from the pastoral care leaders of the mid-twentieth century. From Baxter and his cohorts, however, we might well learn to keep central in our pastoral work a concern for what truly makes possible the good and moral life.

The Age of Voluntarism and Religious Privatism

As the years following the Enlightenment unfolded, the trends begun in the period following the Reformation, now accompanied by the rationalism and secularism of the Enlightenment, created an atmosphere conducive to voluntary participation in church life and thus to religious privatism. By the beginning of the nineteenth century even such a potent theological voice as that of Friedrich Schleiermacher advocated a separation of human social affairs into public and private spheres and placed the life of faith and religious practice within the private sphere.[26]

Particularly in America, but also to a degree in Britain and Europe, the dominance of the established churches linked to state support and control gave way to religious pluralism and church structures organized as voluntary associations. The leap from the church of the Middle Ages as official arbiter of cultural values for the society to the church as private community made up of volunteer believer participants had been completed.

This turn toward voluntarism and the privatization of religious life had profound effects upon the commonly understood role and function of pastoral care in the churches. The role of pastoral care as discipline relative to the control of belief and behavior greatly diminished and in its place the roles of pastoral care as call to conversion and nurture of the religious life were greatly enhanced. The nineteenth century thus became a time of experimentation in pastoral practice. In America in particular new modes of pastoral practice were needed to fit the changed cultural atmosphere as well as the changing social environment of a frontier society now organizing into towns and cities.

As E. Brooks Holifield suggests in his *History of Pastoral Care in America*, a prototypical pastoral figure of this period was perhaps the Reverend Ichabod Spencer, who in 1850 published his *Pastor's Sketches*. A pastor in Brooklyn, Spencer wrote about his conversations with what he called "anxious inquirers." Holifield writes of Spencer's second edition of his *Sketches*:

> Spencer was cautious and even somewhat defensive. . . . Not everyone would approve of his mode of conversation, he wrote. But he assured his readers that he never had knowingly uttered a single sentence that would "wound the feelings." Some expressions might "sound abrupt, and perhaps *severe*," but surely none could be "found offensive to refined taste." His goal had simply been "to cause the *truth* to be understood." Spencer's defense of his conversational method embodied both a presupposition and a problem that typified the cure of souls in antebellum America. The presupposition was that the pastor, in appealing to the will, would accord proper weight to both rationality and sentiment. The problem was in determining how to insist on "truth" while deferring to refined taste.[27]

In Holifield's interpretation of Ichabod Spencer's struggle to find a mode of pastoral care appropriate to religious life in the nineteenth century we can detect significant changes from the situation as Richard Baxter perceived it in 1656. With the volunteer Christian, Spencer felt he must be much more concerned not to offend, while yet trying to speak the truth. By 1850, his authority to command or admonish had diminished. Yet his pastoral concern remained very much the same. He wanted to guide the "anxious" soul through the vicissitudes of living while sustaining the person's relationship to the faith tradition and its worshiping community. He also wanted to share his concern for morality. But he must do it with careful attention to "sentiment." In short, he must become more psychologically astute than had been thought necessary by his predecessors.

It may be useful to reflect on Spencer's pastoral care situation within the structure of pastoral reflection of figure 2. Within that structure we can see that Spencer's care for the tradition as well as his care for the individual to whom he was relating had now to be balanced in new ways, because the community of Christians now understood itself as a group of volunteer participants, each of whom could make a culturally approved decision to take his or her religious practice elsewhere. Likewise, we can see that all three of these pastoral care concerns—tradition, the individual, and the community—were being greatly influenced by the sociocultural situation of the time. Little wonder that Spencer was anxious and somewhat defensive!

According to Holifield, the privatism of the nineteenth century saw the development of a growing interest in self-culture: "The properly balanced self in which the will, the intellect, and the affections moved in harmonious unity."[28] With this development, pastoral care practitioners became even more concerned for the psychological processes by which the self could simultaneously achieve a healthy, balanced sense of self and an experience of salvation. Holifield cites William Ellery Channing as a prime example of this popular mode of pastoral care practice:

> Channing affirmed a continuity between self-culture—the unfolding of one's powers and capacities—and salvation: He finally decided that the "essence of the Christian religion" was God's perfecting our nature "in a career of endless improvement." For Channing, such a process was "the only true good."[29]

With the primary purpose of pastoral care practice becoming the fostering of the culture of the self, the way was opened toward the full-blown appropriation of the rapidly developing psychological sciences. To be sure, there were important transitions yet to be made after the work of William Ellery Channing. By the end of the nineteenth century, two highly significant developments had taken place: one in the style of pastoral presence, and the other in the style of congregational life. In Holifield's interpretation, a virtual cult of vitality—a "muscular Christianity"—took hold of pastoral leadership. This matched the virility of the so-called captains of industry who were becoming the American nation's heroes. Christianity was promoted by its "princes of the pulpit" as a source of power for living. Controversies developed among pastoral leaders over the question of the manly appropriateness of quiet interviews with parishioners. Stout defense of this practice was mounted on the grounds that such conversations fostered the appropriation of Christianity's power for living.[30]

A second development that transformed the context of the church's caring ministry took place within the life of the congregation. Symbolic of that transformation was the coming into vogue of the church parlor. Churches that had previously been primarily centers for worship and evangelism now became centers for community social life. Church facilities were built to house "Sunday school concerts, church socials, women's meetings, youth groups, boys' brigades, girls' guilds, singing classes, reforming societies, and a host of other organizations and activities." The place of gathering for the community of faith became the social center of many communities in America.[31]

Those who tend to think of the development of a psychology of pastoral care as a twentieth-century innovation should remember that this trend has deeper and more complex cultural roots. Interest in psychology on the part of priests and pastors goes back a long way, probably at least to the time of John Chrysostom's interest in the psychology of the Greek Stoics. But with the arrival of the age of voluntarism and its accompanying tendency toward privatism, concern for the psychological implications of pastoral ministry took on greater importance. Thus the developments we shall be reviewing in the next chapter regarding the renaissance of pastoral care through the influence of modern psychology should be seen not so much as brand new innovations as continuations of a trend that began at least two hundred years ago. They are in large part a natural outgrowth of the turn toward the privatization of religion.

The resurgence of interest in the life of the congregation as a community of people who care for one another and for their community likewise has roots in the altered situation of the churches that came with the separation of human affairs into public and private spheres. With those changes the authority of the clergy had to change, and the mutual care of Christians took on a different cast. As a result, *pastoral* care now needs to be considered from a larger perspective. It involves the care of the entire community of faith. Within that perspective, pastoral care as the work of the ordained pastor includes the task of pastoral leadership as well as the individual caring work of the pastor.

The story of pastoral care is indeed a long one with chapters that unfold alongside and within the larger history of the church in the world. In this chapter we have made a quick tour of the long ages of that history, leading to an important resurgence of pastoral care in the twentieth century.

CHAPTER 2

Pastoral Care in the Twentieth Century

Having hopped and skipped rather hastily through more than twenty centuries of pastoral care history in the preceding chapter, we come now to the task of reflecting on the groundbreaking developments that have taken place in pastoral care practice during the twentieth century. This is the story of our most immediate ancestors and their contributions to the pastoral care tradition. They are the persons who have shaped pastoral care as we know it today. In significant ways many of their contributions have become normative for pastoral practice and thus not only set standards by which good pastoral care is measured, but also provide us with many of the basic tools and methods of pastoral care. Though the fundamental commitments to Christian ministry of the pastors we shall discuss in this chapter are in deep continuity with those of the historic figures discussed in chapter 1, they are people of the twentieth century whose consciousness and perceptions of human needs have been shaped by the consciousness and concerns of their culture.

The Turn of the Century: The Psychology of Religion Movement

The most significant developments in pastoral care at the beginning of the twentieth century were in continuity with the turn toward the self that emerged from the rapidly developing privatization of religion in the nineteenth-century West. Religion had become closely associated with self-development. This was the case whether one found affinity with mainline liberal theology, an evangelical theology of salvation by acceptance of Christ as personal Savior, or the moral honing of the self by means of pietistic holiness practices.

Brooks Holifield says of this period, speaking particularly of main-line liberals, that pastoral leaders "concluded that the key to unlocking the mysteries of religion and reality was 'in ourselves.' "[1]

This was also the time of the beginnings of modern psychological science, both in Europe and in America. Wilhelm Wundt established the first psychological laboratory in Europe in 1879 to do basic physiological studies of human mental states following what was termed a structuralist scientific approach. In America, William James began his more functionalist approach to psychological research at about the same time. Soon after that, James combined his interests in functional psychology and in religious experience; in 1902 he published his widely read and influential *Varieties of Religious Experience*.[2] James was soon joined by other psychologists with primary interest in the psychology of religious development: among them G. Stanley Hall, James Leuba, E. D. Starbuck, and later the American pioneer in religious education, George Albert Coe.[3]

Although neither William James nor the other turn-of-the-century psychologists of religion were themselves directly concerned with pastoral care practice as such, their interests being more directed toward the psychology of religious development, their widely read works had considerable influence in further pointing pastoral practice in a psychological direction. Scientific psychology became, particularly for theological liberals, a primary partner in assisting pastors to respond to the culturally shaped concern for the religious development of the self. With the passage of time, the psychology of religion movement waned; however, as we shall see, these psychologists of religion later had great influence on Anton T. Boisen, the man who is often referred to as the father of modern twentieth-century pastoral care.

The Turn of the Century:
The Self and the Recovery of Pastoral Healing

As we saw earlier, the emphasis during the medieval period on pastoral healing faded from the center of attention with the coming of the Protestant Reformation. Reconciling the individual soul to God and neighbor moved to the forefront of the Reformed pastor's attention, although there is also evidence that Reformed pastors worked with small groups and engaged some of the serious social problems of the times. In later epochs an emphasis on the reconciliation of individuals was joined by a preoccupying concern for sustaining the life of the spirit during the rapid changes of the Enlightenment and later the movement toward privatism. However, with psychological science's move to the forefront of pastoral attention at the beginning of the twentieth century came a renewed interest in pastoral healing. Psychology, particularly psychology seen as therapy for the beleaguered self, offered the possibility of enhancing pastoral ability to minister to troubled persons in Christian congregations.

The organization that pioneered the development of this new form of pastoral healing in America was founded by the Reverend Elwood Worcester in Emmanuel Church in Boston between 1904 and 1906, and thus it became widely known as the Emmanuel movement. Worcester was an Episcopal priest who, after graduating in only one year from General Seminary in New York, went to Germany and studied with both Wilhelm Wundt and Wundt's teacher, Gustav Fechner, the founder of physiological psychology. After returning to the United States and becoming rector of Emmanuel Church in 1904, Worcester, impressed and yet deeply troubled by the rapid growth of Christian Science in New England, in 1906 arranged for two psychiatrists to join him in making themselves available at the parish house to consult with anyone needing assistance with nervous or spiritual disorders. To the organizers' great surprise, 198 people came to the first session! Thus began a movement that joined the efforts and expertise of pastoral care practitioners and psychologically oriented physicians in response to people with all manner of functional ailments, from hysteria and hypochondria to alcoholism and moral and spiritual difficulties. The movement soon spread to churches of other, largely mainline liberal denominations as a significant joint activity between medicine and religion, physicians and pastors. The movement flourished through the first twenty years of the twentieth century, but began to wane by 1930 and was dead by 1940.[4] The model of theoretical and practical collaboration in the art of healing of sick and troubled persons, however, became an important one that set a direction for pastoral care practice for decades.

Freud and the Influence of Freudian Psychoanalysis

The late nineteenth century was not only a time of rapidly developing new approaches to human psychology emanating from the laboratories of physiological psychologists and from the more functionalist studies of William James; it was also the period during which Sigmund Freud began his work in Vienna. In the beginning Freud too intended to develop a physiological, even mechanically anatomical grounding for new discoveries about human psychology. Soon, however, his thought turned in a more mental, experiential direction. With the publication of *Interpretation of Dreams* Freud turned his thoughts firmly toward what he hoped would be a complete explanation of the emotional life of persons.

Although Freud himself disdained any interest in religion except as it represented what in Freud's understanding was a cultural neurosis, his work soon began to attract the attention of clergy, both in Europe and America. Oskar Pfister, a Swiss pastor, carried on a lively correspondence with Freud concerning his efforts to develop a psychoanalytically oriented style of pastoral care. Pfister worked to bring together the cathartic powers of psychoanalysis with the healing power of religion to the end of enhancing human development.[5]

In North America, Freud's psychoanalysis drew the attention of both the leaders of the Emmanuel movement and the psychologists of religion. By 1909, Worcester, the Emmanuel movement's founder, announced that he and others associated with the movement had aligned themselves with Freud's theories. In 1909, G. Stanley Hall, president of Clark University and the leading organizer of the psychology of religion movement in the United States, brought Freud to Clark to lecture on psychoanalysis. That event, together with widely publicized lectures in a number of churches on psychoanalysis by the psychiatrist A. A. Brill, brought Freud's work to the center of attention of those who were in the forefront of the psychological renewal of pastoral care in the United States.

As we shall see when we discuss the development of the clinical pastoral education movement, Freudian psychoanalysis continued to have a major influence on the establishment of pastoral care as a psychologically oriented discipline through the early and middle twentieth century, as it does even today. Its foundational status, however, met a number of important challenges from other perspectives.

The Social Gospel Movement

In chapter 1, we schematized pastoral care as a quadrilateral structure involving care of the tradition, care of the culture, care of the individual, and care of the gathered community of Christians (see figure 2, chapter 1). The Freudian thrust of pastoral psychology, as evidenced by the Emmanuel movement, strongly emphasized the individual component of our quadrilateral schema. Psychoanalysis gave pastoral practice a strong nudge in the direction of individual psychopathology, the care of sick souls. What was happening to the other dimensions of pastoral care practice during this period? Freud's psychoanalytic studies of culture seem to have been largely overlooked by the Emmanuel movement. What then about the care of the community and the society?

One answer to that question may be found in what came to be called the Social Gospel movement, whose development closely paralleled that of the Emmanuel movement. Both movements had their origins in the rise of the social sciences during the latter half of the nineteenth century and the accompanying developments in theological liberalism. There was one primary difference between the two movements, which caused them to go in quite different directions. Whereas the Emmanuel movement, along with the psychologists of religion, found its primary social scientific partnership with psychology, the Social Gospel movement was prompted by a developing dialogue with sociology. One might even say that, whereas the Emmanuel movement psychologized the gospel to the end of transforming the cure of souls into a scientific pastoral therapy, the Social Gospel movement sociologized the gospel to the end of transforming Christian social ethics into a scientific cure for society's ills.

From a somewhat different standpoint, we may say that whereas the adherents of the Emmanuel movement embraced the dominant individualism of their time, adherents of the Social Gospel movement sought to stand over against individualism and uncover the social ills that it caused. Impressed with the manner in which the prevailing social system, individual capitalism, tended to create two classes—the haves and the have-nots—the proponents of the Social Gospel movement railed against the injustices of social life and advocated the transformation of social reality. As Josiah Strong wrote in 1893:

> Our existing social system . . . is destined to undergo great changes before the sociological problems of the age are solved. And as their solution must come through the application of Christ's teachings, this surely is the opportunity of the centuries for the church to mold the civilization of the future by taking to heart the teachings of her Lord in all their fullness. The conversion of the church to Christian theory must precede the conversion of the world to Christian practice.[6]

This statement, which places Strong in the center of the developing Social Gospel movement, reveals two things about the movement. First, it reflects the influence of theological liberalism's hope for the progressive realization of the kingdom of God through human efforts to apply Jesus' teachings to human affairs. Second, it reflects the influence of a sociology that came to be called a Christian socialism. From the vantage of historical distance, the Social Gospel movement thus appears to be characterized by a robust Christianity similar to that evidenced by turn-of-the-century pastors who sought to enhance the psychological development of their parishioners. Whereas the pastoral psychologists emphasized the grace and empowerment of God for human individual development, the Social Gospel movement's proponents emphasized God's justice and the social workability of the teachings of Jesus.

The most brilliant spokesperson of the Social Gospel movement was Walter Rauschenbusch, who as a young pastor served a struggling congregation on the edge of Hell's Kitchen in New York City. There Rauschenbusch was deeply impressed with the insecurity, unemployment, abject poverty, malnutrition, and crime that beset his congregation. This experience caused him to turn his pastoral attention to social transformation linked theologically to the biblical image of the kingdom of God. He later wrote:

So Christ's conception of the kingdom of God came to me as a new revelation. Here was the idea and purpose that dominated the mind of the Master himself. All his teachings center about it. His life was given to it. His death was suffered for it. . . .

But in addition I found that this new conception of the purpose of Christianity was strangely satisfying. It responded to all the old and all the new elements of my religious life. The saving of the lost, the teaching of the young, the pastoral care of the poor and frail, the quickening of starved intellects, the study of the Bible, church union, political reform, the reorganization of the industrial system, international peace—it was all covered by the one aim of the reign of God on earth.[7]

For Rauschenbusch and the other social gospel advocates, the care of the church for persons like those caught in the traps of the Hell's Kitchens of the world meant more than simply care for individuals. It meant mustering all forces possible to attack the social structures that created poverty and injustice. It meant caring for the larger world of human affairs by the application of Christian social principles. They thus did not speak much about pastoral care as such, but rather of the transformation of society through the leadership of the church. Their aims were social, not psychological.

To be sure, not all the pastors devoted to the Social Gospel movement were primarily social critics. Some sought to combine their concern for society's ills with a more individual approach to pastoral practice. Charles Sheldon, a Congregational pastor in Kansas, became famous following the publication of his book *In His Steps* in 1897. In this rather simple novel Sheldon attempted to portray what could happen to very ordinary people if before every significant choice or action they asked themselves, "What would Jesus do?" The book became highly popular, so much so that by 1933, Sheldon estimated that 23 million copies had been sold, though Sheldon had sold the rights to the novel for a paltry seventy-five dollars at the time of its first publication.[8] As of this writing the book is still in print; it clearly still holds significant popular appeal nearly a hundred years after its first appearance.

Looking back, we can only lament the apparent separation that took place between the turn-of-the-century pastors who had discovered psychological science and those who were attracted by scientific sociology. Had they not gone their separate ways, the history of pastoral care in the twentieth century might have been very different. The vast and fruitful influence of psychology on pastoral care practice might not have been diminished so as to lose what was gained by the appropriation of psychology's insights. Its individualistic dominance over pastoral care's practices during the middle decades of this century might well, however, have been tempered by the attention to social dimensions of the human condition that were so forcefully, albeit perhaps too optimistically, expressed by social gospel adherents. As we shall see, however, the issues that surround this separation between pastoral psychology and societal transformation do not disappear but continue to be important matters of wrenching concern for pastoral practice in our own time.

The mood of optimism to which I have referred, fueled by the immanentism of liberal theology, permeated both the pastoral psychology and social reform movements during the first several decades of the twentieth century. As Holifield noted in his history of this period, the code word was *adjustment*, a term that bore the imprint of the thought of John Dewey. Pastoral psychologists worked to assist persons to *adjust* to a complicated environment. Social reformers worked to reform the churches and other social institutions in order to better *adjust* them to the needs of the people.[9]

Anton Boisen and the Beginnings of the Clinical Pastoral Education Movement

By the 1920s all three of the movements that had shaped pastoral practice during the transition from the nineteenth to the twentieth centuries—the Emmanuel movement, the Social Gospel movement, and the movement to develop a scientific psychology of religion—had begun to wane. Theological liberalism was also beginning to experience difficulties with the rise of what came to be called neoorthodoxy—a critique of liberalism's immanentism and a response to the brutal realities of world war and the oppression ushered in by the twentieth century. With the publication of Karl Barth's commentary on Romans in 1918, the care of the tradition within the mainline churches took a turn away from liberalism's optimism and idealism toward a darker, more sober concern with human sinfulness and need of salvation from outside the self. Neoorthodox theologians such as Barth and, later, Tillich, Bonhoeffer, and the Niebuhrs, believed that only a return to the theology of the Reformation and the Bible could offer a realistic Christian understanding of God and human life.[10]

In the midst of this transition arose a new development within the field of pastoral care that was to have a monumental impact on the caring practices of the churches for decades and remain a significant factor in determining the scope and methods of pastoral care right up to the present time. It had its beginnings in the tortured but creative mind of one man, though there were numerous others who shared similar interests and thus supported the development of a movement that gathered momentum during the decades of the 1920s to the 1960s.

Anton T. Boisen, generally recognized as the founder of what came to be called clinical pastoral education, was a Congregational-ist pastor who, having been unsuccessful in several rural pastorates, suffered an acute mental illness resulting in his hospitalization in a Massachusetts state psychiatric hospital. Boisen emerged from his psychotic illness with two deep convictions that gave to his disor-ganized life a powerful and persistent sense of mission. Boisen believed that he had undergone a profound religious experience in his battle with mental illness and thus that there was an equally profound connection between religious conversion and mental an-guish. That connection needed somehow to be researched and brought into dialogue with theological inquiry. He likewise believed that the church had badly neglected its ministry to mentally suffer-ing people and that his own future ministry should be among his fellow sufferers.

Supported by Richard Cabot, a prominent Boston physician and churchman, and others primarily within theological education, Boisen was appointed as chaplain of Worcester State Hospital in Massachusetts and was able in 1925 to bring the first of a number of small groups of theological students to the hospital to study with him. In this position he developed his case-study method of research and teaching that became the prevailing model of inquiry in the new movement, though it was later supplemented with the use of so-called verbatim reports of conversations between pastoral care students and those for whom they were seeking to care.

Boisen and Cabot eventually parted ways over the issue of Boisen's psychological views of psychotic experience. Cabot held to a strictly organic view of mental illness; he eventually withdrew his support of Boisen's work over this issue and instead invested his interest in pastoral training at Massachusetts General Hospital, where pastoral students focused their ministry on the care of physically ill patients. Subsequently Boisen, after another painful psychotic episode, moved his work to Elgin State Hospital in Illinois, where he continued his work with students from Chicago Theological Seminary.

From this beginning, the clinical pastoral education movement spread across the United States and later throughout the world as a generally accepted, standard approach for the socialization of clergy into the role of pastoral care with not only sick and troubled persons, but also with prisoners, the aging, children and youth, and others with particular needs for pastoral care. Boisen's students soon took clinical pastoral training to other psychiatric and correctional institutions across the country. Meanwhile, the work Cabot had begun at Massachusetts General Hospital developed into a close-knit network of training programs in medical centers in New England. Two organizations were formed around these two models of clinical education: the Council for Clinical Training (the group emanating from Boisen's work, focused primarily on psychiatry and pastoral care) and the Institute of Pastoral Care (the New England group, focused at first primarily on pastoral care of the physically ill, though later including psychiatric and other forms of human difficulty). Much later, in the 1960s the two groups finally united, along with similar groups founded by Lutheran and Southern Baptist pastoral supervisors, to form the Association for Clinical Pastoral Education.

Before moving on to discuss the insights and methodologies that sprang from the clinical pastoral education movement, it is important to pause to recognize Boisen as a significant transitional figure in the history of pastoral care. Although his theological training had been at Union Seminary in New York, his theological proclivities had more affinity with the empirical school of liberal theology developing during his time at Chicago Theological Seminary. He desired to apply empirical methods of research to the study of religious conversion and mental illness. Thus, although he was a theological liberal who in significant ways stood over against re-formed theology's biblicism and return to the historical documents, he rejected the optimism and progressivism of much of early-twentieth-century liberalism as found in the Social Gospel move-ment. Rather, he thought of his project as an empirical study of "sin and salvation."

In this regard, Boisen also had great affinity with earlier psycholo-gists of religion, most particularly with William James, who had also pursued his interest in the phenomenon of "twice-born" converts to religion. Yet Boisen was also in certain respects a social advocate, not simply a researcher. He argued vigorously for changes in the care of the mentally ill and in pastoral theological education. Often brood-ing and cantankerous in his relationships, he was preoccupied with his own and others' inability to "live up to the best." Thus he emphasized concerns about human failure not unlike those of the emerging neoorthodox theologians.

Clinical Pastoral Education Comes to Maturity

The decades of the 1930s and 1940s were increasingly a time of growth of the clinical pastoral education movement, leading up to its maturation during the 1950s and 1960s as a dominating force in pastoral care education within and outside the theological schools. At the beginning of the 1930s the psychology of adjustment still dominated most pastoral care literature. What pastoral care teaching occurred in the seminaries was done primarily by religious educa-tion professors whose interest in psychological development in-cluded adjustment theories.

The Freudian influence on pastoral care theory was just beginning in the early thirties, but that was to change significantly by the end of the decade. In 1936 Boisen published his *Exploration of the Inner World*, the result of his reflection on his own life experience and his study of psychopathological religious experience among the men-tally ill.[11] Though Boisen had misgivings about Freud's emphasis on sexual dynamics, feeling that emphasis too short-sighted and lack-ing in concern for moral issues, much of Freud's theory of the nature of unconscious conflict fit with Boisen's focus on the inner life of the individual. Boisen's students, who were then becoming leaders of the clinical pastoral education movement, embraced Freudianism much more enthusiastically, so much so that many of the clinical pastoral methods being taught in the clinical centers were heavily weighted toward Freudian theory. As might be expected, this was more true of the centers affiliated with the Boisen-originated "New York group" than it was of the medical hospital centers in and around Boston.

The year 1936 also saw the publication of *The Art of Ministering to the Sick,* by Richard Cabot and Russell Dicks, the first chaplain at Massachusetts General Hospital and the originator of the use of verbatim reports of pastoral conversations in clinical pastoral education.[12]

That book popularized the notion of a "growing edge" within individuals toward which the efforts of the pastor should be directed—a notion that, while echoing theological liberalism's optimism, later in the 1960s and 1970s developed into an important metaphor for many in the pastoral care field, most notably Howard Clinebell, who developed his highly popular theory of pastoral care and counseling around the primary metaphor of "growth counseling."[13]

In 1939 an early and widely read pastoral counseling text was written by Rollo May, a theologically trained psychologist who later became one of the exponents of "existential psychoanalysis." The book, *The Art of Counseling,* proposed a method of counseling that embodied certain of the insights of psychoanalysis blended with some of the practical suggestions then being made popular by the "mental hygiene" movement—mental hygiene being a loose term applied to the transitional emphases of the adjustment psychologies now being influenced by more dynamic psychological principles.[14]

The decade of the 1940s was an important time of establishment of pastoral care as a recognized member of the family of practical theological disciplines, particularly in the United States. The bases for this recognition and forward movement of specialized interest in the care of persons were several, the foremost being that this was a time when the mental health movement began to have an important impact on American culture generally. Psychiatry and psychology had become necessary and important societal responses to the countless psychological casualties of World War II and its aftermath. Pastoral care practitioners serving in military and civilian health facilities joined with other mental health professionals in response to this recognized need. Pastoral care began to be recognized as a specialized ministry to individuals in need of care of all sorts. On a wider scale, Freudianism was beginning to have a significant impact on the culture, particularly of the educated middle class in America. Parishioners in the mainline churches were beginning to expect that their pastors would not only be available to them to converse about their problems of living, but that they would be knowledgeable about the new understanding of human development and interpersonal relationships emanating from the Freudian cultural revolution quietly creeping across the land.

On another, more subtly theological level, particularly among some younger clergy, pastoral care was beginning to attract a renewal of theological interest in human religious experience. For some, this theological quest represented dissatisfaction with the radical transcendentalism of certain forms of neoorthodoxy that appeared to disdain any human capacity to transform life through the exercise of human powers. For others, it was simply a continuation of the pursuit of an essentially liberal approach to theological reflection. In either case, human experience, particularly human relational and developmental experience, was once again becoming a subject of theological fascination. Human pastoral experience likewise began to make gains in theological relevance.

Particularly in its methods of relating to individuals, the evolving clinical pastoral tradition was meanwhile beginning to appropriate a newly developing offshoot of psychotherapeutic psychology not connected to Freudianism. Its originator and chief spokesperson was the American phenomenological psychologist, Carl R. Rogers. Like Rollo May, Rogers had pursued theological training, but turned away from theology to receive a doctoral degree in academic psychology. In 1942 he published his widely acclaimed *Counseling and Psychotherapy*, the book in which he first proposed his "non-directive" method of counseling.[15] In 1951, Rogers slightly altered the terminology of his method to that of "client-centered therapy."[16] As both terms indicate, Rogers, not unlike the liberal theologians of the late nineteenth century described earlier in this chapter, believed that the solution to most of the human relational problems that beset persons under his care lay within the person's own self. The task of the psychological helper was to create a relational context within which those inner solutions could come forth and thus overcome the "subceptions" of the self that had been created by the insistent dominance of parental and other authoritative perceptions of self and reality over the individual's own "organismic responses." Reflective responses that encouraged the evocation of the troubled person's own perceptions, values, goals, and purposes were what was needed from the helping counselor or therapist.

Rogers' methods of counseling soon took hold in members of the budding clinical pastoral education movement, even though many, particularly of Boisen's followers, continued to utilize Freudian theory as their primary orientation to understanding the developmental dynamics of their own and their parishioners' and clients' problems of living.[17] Learning to make the nondirective response in pastoral conversations became the sine qua non of learning to give good pastoral care during this period. In large part that remained the case through the 1950s and much of the 1960s.

It is important to note that the clinical pastoral movement in the 1940s retained vigorously Boisen's commitment to prophetic ministry with regard to the care of persons who were being overlooked or neglected by the society of post–World War II ebullience. It was during this period that the prophetic dimension of the movement gathered to itself a wide range of concerns for differing forms of human difficulty. In hospitals and other medical centers it focused on a more empathic response to persons undergoing the crises of physical illness, death, and bereavement. In psychiatric and other mental health centers it sought a more humane and caring response to the victims of mental illness. In prisons and criminal justice centers it established ministry programs that avoided participation in the ethos of punishment, but rather sought to respond to the needs and concerns of those imprisoned. In these and other ways the emerging interest in pastoral care took hold of a primary criterion: pastoral care meant response to persons experiencing particular forms of human need.

The Academic Study of Pastoral Care and Counseling

Although to a considerable degree the clinical pastoral care movement received much of its initiative from outside the theological schools, by the latter half of the decade of the 1940s one by one the mainline Protestant seminaries in America began to establish departments of pastoral care or pastoral theology rooted in the developments that were taking place in the clinical centers. Four of these newly appointed pastoral care faculty members, each with primary academic training in other theological disciplines, pioneered in formulating basic academic texts for the newly recognized field of pastoral theology and ministry.

Paul Johnson, trained as a philosopher of religion in the Boston personalist school, became the first professor of psychology and pastoral counseling at Boston University. Johnson was an admirer of the turn-of-the-century psychologists of religion and in 1945 wrote his own version of religious psychology upon which much of his later work was built.[18] Johnson desired to combine his interest in personalist thought with his growing interest in Freudian psychology. This led him to extend his psychological interests in an interpersonal direction, making use of the ideas of the interpersonalist neo-Freudian Harry Stack Sullivan. In 1953 Johnson published his *Psychology of Pastoral Care*, a book widely read by pastors that drew heavily on Rogerian methodology. Later in the sixties, Johnson departed from his use of Rogers' nondirective techniques and sought rather to build a thoroughgoing interpersonal model of pastoral care grounded in personalist theology, dynamic interpersonal psychology, and the thought of Martin Buber.[19]

A second pioneer in the academic study of pastoral care, particularly as that study had to do with developing a practical theological grounding for pastoral practices, was Seward Hiltner. A student and admirer of Boisen, Hiltner had been one of the leaders in the clinical pastoral education movement during the 1930s, having been executive secretary of the Council for Clinical Training of Theological Students for several years. He then became executive secretary for pastoral services of the Federal Council of Churches, a position he held until becoming professor of pastoral theology at the University of Chicago in 1950, moving to Princeton Theological Seminary in

1961. Probably the most widely used pastoral care text during the decade of the 1950s was his *Pastoral Counseling*, published in 1949. Trained in theological ethics, Hiltner sought, like others of the time, to use Rogerian techniques while maintaining a steady eye on issues of ethical clarification and pastoral theological identity. In 1958, Hiltner produced his *Preface to Pastoral Theology* as the first comprehensive effort to establish a mode of theological reflection on the "operations" of the pastor with a view toward making a contribution to theological inquiry itself. It was Hiltner who formulated for pastoral care in the twentieth century the image of pastoral care as the fulfillment of the "shepherding" role of the pastor.[20]

Another of Boisen's early students who, while utilizing Rogerian counseling methods, made significant contributions to the now burgeoning mental health counseling movement, was Carroll A. Wise. Wise succeeded Boisen as chaplain at Worcester State Hospital in Massachusetts and earned his doctoral degree in theology from Boston University. Like Johnson, Wise was theologically oriented toward the personalist school. Not long after his service at Worcester State Hospital, Wise became a full-time pastoral counselor on the staff of a large Methodist church in Minneapolis, Minnesota. In 1947 he went to be the first professor of pastoral psychology and counseling at Garrett Biblical Institute in Evanston, Illinois.

Wise's two most influential books were his *Pastoral Counseling: Its Theory and Practice*, published in 1951 at the same time that Johnson and Hiltner brought forth their introductory texts, and *The Meaning of Pastoral Care*, published in 1966.[21] Wise sought diligently to combine a thoroughgoing Freudian dynamic psychology with an equally thorough immersion in Rogerian client-centered methodology. From a theological perspective, Wise argued that pastoral care is fundamentally relational and involves the "communication of the inner meaning of the Gospel to persons at the point of their need" by means of an accepting, caring relationship.[22] A leading critic of academic theology, Wise was primarily interested throughout his life in psychology and psychotherapy. He often crossed swords with Hiltner on these issues and was one of the founders of the American Association of Pastoral Counselors in the 1960s, a development Hiltner strongly opposed on the basis that pastoral counseling needed to be more closely tied to the work of the parish pastor.

For conservative, evangelical pastors, the primary spokesperson both academically and through his wide-ranging continuing education efforts with parish pastors was Wayne E. Oates, longtime professor of pastoral theology at Southern Baptist Theological Seminary. Somewhat less wed to Rogerian methodology than were other pastoral care writers of the time, Oates built his conception of pastoral care around the image of the caring pastor as representative of the care and acceptance of Christ for persons in need of the saving grace of God. The first of his many books, *The Christian Pastor*, came out in 1951. It underwent several revisions and is still widely read as a basic description of the caring role of the Christian pastor. In 1962 Oates published *Protestant Pastoral Counseling*, in which he formulated his understanding of pastoral counseling within the Protestant free church tradition.[23] Oates declared the defining marks of pastoral care to be theological: "An affirmation of the lordship of Christ, of the personal dialogue between Creator and creature, of the priesthood of all believers, and, above all, of the power of the Spirit." These criteria enabled Oates to draw freely from modern psychotherapeutic theories while modifying them to suit the pastoral context.[24]

From Europe arose another strongly theological perspective on pastoral care, this one in opposition to the prevailing interest in the psychological and psychotherapeutic sciences. This voice spoke powerfully out of the climate of neoorthodoxy that dominated European ministry theory during this period. In a widely read but highly controversial book published in English translation in 1962, Eduard Thurneysen, professor of practical theology at the University of Basel, Switzerland, proposed that pastoral care necessarily had to do with the explicit proclamation of the Christian gospel. Thurneysen left little room for the communication of Christian meanings through relationships that sought to embody those meanings. Rather, he likened the discipline of pastoral care to that of homiletics: it involved the speaking of explicit Christian language by the pastor in a one-to-one relationship. Thurneysen was well acquainted with Freudian and other depth psychological perspectives, but he thought that the utilization of psychotherapeutic techniques was only prefatory to the practice of pastoral care in its own specific Christian language.[25]

Pastoral care theorists and practitioners in America by and large rejected Thurneysen's point of view, instead building their theological connections by means of the symbolic representation of Christian meanings in the person of the pastor and in the manner of the pastor's relationships. Here the Rogerian concept of "unconditional positive regard" was often linked with such concepts as Paul Tillich's understanding of the gospel as God's acceptance of humans in spite of their unacceptability. American pastoral care practitioners of this period found Tillich's brand of existential neoorthodoxy more to their liking than the radical transcendentalism of Karl Barth.[26]

There was, however, one notable exception to this majority American opinion concerning Barthian neoorthodox theology and pastoral care. The pastoral theologian Thomas Oden, in two books published in the mid-1960s, attempted to correlate Barthian theology with Rogerian psychotherapy. He asserted that the Christian kerygma is "implicit" in the atmosphere of acceptance created by the Rogerian therapist, but that it can only be made explicit and thus clearly known through revelation as understood by Barth and his neoorthodox followers.[27]

Post-Rogerian Pastoral Care

If the thirty-five years from 1930 to 1965 were the years in which the leaders of the clinical pastoral movement strove to appropriate Freudian and neo-Freudian dynamic psychology and integrate those insights with the nondirective methods emanating from Carl Rogers, the years after 1965 were years in which pastoral care teachers and practitioners sought to adopt a virtual plethora of methods that became available on the psychotherapeutic market. Family therapy, transactional analysis, reality therapy, cognitive therapy, the logotherapy of Viktor Frankl, the gestalt therapy of Fritz Perls, and numerous other therapeutic modalities came into being and were presented as modes of therapeutic response to human relational difficulties. Not surprisingly, this was also the time in which pastoral counseling as a specialized form of ministry apart from parish pastoral care took form and was organized as a professional guild, the American Association of Pastoral Counselors.

The undoubted leader in the movement within pastoral care to adopt these new resources for their use by clergy was Howard Clinebell, professor of pastoral counseling at Claremont School of

Theology and the first president of the new association of pastoral counselors. Asserting that although much had been gained for the work of pastors with troubled persons during the Rogerian period, the nondirective method remained too passive to meet the needs pastors encountered. Clinebell proposed that pastors needed to learn to be more versatile. In his highly popular *Basic Types of Pastoral Care and Counseling,* Clinebell proceeded to do just that.[28]

With chapters on a variety of approaches to differing problems, such as "supportive care and counseling," "bereavement care and counseling," "marriage enrichment and marriage crisis counseling," "referral counseling," and "pastoral psychotherapy," Clinebell offered a toolbox approach that invited pastors to select the proper type of counseling to fit the particular human problem at hand. Learning to do competent pastoral care, under Clinebell's tutelage, meant learning to make a careful diagnosis and then utilize the technique that best fit that type of problem. Most of these techniques were drawn from the standard secular therapies available at the time.

The organizing theme for Clinebell's approach was *growth*. Pastoral care represents the pastor's effort to assist people to grow personally, relationally, and spiritually. Although Clinebell did not delve deeply into the theological grounding for his approach, a careful reading of his work uncovers echoes not only of the 1930s theme of the "growing edge," but also of the optimism and progressiveness of the theological liberalism of the turn of the century. In the 1984 revision of his *Basic Types of Pastoral Care and Counseling,* Clinebell sought to relate his conception of growth counseling to liberation and feminist theology, though the themes of progressivism and human potential for growth remained at the center of his thought.

Pastoral Care in the 1970s and 1980s:
Counsel for the Individual or
Care for the Community and Its Tradition?

To understand what was taking place in the continued growth of the pastoral care tradition during the 1970s and 1980s, we need to return to the structure of analysis of pastoral care's history formulated in chapter 1: the quadrilateral structure of care of the tradition,

71

care of the culture, care of the individual, and care of the Christian community. Important and sometimes contradictory developments were taking place in each of these arenas that made for a time of sometimes confused, often conflicting, but nevertheless promising epigenesis of the pastoral care movement.

At the level of the care of the individual, particularly as in the recent past, the individual with some special need for expert care, a broad range of developments was taking place, each producing a literature of practical, methodological suggestions for use by pastors and lay counselors. Books came forth about how to do grief ministry or ministry to the dying, pastoral care of youth and the aging, the care of AIDS victims, how to relate to victims of spousal and child abuse, the care of substance abusers and their families, and many other specialized situations of need that come to the attention of the pastor. As was the case earlier with Howard Clinebell's *Basic Types of Pastoral Care and Counseling*, most of these books and journal articles sought to make available to pastors the results of developments in the secular helping professions. Thus, most gave only cursory attention to issues of the theological grounding for pastoral care, choosing rather to focus simply on practical matters of diagnosis and ways of providing psychologically informed care. Parish ministers interested in enhancing their skills in the care of persons with special needs in their congregation turned to these "how-to" books for practical guidance in their ministries.

Meanwhile, still at the level of the care of the individual, the specialization of pastoral counseling was proceeding apace. The movement to establish pastoral counseling centers grew rapidly, some sponsored by individual parishes or groups of churches, some developed as church-oriented nonprofit community agencies, still others as affiliates of a franchised "chain" of community-based centers. Some of these centers took form as loosely structured inter-disciplinary programs variously involving the cooperative efforts of pastoral counselors, psychologists, social workers, family therapists, or physicians. Others employed only appropriately certified pastoral counseling specialists, many of whom sought credentialing not only as pastoral counselors, but also as family therapists or psychologists. Though it was by no means unanimous, many of these pastoral counseling specialists began during this period to refer to themselves as pastoral psychotherapists. Pastoral counseling became more and more defined as a specialized referral service to be used by pastors and others as a means of ministering to persons whose needs lay beyond the competence and time limits of the parish pastor.

It was also during this period that the notion of mutual care of individuals with similar problems took hold in the churches. With its origins in all probability lying with the relative success of Alcoholics Anonymous, this movement, frequently although not always based in the churches, soon spawned mutual help groups for the bereaved, recently divorced, singles, families of Alzheimer's victims, the aging and their families, and the like. Most of these groups were formed with lay leadership; often they sprang up quite spontaneously without formal leadership from the clergy.

At the same time that the increasing specialization and particularization of pastoral counseling was taking place, at another level some pastoral care leaders began to turn away from the heavy influence of individual psychology and psychopathology that had marked the pastoral care enterprise since World War II, toward a renewed concern for and interest in the care of the community of Christians. Focusing on the values to be found in the nurturing of a communal context of care, these pastoral caregivers began to gather data that suggested that, while pastors often are important symbolic caring figures in the community, the primary care of the church for persons is provided by the family and group interactions that take place in the life of the church.[29] For them the focus began to move beyond the one-to-one caring relationships of the pastor toward the network of care to be provided by the church as a living community. Within this movement, the concept of pastoral care began to take a turn toward pastoral leadership that nurtures certain qualities of life in the members of the community. Some in this movement joined forces with sociologists and anthropologists of religion to form an interdisciplinary cadre of people focusing on the study of the congregation, its history, its identity, and its dynamics of interpersonal interactions.[30]

At the level of care for the society and its culture (and reciprocally, the influence of the culture on the meaning and quality of care), other important developments were taking place during the 1970s and

1980s. In an important book published in 1976, *The Moral Context of Pastoral Care*, the pastoral theologian and ethicist Don S. Browning made a strong argument for his observation that the changing cultural context of the societies of the West had so eroded a previously taken-for-granted consensual moral context that the practices of pastoral care that had been dominant in the decades of pastoral care's resurgence needed to be altered. No longer was it possible, said Browning, simply to temporarily set aside issues of morality and ethics in order to communicate acceptance and forgiveness, knowing that there was a relatively stable cultural moral context to which both pastor and help-seeking parishioner would return. That context had become so unstable that primary issues of morality and ethics needed to be attended to in the pastoral care relationship itself. Pastoral care practitioners needed to become more sensitive about and openly responsive to the moral and ethical implications of their and their help-seeking parishioners' actions and decisions.[31]

A number of other large-scale cultural developments took place during these two decades that had varying degrees of impact on the pastoral care enterprise. Though space will not allow for their adequate elaboration, simply to enumerate them is to recognize that the issues pastoral care theorists and practitioners must now confront are both extremely complex and of a level of significance that cannot be ignored.

There is a growing awareness, for example, on the part of pastors and laity alike of the powerful, often insidious, ways in which the societal structures of our culture shape and even determine many of the human problems that are confronted in the caring work of the pastor and the congregation. The structures of poverty and affluence, race and class, exploitation of the materially poor by the materially wealthy, ageism and sexism, bottom-line economics with its disregard for the basic human needs of workers and consumers— all of these societal inequities and problems compound human pain and need beyond the capacity of pastoral care to alleviate. In short, the awareness of need for societal transformation that prompted the Social Gospel movement earlier in the century has returned with greater, more widespread force. Thus the task of pastoral care needs to be more holistically integrated with the task of social transformation. The concerns that separated the followers of the Social Gospel movement and the followers of the Emmanuel movement at the turn of the century need to be brought closer together.

Feminist perspectives have forced upon us an awareness of the long history of oppression of women by a culture of patriarchy. That new awareness drastically alters the task of pastoral care and communal care of women as they not only enter the workplace in increasing numbers, but also strive to gain equity in the human relationships of home, church, and community. It also alters the task of care of men and likewise of children. Feminist perspectives on the meaning of care itself need now to be correlated with more traditional, often hierarchical, images of care.[32]

If a renewed awareness of our own Western culture and its injustices and inequities has affected the pastoral care field during the 1970s and 1980s, so also has an enlarged awareness of the pluralism of cultures in the United States and the larger world. African American cultural differences assert themselves, now with independence and pride rather than simply a wish to join the dominant white culture. So also with Hispanic and Native American cultures.

We are just beginning to experience a heightened awareness of the world's many cultures with their often differing values, ways of scheduling human development, and criteria for measuring the quality of care. No longer can it be assumed that the white, middle-class cultural standards of the West are the measure by which all other societies are to be judged. Both greater knowledge of and critical capacity for evaluating differing cultural modes of living are needed by pastors, who now often encounter in their own congregations persons from widely varying cultural backgrounds. Thus a sophisticated pastoral care must become more globally aware than was the case in previous generations.[33]

Changing Patterns in the Care of the Tradition: Pastoral Care and Postmodern Theologies

The twentieth-century pastoral care movement was not only influenced by consciousness-altering sociocultural changes during the 1960s, 1970s, and 1980s; it was also influenced by changes taking place as the disciplined care of the Christian tradition moved ever deeper into essentially postmodern ways of evaluating and interpreting traditional thought. For some pastoral theologians this meant that the models of pastoral care rooted in the liberal humanism symbolized by Rogerian and other humanistic methods emphasizing the embodiment of the Christian gospel in pastoral relationships were no longer adequate. Their apparent avoidance of Christian language in pastoral care interactions came under suspicion. The substitution of psychological for theological language seemed to these pastoral theologians to be evidence of a loss of an essential critical edge grounded in Christian understandings of the human condition.

At the same time, to many of these pastoral theologians, the pastoral methods rooted in the neoorthodoxy of Karl Barth as advocated by Eduard Thurneysen, Thomas Oden, and others seemed likewise unsatisfactory. Their insistence that the human relational aspects of pastoral work and life in the Christian community only "prepared the way" for the speaking of a narrowly defined Christian language, which alone could be designated as "pastoral" care, seemed unnecessarily narrow and confining. As the postmodern theologians asserted, a new way needed to be found whereby the traditional language of the Christian community could be asserted and given credence in open and public dialogue with other ways of speaking about the human condition.

For pastoral theologians, that meant finding ways to open dialogue between Christian ways of speaking and the ordinary language of the people. Pastors needed to become more proficient interpreters: interpreters of the Christian language and its ways of seeing and evaluating the world of human affairs, and interpreters of the cultural languages that shape much of everyday life. Christian communities needed to become more self-aware in their Christian identity as they lived out their lives in a world of many languages and ways of speaking.

Having traced the history of pastoral care from its beginnings in biblical times to the present, we need now to turn our attention toward the future—both the immediate future and the long-term future. Is there a model for pastoral care that can value and preserve the gains that have been made in pastoral care's history while yet facing with clarity the issues and problems that confront pastoral care in a changing world? Is there a model that can give balanced attention to the ongoing care of the tradition by which we as pastors and Christian people are identified, the fluid changes that are taking place in a world of many cultures, the responsibilities we have for the preservation and nurture of communities of Christians, and the diverse needs of individuals and families who look to us for care? I believe that there is such a model. Its basic framework emerges from the history of the pastoral care tradition. Like all traditions, the pastoral care tradition will remain alive and lively only as we tend it carefully in open dialogue with new issues as they emerge.[34]

CHAPTER 3

New Directions in Pastoral Care

In our survey of the history of pastoral care, some events and pastoral contributions were inevitably given greater attention than others. I focused on those innovations and persons that seem now to have made positive contributions to the pastoral tradition rather than on those times when pastoral care languished or took a turn in what seemed a wrong direction. I made those decisions guided by a particular vision of the whole of pastoral care's history and the directions our pastoral tradition needs to take today as we move into the future. Another reader of pastoral care history might well have focused on other developments, other pastoral ancestors.

Before proposing new directions for pastoral care practice, I will highlight some of the major contributions of remote and recent eras of pastoral care history that we need to carry with us as we enter the twenty-first century. Some of these practices from the past will need to be modified to fit the changing situation of the time ahead, but their preservation is important because they have shaped the tradition of what it means to be a faithful pastor of God's people. We may think of these contributions as models, images, and functions that we can tuck away in our packs as we set off on pastoral care's journey into the future. What of our heritage, both ancient and modern, do we want to take with us?

The Heritage of Ancient Israel: The Pastor As Priest, Prophet, and Wise Guide

First, we need to carry with us the balance that our Old Testament Israelite ancestors struggled to achieve among the functions of pastoral leaders as priests, as prophets, and as the wise guides of the people. The Israelites sought that balance by a rough-hewn division of institutional labor that at times resulted in a contest for dominance. Later pastoral ancestors tended to emphasize one or another of these role models. Most recently, as I said earlier in chapter 1, the function of wise guidance has been predominant for pastoral care practice. Recovery of the role of priestly care through the ritual practices of the church as well as the educational function the priests played for the people of Israel needs now to be undertaken with care and imagination. Likewise, the exercise of prophetic imagination in the day-to-day work of pastoral care takes on greater importance in a time such as ours, when we are becoming more aware of the human suffering all around us brought about by oppressive societal structures and practices. We are likewise becoming more aware of the ways in which even those of us who live in cultural and economic privilege have our lives shaped by sociocultural forces that subtly tell us who we are to be and how we are to act. Achieving a new and creative balance among these three roles will be one of our tasks in the days ahead.[1]

The Pastor As Shepherd of the Flock

More than any other image, we need to have written on our hearts the image most clearly and powerfully given to us by Jesus, of the pastor as the shepherd of the flock of Christ. Admittedly, this image originated in a time and place in which the shepherd was a commonplace figure, and we live in a social situation in which shepherding is a scarcely known, even marginalized vocation. Nevertheless, the New Testament depiction of Jesus as the good shepherd who knows his sheep and is known by his sheep (John 10:14) has painted a meaningful, normative portrait of the pastor of God's people. Reflection on the actions and words of Jesus as he related to people at all levels of social life gives us the model sine qua non for pastoral relationships with those immediately within our care and those strangers we meet along the way.[2]

We need also to take with us our memory of those pastors of past eras who distorted the image of the pastor as Christ's shepherd by assuming the authority to judge and direct God's people—an authority that rightfully belongs only to Christ himself. Particularly in the time of the church's rise to power during the Middle Ages, but also in the time of Richard Baxter and his rationalist cohorts, the pastor tended to take on authoritarian power over the people in ways that corrupted the consciousness of the people—and all in the name of Christ! The better, more lively exemplars of the pastor as the shepherd of Christ's flock have been those of our ancestors who exercised their shepherding authority to empower the people and offer care for those who were being neglected by the powerful of their communities. In important respects the monks of the desert and the St. Francises of our heritage were better models of the good shepherd than were the Gregory the Greats, who used their pastoral authority to control and direct. Here Seward Hiltner's definition of proper shepherding as "care and solicitous concern" becomes an apt guideline for our efforts to embody the model of the shepherd in our pastoral work.

The Pastor As Mediator and Reconciler

Although our pastoral posture toward the people whom we serve will greatly differ from that of the early leaders of the church in New Testament and post–New Testament times, we will want to keep before us the ancient function of the pastor as mediator and reconciler between individual believers and the community of Christians. In the New Testament, no one is a better model of this role than the apostle Paul. To read the Pauline letters is to listen in on long conversations between the great missionary apostle and the diverse people who made up the congregations he visited—conversations that sought to reconcile people to one another, to the gospel as Paul had received it, and most of all, to Christ, the head of the church.[3]

By the time of the post–New Testament Roman persecutions, the pastoral role of reconciler had, as we saw in chapter 1, become institutionalized into a role of administrator of formal processes of exomologesis and penance. Under the pressure of persecution and threat by secular authority, the pastor's role as reconciler in many cases became authoritarian and arbitrary. We can be thankful that the passage of the centuries has eroded that authority to command and exclude. Our methods of reconciliation must now more nearly follow the manner of listening, invitation to consider, and clarification of commitments. It is in certain respects even a gentler role than that fulfilled by the apostle Paul with his churches. Yet the function of reconciliation must, if we are to remain true to the deep sources of our pastoral tradition, keep those sources central to the background of our work as pastoral caregivers. Like Quintus Tertullian and John Chrysostom, we will often find ourselves located somewhere between the community of faith and its individual members, tending the boundaries of the community while maintaining our central concern for the individual.

Care and Sacrament: The Pastor As Ritualistic Leader

What do we desire to take with us from our ancestors of the Middle Ages? Probably not their tight-fisted control of the keys to salvation: the right to administer indulgences or the giving and withholding of the sacraments. Those devices for the exercise of pastoral care authority are no longer available or appropriate for pastoral work in our time. Yet there is something of the sacramental, liturgical, ritualistic expression of care by the community of Christian believers to be learned from the church of the Middle Ages. Liturgical tradition can be preserved only by careful administration by pastoral leaders who carefully tend the connections between liturgical practice and life experience. Important as it is, not all care can be expressed through the medium of conversation. Some care can only be given the power of deep connection with communal meanings by way of corporate participation in the symbolic acts of receiving bread and wine, the laying on of hands, and the administration of the water of baptism. Singing together can express care and acknowledge our mutual need for care. Praying together can search for and celebrate the receiving of the care that only God can provide.

The Middle Ages also left us the imagistic legacy of the pastor as the physician of the soul. That image conveys to us that it is not enough for our care simply to express a superficial goodwill toward others. It is not enough simply to wish our parishioners well or to express our desire that they "have a good day." No, from some of our medieval priestly ancestors we learn that to be a good pastor is to seek to understand the deepest longings, the secret sins and fears of the people so that the healing unction of our understanding may communicate that we and the God we serve care deeply and intimately for them.

On one of my daily walks through the neighborhood, I happened by the home of Margaret Algood and her husband, Robert. In their early sixties, the Algoods had, I knew, been suffering gallantly, but with increasing difficulty, from a drastically altered life since Robert suffered a devastating stroke several years ago. Virtually speechless, nearly unable to see, and unable to get around without physical support, Robert, once physically active and creative, had been restricted to spending time in bed and in his hammock on the porch, needed assistance with the most elementary bodily functions, and suffered profound depression. Margaret meanwhile had seen her life, once highlighted by a job she enjoyed, tending her garden, vigorous daily walks and weekly tennis, together with frequent trips and outings with her husband, reduced to twenty-four hour nursing care, punctuated by occasional, frantically difficult trips to hospitals and medical clinics and the frustration of trying to keep up with health insurance forms and doctor bills.

As I approached the Algood home I saw Margaret struggling to mow their lawn, a job neglected for several weeks because she had been virtually living at a hospital some hundred miles from her home; Robert had become sick and dehydrated during a difficult but necessary visit to Margaret's mother, the responsibility for whose care Margaret shared with a sister.

Like any good neighbor, I inquired as to how things were going, wanting to express neighborly concern. Margaret asked if I had a few moments to come with her to the porch, where we could talk. We had talked casually before, but not like Margaret needed to talk now. She knew me primarily as a neighbor and as the husband of a friend. But she also knew that I was a pastor and teacher of pastoral care. Before I had time to catch my breath, she began to lay bare some of the deepest questions and agonies of her soul. Was it time to give up on her battle to prolong Robert's life? How could she possibly continue to care for him? How was she to deal with the exhaustion and discouragement she felt so deeply but had not been able to express to anyone before? What did God want her to do? What would Robert want her to do? Whereas up to now they had been able to communicate, albeit only fragmentarily and with difficulty since Robert's stroke, now he seemed "out of it." Was it wrong for her to feel she just had to get away now and then to be by herself and do something besides empty bedpans and try to force fluids down Robert's unwilling throat? It was all the more painful for her because of the many happy memories she had of her life with Robert, gone after he suffered his devastating stroke.

There is no better way to speak of the conversation between Margaret Algood and me than as a pastoral effort to offer her care for her soul. She spoke of the deepest issues she faced. She revealed patterns of interpreting the events of her life and convictions about who she was and who she sought to be that came from the depths of a lifetime of self-formation. Margaret had not been formed in isolation, but by participation in a community of faith and a culture that had forced upon her certain meanings, certain questions, certain ways of seeing and judging her behavior.

Perhaps because this incident of human anguish and reaching out for care occurred as I was working on the opening chapters of this book, I found myself as I suffered along with Margaret for a brief time very much identifying with my medieval priestly ancestors. This is what they meant by the care and cure of souls—the pastor as physician of the soul. The experience conveyed to me in a profoundly moving way the depth and richness, the pain and difficulty, and the privilege of this ministry. It is a heritage those who pastor need to cherish and to hone with humility.

Pastoral Care and the Moral Life of the People

Important as the theme of the care and cure of souls has been throughout the history of pastoral care, it has consistently been paralleled with another theme: the image of the pastor as caretaker of the moral life of the people. This was the primary self-image of the prophets of Israel. To care pastorally for the people, both individually and as a community, was to consistently inquire about and help the people to consider the morality of their actions. Thus developed the tradition of the law, the collection of definitions that set the moral boundaries within which the life of the people of God must be lived. Care had to do with a certain ordering of human actions and relationships. To call the people back to those boundaries became from very early in the life of the Old Testament community a central role of pastoral care.

The care modeled by Jesus in the Gospels likewise was concerned with the lawful ordering of life. Contrary to the way Jesus is often portrayed—as one who stood over against the Pharisaic tradition of the law—his stated and lived purpose was to "fulfill" the law, to flesh out the law's ordering of life to its fullest possibilities. Jesus, however, did not hesitate to challenge and transform traditional understandings of the moral life in the Jewish community as he embodied a higher and fuller stance toward its implications. "Do not think that I have come to abolish the law or the prophets; I have come not to abolish but to fulfill" (Matt. 5:17).

This concern for the moral life received originally from pastoral care's Hebrew ancestors continues throughout history. It was a major theme of Paul's pastoral writings to the New Testament churches, even though Paul struggled mightily with his sense of caughtness in the law. It was present in the pastors who attempted to hold together the ancient Christian communities during the Roman persecutions. It is a central theme found in the fragmentary records we have of the pastoral work of the desert *Ammas* and *Abbas*, even though the care offered within these early monastic communities was not as legalistic as had been that offered by their earlier counterparts during the persecutions.[4]

The image of the pastor as moral guide persisted right up into the twentieth century. As the therapeutic paradigm for pastoral practice gained dominance, however, this theme was muted. All too often the motifs of acceptance and forgiveness have in recent years been set over against the pastoral theme of moral guidance. By tucking that theme back into our pastoral packs, we will be involved in a recovery, a rehabilitation of the role of pastor as moral guide. It is useful to remember that in the minds of most of the laity the image of pastoral moral guidance is still very much alive and well. When my neighbor Margaret Algood bared her soul about her desperate situation, as much or more than anything else she wanted moral guidance.[5]

Pastoral Care and the Life of the Spirit

If the theme of moral guidance came down to us from Hebrew sources, the themes of spiritual search, mystical desire for union with

God, the pastor as spiritual guide, probably came to us from Christianity's Greek sources. To be sure, the mystical tradition is to be found in the Bible, most particularly in certain of the Psalms (27, 42, 63, 139, for example), in the writings of the Isaiahs, and in the Johannine writings of the New Testament. However, its full appropriation as a theme for the pastor's care of the people originates from Christianity's dialogue with Greek Platonic and Neoplatonic thought.[6]

At its best, the theme of spiritual search has expressed the dependence of human life on the mystery of divine grace. Quite apart from the necessity to order human ways of living, all human living is made possible by God's faithful and continuing activity on human behalf. When humans fail, God's forgiveness is mysteriously available. Thus it is by God's grace that human life is empowered, redeemed, renewed, and reformed. By God's grace likewise particular gifts of discernment and healing are granted to individuals: graces known as the gifts of the Spirit. The Christian community down through the ages has valued and cultivated its spiritual leaders as well as its moral leaders.[7]

In the early years of the Christian community, spiritual direction was informal and common in the practice of pastoral care. Later in the Middle Ages it became more formalized, its practices more rigidly prescribed. Thus it became separated from the day-to-day care of the people in relation to their problems of living within the community of faith. With some exceptions this separation has continued to the present. Practitioners of spiritual direction have suggested that pastoral care offers merely temporary solutions to immediate problems, whereas spiritual guidance offers "more positive guidance aimed at the development of creative gifts of the spirit."[8]

Practitioners of pastoral care have made an equally biased distinction by saying that whereas pastoral care deals with the "real problems" of individuals, spiritual direction only encourages navel gazing and Gnostic searching for the Christ who is better found where people are in pain.

In recent times there are signs that these two long-separated pastoral traditions may be seeking a new rapprochement. As readers will see, I propose future directions in pastoral care that take seriously the task of restoring a language of spiritual discernment in the care practices of pastors and in the community of Christians. Some spiritual direction centers have begun to appropriate some of the more nondirective, person-centered modes of conversation with seekers of spiritual enlightenment that once characterized the psychologically oriented discipline of pastoral counseling. Be that as it may, one aspect of our pastoral heritage that we need to tuck away in our packs for the journey ahead has to do with discerning the Spirit at work in our own lives and in the lives of our people.

What Needs to Be Preserved of Our Twentieth-Century Heritage?

The twentieth century has, perhaps above all else, seen the full flowering of pastoral care's sophisticated awareness of human development—the primary importance of individual historical experience. Indeed, when difficulties or conflicts arise in the lives of adult parishioners it has become commonplace for pastors to wonder about and make inquiry concerning earlier life experience. We are now convinced that present difficulties can often be illuminated by what happened much earlier in the lives of those experiencing difficulty. This tool of inquiry, which can allow pastoral caregivers to postulate a certain historical logic to otherwise often baffling human dilemmas, is a valuable one that needs to be preserved. When not applied woodenly or with amateurish lack of restraint, it can enhance the pastor's ability to respond to the specificity of human need. In order to preserve this tool, every practitioner of pastoral care needs to master a well-developed theory of human development, a psychological, theoretical framework within which to consider the developmental issues facing those who are to receive our care.[9]

The perspectives that have been brought to bear on human development in the twentieth century are many and varied. The earliest contributions were made by the turn-of-the-century psychologists of religion, with their psychological interest in religious formation. With the appropriation of Freudian theory by pastoral practitioners, inquiry into religious development took a sharp turn in a psychodynamic direction, and thus it put aside much of its specifically religious aspect. Now accompanied by a preoccupation with psychopathological characteristics—so-called abnormalities of development—psychologically oriented pastoral care began to see itself primarily in terms of pastoral counseling and the care of troubled persons. Examining personal histories began to mean examining them for what was faulty, the historical root causes of present difficulties. With this move toward preoccupation with psychopathology and pastoral care as counseling, inevitably the discipline of pastoral counseling became more and more specialized; the movement toward pastoral psychotherapy began.

Important as this twentieth-century focus on pastoral counseling as ministry to troubled persons has been, it has unfortunately meant at times a concomitant lack of focus on nurturing the development of more ordinary, relatively healthy people. Pastoral care needs to have as its primary focus the care of all God's people through the ups and downs of everyday life, the engendering of caring environments within which all people can grow and develop to their fullest potential. Not all of God's people will need pastoral *counsel*; all people, however, need the nurture and support of a *caring* environment.

Pastoral Listening to the Inner Life of Individuals

Having warned against focusing too much attention on counseling as the central task of pastoral care, I need now to temper that caution. Certainly some elements of pastoral counseling must be preserved in the future of pastoral care. The first element is pastoral counseling's emphasis on psychodynamics and the inner life of persons. As Carroll Wise said so well in the mid-1960s, it is the communication of the *inner meaning* of the gospel to persons that defines the intention of pastoral care at its best.[10]

That means that good pastoral care is not simply talk about the gospel or some general statement of its applicability to people's lives. Rather, good pastoral care embodies the gospel in relationships by speaking to the inner being of individuals. Good pastors seek to relate to persons in ways that make possible what the theologian H. Richard Niebuhr calls "moments of revelation."[11]

What is communicated in the relationship makes a connection with the internal history of the person in a new and potentially transforming way.

In order that pastoral relationships at every level may open up and invite this level of connection, pastoral leaders need both the skills and the discerning sensitivity to relate to people's inner lives. A well-appropriated knowledge of psychodynamics greatly facilitates the pastor's success in this area. To be sure, a knowledge of psychodynamics needs to be supplemented by a knowledge of spiritual dynamics—the dynamics of the individual's internalization of knowledge of God and the life of the Spirit.

Pastoral counselors of the recent past have enhanced their knowledge of psychodynamics by the appropriation of theories that focus on family dynamics and family systems theory. That form of counseling has likewise become a specialization in ministry. Although it may not be appropriate for parish pastors to seek to become family therapists in a specialized sense, sensitivity to the dynamics of family life among their parishioners can greatly enhance their ability to communicate the gospel to persons in families at the point of their need.[12]

Pastoral Care of Those in Special Need

A second element that needs to be preserved from the tradition of pastoral counseling is its sense of mission toward neglected or overlooked persons. As we learned in chapter 2, Anton Boisen and others of the clinical pastoral care movement had a profound concern for the mentally ill and the imprisoned: society's forgotten outcasts.

Unfortunately, as pastoral counseling has become increasingly specialized under the influence of psychotherapy, more and more of its recipients come not from the margins of society, but from the affluent middle and upper classes. Pastoral counseling has increasingly become counseling only for those who can afford it! So it is that, as the discipline of pastoral care moves into the future, it must renew or recover its earlier sense of mission to those whose needs are great while their ability to seek out the care they need is small. We must find new ways to make care available to all people in need and not simply to those who are affluent and sufficiently psychologically sophisticated to show up at the pastoral counselor's office. This may mean finding ways to bring care to these marginal persons other than counseling in the strictly psychotherapeutic sense.

Pastoral Concern for Persons
and for Social Situations

Pastoral care at the turn of the twentieth to the twenty-first century must find new ways to give equal emphasis to concern for the individual and concern for the larger social environment that surrounds the individual.

One cannot think of the pastoral heritage of the twentieth century without remembering the split that took place early on between the Emmanuel movement's individualism and the Social Gospel movement's dedication to social transformation. From that period on, the development of pastoral care in North America has been dominated by psychological individualism. The circle of interest was drawn more or less tightly around the question of what was of concern to the individual who was the immediate recipient of pastoral care. During the period of the adjustment psychologies' popularity, pastoral care practitioners tended to take for granted that the larger social situation could be counted on to support self-realization. But by the end of World War II, that mood had changed under the influence of such neo-Freudian psychologists as Erich Fromm and Karen Horney. These psychologists and their pastoral followers tended to "view most social institutions as bureaucratic impositions on human freedom and dignity."[13]

Pastoral care's focus on the individual and, in some cases, the family of the individual, deepened. The advent of pastoral counseling as the dominant mode of pastoral care brought with it a characteristic stance toward persons coming for care that included efforts to assist the individual to survive in and surmount the intrusions of their social situation.

Meanwhile, as we found in chapter 2, the Social Gospel movement—a product of theological liberalism's optimism about the possibility of transforming social reality into social life governed by the rule of God's righteous kingdom—gradually gave way to the realism of neoorthodoxy. Still later came the rise of liberation theology with its focus on social transformation by means of social empowerment of the oppressed. None of these movements within theology has, it would appear from a pastoral care perspective, offered a fully satisfactory way to combine concern for the individual and concern for social transformation. The split between these two concerns that took place nearly a hundred years ago in large part remains.

For the pastor involved in day-to-day relationships with persons at all levels of social life, at least two observational capacities are of crucial importance, each of which has been emphasized by one or the other approach—concern for the individual or concern for the community—during the twentieth century. The first is the art of listening. It is this, above all else, that the twentieth-century clinical pastoral care movement has taught pastors. Listening involves more than simply hearing the words that people say. It means being attentive to the emotional communication that accompanies the words. It means listening for the nuances that may give clues to the particular, private meanings that govern a person's inner life. It means listening for hidden conflicts, unspoken desires, unspeakable fears, and faint hopes. First and foremost, pastors must be listeners who invite self-disclosure and thus communicate acceptance and nonjudgmental care.

The second observational capacity, which has been fostered more by the descendants of Walter Rauschenbusch and the Social Gospel movement than by the clinical pastoral care movement, might be called the capacity to observe. It asks that pastors look carefully at and make evaluative judgments about the social environment that surrounds those who are the subjects of pastoral care. We might say that this capacity asks that we look around in addition to looking within. What in the social situation of the people receiving our care may be causing or exacerbating people's distress? Are the social structures that surround the lives of those under our care providing the social supports that people need in order for their lives to flourish?

If those of us who are to offer pastoral care in the future are to learn both the capacity to listen and the capacity to observe fully, we will find ourselves called equally into a ministry of care and nurture of individual and family life, and into a ministry of social and cultural transformation. A ministry of social and cultural transformation will involve not only advocacy on behalf of oppressed and injured individuals, but also efforts, as biblical scholar Walter Brueggemann has said, to "nurture, nourish, and evoke a consciousness and perception alternative to the consciousness and perception of the dominant culture around us."[14]

Pastoral Care of and
Within the Congregation

This brings us to the most recent and in certain respects less-developed emphasis within twentieth-century pastoral care, namely, the rediscovery of the congregation as a primary context and agent of care for the people of God. I speak of this as a *re*discovery because, in a sense, we who have from generation to generation made up the Christian community have always known that the primary source of Christian nurture and care lies in the gathering together of God's people. That was true for the earliest primitive communities of Christians and has been in large part true ever since. However, the church through the centuries has likewise always given a special significance to the relationship of care of the ordained leaders of the community. Thus, although emphases have fluctuated from time to time, the ordained pastor's care for individuals has usually been given a dominant emphasis. Furthermore, in the recent history of pastoral care, in large part because of the influence of individualism and psychotherapeutic psychology, the organizing conceptualization of pastoral care has focused on the individual care of the pastor for individual persons.

In our effort to reappropriate our history, it is important to remember that the meaning of the term *pastoral* as it has been used within the Judeo-Christian tradition has had a fundamentally communal connotation. Pastoral care thus denotes the care of a community for its members. As Ronald H. Sunderland has pointed out, "It derives from the figurative language of Jewish scriptures and, supremely, from the Lord's care of Israel (Psalms 23, 80)."[15]

From very early in the life of the Israelite people, images, themes, and narratives appeared that held before the people their obligation to care for one another and for the stranger in their midst. That standard was reemphasized in the New Testament, most particularly in the Fourth Gospel and the Johannine Epistles, "where the members' love for one another, by which the world will know that they are truly the Lord's disciples, is the highest expression of the evangel. Through their ministry to each other, they are to exemplify Jesus' ministry to his disciples."[16]

The renewed interest in congregational care as a primary structure of care for God's people in recent times is an aspect of a broad and multifaceted movement to study the congregation as an ethos within which the meaning and practice of the Christian life is lived out at the grassroots level. A number of differing approaches have been proposed as avenues of investigation for understanding the dynamic relationships within local congregational life.[17] While most of these approaches appear to be based on a presupposition that people within congregations are there at least in part because they care for and are cared for by the other members of the community, only a few researchers have sought systematically to investigate that presupposition.

So it is that, as we carry forward this renewed interest in the congregation as a primary locus for the care of individuals, we will need to do so with both a research agenda and a renewed concern for pastoral leadership of the community of faith. We need to know more about just how care is communicated within a local community of faith. Preliminary studies, such as the Lutheran study to which I referred in chapter 2, seem to indicate that the basic matrix of care is communicated within a community largely in informal, even relationally casual ways. Here the ethnographic methods developed by James Hopewell can be usefully applied by pastors who wish to know more about the informal caring network within a given congregation.[18]

Renewed attention to communal aspects of pastoral care will also involve giving greater attention to the importance of ritual acts and liturgical practices that corporately express God's care for the welfare of God's people and their care for one another. The symbolic meanings of community are best displayed in public actions that express in ritual and liturgical forms the meanings that give ordinary events their significance. The power of ritual actions to communicate care is greatly dependent upon the informal atmosphere of care within the community that surrounds those actions. Pastoral leadership must therefore give adequate attention to both these dimensions of care.

Pastoral Care As Pastoral Education

Hidden within most of the significant developments of each era of pastoral care's history lies a function of care that I have not yet fully acknowledged. Stated simply, it is the function of pastoral education, a function that in the twentieth century has usually been assigned to other subspecialties within the role of ministry. At each step along the way of the history of pastoral ministry, priests and pastors were formally or informally teaching the people about what it means to care—for the tradition of faith, for the community of believers, for individuals and families, and for the sociocultural milieu of the believing community.

In his visits to New Testament churches and in his letters to them in his absence, Paul was constantly teaching people about the meaning of the gospel and the expectations that were to be fulfilled if people were to be a faithful community. Pastors in the primitive post–New Testament church were teaching their people about the necessary boundaries between life in their community and life in the surrounding pagan culture. The medieval priests combined their sacramental pastoral practices with teaching the people about the use of those practices to give meaning to the events of their life and death. So it went through the centuries. Each new turn that the history of pastoral care took intentionally or unintentionally involved the care-filled teaching of the people about the meaning and context of care.

At no time has this pastoral function of the teaching of care been more powerful in its significance nor more obscured than during the recent time of the dominance of the psychotherapeutic paradigm. Pastors who became acquainted with psychological and psychotherapeutic ways of thinking about human problems, sometimes with intention and deliberation, more often informally through the use of the psychological idiom abroad in the land, have acted as pastoral psychological educators. They have taught their people psychological ways of speaking about everything from the childhood origins of adult human difficulty to the stages in the processes of death and bereavement. Through preaching that in various ways combined the imagery of the gospel with themes and images that expressed the modern psychological idiom, through programmatic efforts to give support to healthy individual and family life, and through the use of psychological concepts in pastoral conversations, pastors have been educators and participants in inculcating popular psychological notions into the lives of many people. At their best, these pastoral activities have been able to bring the values and meanings of the Christian tradition into productive dialogue with contemporary culture. At their worst, these activities have tended to subordinate the gospel to the latest package of popular psychology. In either case, pastors have acted as pastoral educators in their caregiving.

As we shall see, a primary intention of this book is to bring more clearly to the fore this educative aspect of pastoral care and leadership. This means that it is not enough for pastors to become relatively competent psychologists and therapeutic counselors if they are adequately to perform their pastoral role. They need also to become competent in helping people make connections between their lives of faith within the community and tradition that identifies us as the people of God, and the day-to-day individual, social, and cultural realities of our lives.

In the next chapter I will propose a model of pastoral care that seeks to make these connections. In a certain sense it is a new model, in that it involves a departure from the psychotherapeutic counseling paradigm that has so dominated pastoral care practice of the recent past. But in a larger sense it is a model that grows out of and is dependent upon the long tradition behind pastoral work in the present. It draws upon the developments of all the earlier epochs of pastoral care practice, including the most recent psychotherapeutic epoch. Thus what we seek is in certain ways a synthesis of the strengths of the pastoral tradition as a model for the present and the future. A certain dialectic will govern its structure—a dialectic between faithfulness to the tradition and attentiveness to the demands of life in the present.

CHAPTER 4

The Stories of Our Lives and the Christian Story

In this chapter, the tense of our work changes. Now we turn our attention to the present and, as far as we can foresee, the future. As we have already noted, the flow of time and history inevitably brings change alongside the continuing power of traditions formed out of earlier human experience. Is there a model for pastoral care that builds on past history yet listens for the issues of the present? Is there a model for pastoral care that can inform and shape the practice of pastoral ministry in ways that fit people's needs in our time and the time just ahead? Are there human needs that have come to the fore in the lives of late-twentieth-century people that make peculiar demands upon pastoral care? Do those needs call for some revision of the basic paradigm for pastoral practice that has in many ways worked so well during the middle decades of our century?

These very questions suggest that the human needs toward which our pastoral care is directed have indeed altered their shape. The cultural context within which ministry must take place has changed in very significant ways; aspects of that cultural context that have been present but somehow hidden in the past have now become apparent and demand a fresh response. In part because of these cultural changes, the situation within Christian communities has likewise been altered.

As we have already observed of other times during which patterns of pastoral practice have changed, changes in the larger social situation alter the shape of Christian communities and thereby alter the requirements and modes of pastoral practice. Thus, to speak of a paradigm shift in pastoral care practice implies that there have been shifts in human cultural consciousness and practices that present pastoral practitioners with an altered context for their ministries. Though the changes that have taken place within the relatively short span of the past fifty or so years may not appear to be as radical or far-reaching as those of earlier periods, they nevertheless are substantial enough to prompt us to reconsider our current paradigm.

There are many who would disagree. They may concede that the psychotherapeutic paradigm for pastoral care needs to be elaborated somewhat, its range of skills expanded to take into consideration such new human ills as AIDS and the increase in such human aberrations as drug abuse or violence toward children, spouses, and the elderly. But the basic paradigm focused on the dialogue between pastoral care and counseling and psychotherapeutic practice remains secure for those pastoral care theorists. It is my conviction, however, that although the psychotherapeutic pastoral model has many strengths that need to be preserved, it is inadequate to meet the needs and address the issues that confront pastoral care practice today.

The Case of Robert and Margaret Algood Revisited

In the previous chapter, we looked briefly at the agonizing situation of Margaret Algood, whose life had been drastically altered by a sudden, devastating stroke suffered by her husband, Robert. I spoke of my impromptu ministry with her as a response to the deep cries of her soul. A second look at Margaret's situation can, I believe, provide us with a useful glimpse of some of the factors that seem now to be pressing for significant change in the normative model for pastoral care practice.

If I were to respond to Margaret from what I have called the psychotherapeutic pastoral care paradigm, my focus of attention would be primarily on Margaret's conflicted feelings: her love for her husband; her anger and frustration with his increasing limitations and his inability to communicate as he once had; her similar frustration and anger at Robert's doctors, who seemed both unable to make Robert get better and confused in their messages to Margaret about his condition and prognosis. I would also seek to uncover and respond to Margaret's overpowering sense of loss.

In my response to that confused array of feelings I would attempt to piece together a sketchy history of Margaret's life and especially her life with Robert. In short, my response would be focused primarily on Margaret's psychological and relational conflicts and her ambivalent emotions. My hope would be that by providing a sensitive, listening ear—a sounding board for the expression of her confusion—I could convey acceptance and reassurance that I and the God I represented cared for her.

All of this, had I been successful, would have been true to the exercise of the psychotherapeutic model for pastoral care. To that extent it would have been both helpful to Margaret and implicitly true to the Christian gospel of love and acceptance. It would have been authentic ministry. What then, you may ask, is missing that would point toward a need for change in pastoral care models?

My response to that question is complex and multifaceted. First, the psychotherapeutic model, if followed closely, does not give enough attention to the very real and complex ethical issues that Margaret faces. Should she give up on her valiant efforts to prolong Robert's life at the expense of the continuing depletion of her psychological and monetary resources? What is best in terms of Robert's own welfare? How are the relative values of his welfare and her own to be adjudicated? Margaret deeply wants to do what is right in her situation, but how is that to be determined? In short, how is their life now to be ordered?

Second, the narrative hermeneutical perspective within which I am working in this book would argue that there was something going on here that should be stated in terms larger than those of moral choice. As the narrative approach might state it, Margaret was having difficulty making sense out of the story she found herself living out with Robert, his doctors, and others in her situation, in relation to the story of how life is supposed to be, according to the social and religious narrative that in conscious and unconscious ways governs her life. Her appropriation of that larger Christian narrative is apparent in the way she frames her questions. What does God want me to do? Is it wrong for me to want to get away sometimes? Should I be judged guilty for my feelings and wishes? She automatically uses a certain grammar when talking about her situation. That grammar comes from a particular community's way of speaking about life. It is a way of speaking that she has learned from being a part of a religious community that uses its language to make sense of the world and of life in the world. How is that grammar now to be applied to what is happening to her and to Robert? Her use of that grammar is confused and fraught with doubts and questions.[1]

Third, while not speaking directly about it, Margaret is also groping for ways to renew her connection with the religious community from which she learned the deep grammar by which she is trying to make sense of her difficult life situation. As much or more than anything else she needs the support and nourishment of a community so that she will not be alone with her dilemma. As her neighbor, I could in a limited way represent such a community. To the extent that she saw me as a Christian pastor, I could represent that community in a large, symbolic sense. But she needs more than I as an individual can give her. She needs to be surrounded—enfolded, "nested," so to speak—in a living community of faith and care.

Helpful as the psychotherapeutic model of pastoral care is, it offers little help with these issues in Margaret's situation, and whatever help it offers tends toward the translation of her concerns into a grammar that emerges from psychotherapeutic rather than religious ways of speaking. The issues she speaks of clearly call for another level of conversation, a compatible model of response.

These reflections on the case of Margaret and Robert Algood begin to open up a line of argument for something more than simply an expansion of the model for pastoral care recently appropriated from psychotherapy. Examples discussed in later chapters will place before us other aspects of the argument. Now, however, I want to turn to a somewhat more general and abstract discussion of the "signs of the times" that point to the need for such a change of paradigms for pastoral practice.

Signs of the Times Pointing to Need for Change

1. Changes in the Variety and Level of Human Suffering Within the Society

Beneath and hidden within psychological and relational problems lies a deeper and more pervasive malaise that afflicts not only persons caught in extreme and blatant forms of human misery, but also many if not most of the people in our communities who go about their work, their family life, and their play relatively responsibly— even, as in the case of Margaret Algood, courageously. It is a malaise that infects the entire Western culture and, because of the Western-ization of more and more of the world, has become invasive in many other cultural contexts as well. For want of a better descriptive term for this distress that infects our culture, I shall call it a loss or fragmentation of a consensual structure of meaning and value that can give order and purpose to people's lives.[2]

A concise, albeit somewhat simplistic definition of what I mean by consensual structure of meaning involves all those meanings that people of a given culture take for granted as true, right, or good. It also, of course, includes what a given culture takes for granted as being untrue or wrong. When a society loses that consensual set of meanings, it is in danger of becoming fragmented, unsure of itself, and less able to cope with the diversity and pluralism inherent in a world that is becoming more and more a "global village."[3]

The symptoms of meaning fragmentation in contemporary West-ern society include individual and social problems that at first glance seem unrelated. I have already mentioned two or three of these symptoms: the increase of violence of all kinds, the extent of drug and alcohol abuse, and even the epidemic extent of the AIDS crisis.[4]

Further evidence of the fragmentation that besets North Ameri-can society can be found in the literature that has emerged from the psychiatric community in recent years. Whereas that literature fifty years ago was dominated by discussions of various forms of intra-psychic, conflict-based neurotic problems that produced guilt and anxiety (problems created by an environment that overemphasized control and conformity), more recent literature is predominantly concerned with problems such as so-called borderline conditions and fragmented or undeveloped sense of self.[5] The social implica-tions of that literature are fairly clear: if persons are to develop a sturdy and authentic sense of self, they must be surrounded by a consistent set of nurturing relationships, a "good enough" holding environment, as they develop.[6] The fact that a great proportion of the people who appear at the psychotherapist's office today evi-dence a lack of such consistent care and nurture in their histories points toward a breakdown of relational meanings that legitimate and make possible such "good enough" nurture.

It is important to recognize that all these problems have both individual and social dimensions. They represent social and cultural trends in which we, both pastors and congregations, participate. As such, they are beyond the capacity of one pastor or congregation to control. They represent the time and place by which we are surrounded, and we are no more able to control them than the medieval church was able to control the breakup of the Roman Empire.[7]

It is also important to keep in mind that a time of crisis, whether an individual or a social crisis, offers both danger and opportunity. Crises virtually always occur when old social structures or structures of personality cease to be adequate to assimilate new experience. Transformation is necessary, but it will always invite resistance from established patterns that seek continuity with the past. In many ways the tension between continuity and change in human individual and social relationships is an essential dynamic. It keeps the lives of individuals and societal structures from becoming stagnant or moving toward chaotic anarchy. But when the tension becomes so great that it cannot be contained easily and smoothly, crisis occurs.[8]

2. Changes in the Nature of Problems Confronting Christian Congregations

I have spoken earlier of the rediscovery in recent years of the vital importance of the local Christian congregation as the basic context within which persons of all ages and circumstances receive care from their fellow Christians. It is now generally understood that person-to-person care given directly by the pastor is, while symbolically important and crucial during times of crisis and stress, in many ways secondary to the care informally given and received among fellow believers within the community of faith. Care of persons within the congregation means something larger and more comprehensive than the care given by the ordained pastor. It is the work of all members of the community.

The psychotherapeutic pastoral care model, despite efforts to "train" some laity to "assist" the pastor in the work of care, has from its beginning focused on one-to-one counseling, one-to-family counseling, or small-group ministry led by the ordained pastor or other ordained ministers and lay leaders. Useful as that focus has been in emphasizing the importance of caring relationships, it has by and large failed to give adequate attention to the everyday aspects of care within the congregation. In a broad sense, ordinary friendly relationships are mutually helpful and therefore therapeutic in certain ways, although they are seldom spoken of in such terms by the laity . Such symbolic expressions as "fellowship," "communion," and "fellow feeling" are more likely to be used in the common life of the people. This level of care is apt to be expressed not so much in words as in an arm on the shoulder or, in the case of bereavement, the provision of food or flowers.

Because of its emphasis on counseling and problem solving, pastoral care within the psychotherapeutic model fails to give adequate attention to the place of ritual and liturgical practices of the congregation as symbolically setting in place a meaning context that gives Christian care its peculiar way of speaking. It fails to recognize that one of the most basic caring functions that a community of faith can offer is a storied context of ultimate meaning within which life can be lived. Expressed another way, one of the fundamental structures of care that life in a community of faith can and should offer is a story or a grammar—a way of speaking about people's circumstances—that can connect people's life experience with the ultimate context of meaning contained in the Christian gospel.

The topic of the language structure of Christian care will appear in a variety of ways in later chapters of this book, most particularly in part 2. Meanwhile, given the context of the present discussion, I need to point out that the makeup and location of congregations have changed and continue to change in the course of recent decades. These changes have in most cases made the church's life at all levels both more complicated and more problematic.

Some of these changes have come about simply because of the process of urbanization in Western society. Whereas a hundred or more years ago most Americans lived in rural areas or in small towns, today the majority of American people live in metropolitan communities. Concomitantly, their close friends and associates are generally no longer their nearby neighbors, but their fellow workers or professionals, who may live at some distance from them in scattered neighborhoods. The same may be said of the churches in many urban communities. Fellow church members often do not live close to one another. Even if they do, they may not be close associates in daily life. Memberships of urban churches likewise tend to be socially and economically diverse so that an authentic sense of community is difficult to attain.

While all these societal changes have been taking place, the basic model for congregational care has been based on a relatively small (three hundred members or less) local church community made up of people who know one another and meet one another in their daily life. This model has assumed that the pastor will be able to become well acquainted with most if not all of her or his congregation. In the urban or suburban churches of today this becomes increasingly difficult, particularly for churches that are no longer located in distinct neighborhoods that look to the church as a center of community life.

Although the psychotherapeutic model of pastoral care and counseling was developed primarily within institutional contexts other than the local church (hospitals, mental health treatment programs, and more recently, pastoral counseling centers), its applicability to pastoral care ministry in the parish has been assumed. As stated earlier, its focus has been primarily on the one-to-one and one-to-family ministry of the pastor. Hidden within that focus has been the tacit assumption that the local church is a relatively small community with few enough members that the pastor can get to know everyone well and, when necessary, work with them on a one-to-one basis. When numbers make one-to-one ministry difficult, it has been assumed that the pastor will minister to persons in acute crisis and make use of referral resources if and when his or her time or skill is exceeded. Persons not in such crises are assumed to be able to "take care of themselves."

Clearly, a more communal model of pastoral care is needed. The problems of congregational life, however, have become highly complex. Those problems and pastoral approaches to working with them will be explored in part 2 of this book.

3. Changes Taking Place Within Theology that Affect Pastoral Care Practice

In our study of earlier epochs in the history of pastoral care, we have seen that pastoral practices in vogue during any particular time in history have most often been closely related to or been a direct outgrowth of emphases in theology that characterized the time. Thus, for example, the sacramentalism in pastoral practice during the Middle Ages was a direct outgrowth of the theology of the church that dominated that period. The Reformation theology of Martin Luther turned pastoral practices in new directions away from sacramentalism. Likewise, the liberal theology that dominated Protestantism toward the end of the nineteenth and early twentieth centuries fostered pastoral care's focus on self-development and a culture of the self.

The present epoch in theology may justifiably be called a time of transition, controversy, and search for new approaches to theological work. No one school of theology can be said to be dominant in either Roman Catholic or mainline Protestant circles. Not only are the voices of liberation and political theology being heard strongly throughout the churches, but the multiple voices of feminist and black theologians are becoming increasingly articulate. Roman Catholic theology has not only felt the impact of Latin American liberationist thought, but has also undergone wide-ranging changes since Vatican II that have opened the way toward greater emphasis on pastoral theological reflection.[9] Meanwhile, evangelical neofundamentalism has enjoyed a resurgence among Protestants, and at least one leading pastoral theologian has called for a return to classical orthodoxy.[10]

It is little wonder that the field of pastoral care is in a time of transition and controversy. How to sort out all of the diversity within theology and make use of it in setting new directions for pastoral care practice becomes an interesting but difficult problem! It certainly suggests that whatever paths in pastoral practice are taken toward new horizons need to be kept open-ended and flexible, able to accommodate further new developments.

A Typology of Approaches to Theological Work

As I have worked through these issues with regard to the urgent need for a new model for pastoral care practice, I have found the typology of theological models developed by the historical theologian George A. Lindbeck extremely useful and illuminating.[11] Stated very briefly, Lindbeck proposes that all theologies tend to develop along the pattern of one of three models: *propositionalist, experiential-expressivist,* or *cultural-linguistic.* Lindbeck's terms are technical and, on the surface, formidable. But the content he pours into these terms clarifies the issues involved.

Theologies that follow the *propositionalist* model, which includes all of traditional orthodoxy as well as some forms of neoorthodox theology, "function as informative propositions or truth claims about objective realities. Religions are thought of as similar to philosophy or science as these were classically conceived."[12] This model contests the notion that to speak about God or ultimate reality is always to speak in metaphoric or poetic language. By contrast, the propositions of this model are thought to directly correspond to what is real and true. They simply describe what is.

According to this model, to be a "true believer" is to accept the truth of certain theological propositions. Therefore, a fundamental purpose of pastoral care within the model naturally follows: namely, to articulate the propositional truth that is applicable to the situation at hand in the expectation that the hearer will accept and believe it. This is the logic behind such methodologies of pastoral care practice as that propounded by the Swiss Barthian pastoral theologian Eduard Thurneysen in his widely read *Theology of Pastoral Care.*[13] Although Thurneysen was well acquainted with the psychological theories of Sigmund Freud and embraced aspects of a relational approach to pastoral care practice, he insisted that whatever was involved in pastoral practice informed by these ideas was preliminary and secondary to the real work of pastoral care, which involved articulation of theology's propositional truth. An American pastoral theology text that expresses somewhat the same position as Thurneysen's is that of the Southern Baptist Edward Thornton. Thornton speaks of pastoral care as "preparing the way."[14]

George Lindbeck's' second model is rightly named *experiential-expressivist.* Rather than being based upon an assumption of the objective truth of certain propositions, it is rooted in the assumption of a common core of human religious experience that may have diverse forms of expression in various cultural contexts. Theological doctrines are thus "noninformative and nondiscursive symbols of inner feelings, attitudes, and orientations."[15] In this model theological tenets are less analogous to scientific statements than to art, poetry, and aesthetics. Lindbeck cites the Catholic theologian Bernard Lonergan as perhaps the clearest example of experiential-expressivism in theology, although he also makes reference to Paul Tillich and others.[16]

This mode of doing theology undoubtedly had its roots in the turn toward the self that, as we saw in chapter 1, began with the coming of modernity. In significant ways it characterized the work of Friedrich Schleiermacher, the nineteenth-century theologian who is often spoken of as the father of modern Protestant theology. Schleiermacher grounded his theology in the common human experience of complete and utter dependence. Or, as Paul Tillich's method of correlation put it, human experience prompts the questions that theology seeks to answer. And, as Lindbeck points out, "The structures of modernity press individuals to meet God first in the depths of their souls, and then, perhaps, if they find something personally congenial, to become a part of tradition or join the church."[17] Experiential-expressivism thus lends itself to the dominant individualism of our time. But, as Lindbeck goes on to say, "Thus the traditions of religious thought and practice into which Westerners are most likely to be socialized conceals from them the social origins of their conviction that religion is a highly private and individual matter."[18]

Much of the twentieth-century pastoral care that has not followed the neoorthodox path laid out by Thurneysen has, wittingly or unwittingly, followed the experiential-expressivist model insofar as it has been theologically grounded. Twentieth-century pastoral care's focus on the concrete experience of individuals and families has quite naturally, if often unselfconsciously, lent itself to a sometimes rough-hewn experiential-expressivist dialogue between the specifics of an encountered human experience and the meanings of certain theological symbols. Most often the so-called common human experience has been described in psychological language, and then a theological symbol that correlates with this psychologically denoted experience has been sought. Thus for many pastoral caregivers, Tillich's model of correlation has been made applicable, albeit often rather loosely.

George Lindbeck's third model, the one he prefers over either of the others, he calls a *cultural-linguistic* model. Within this model for doing theological work, "religions are seen as comprehensive interpretive schemes, usually embodied in myths or narratives and heavily ritualized, which structure human experience and understanding of self and world."[19] Whereas propositionalist modes of doing theology may be seen as analogous to science (theology as science seeks to assert facts about reality), and experiential-expressivism as analogous to poetry and the arts (theology as art or poetry seeks to express what human beings universally experience), the cultural-linguistic model of doing theology is analogous to culture (theology as the attempt to objectify a particular religious culture and its embodiment in narrative and ritual).

This latter is the model from which I appropriated the term *grammar*. To belong to a religion is to adopt a certain grammar, a way of speaking, an interpretive schema that structures one's understanding of oneself and one's world. The story of one's life is stitched into the larger narrative of the Christian story.

Lindbeck goes on to describe the cultural-linguistic model in more technical terms:

> It is not primarily an array of beliefs about the true and the good (although it may involve these), or a symbolism expressive of basic attitudes, feelings, or sentiments (though these will be generated). Rather it is similar to an idiom that makes possible the description of realities, the formulations of beliefs, and the experiencing of inner attitudes, feelings, and sentiments. Like a culture or language, it is a communal phenomenon that shapes the subjectivities of individuals rather than being primarily a manifestation of these subjectivities. It comprises a vocabulary of discursive and nondiscursive symbols together with a distinctive logic or grammar in terms of which this vocabulary can be meaningfully deployed. Lastly, just as a language (or "language game," to use Wittgenstein's phrase) is correlated with a form of life, and just as a culture has both cognitive and behavioral dimensions, so it is also in the case of a religious tradition. Its doctrines, cosmic stories or myths, and ethical directives are integrally related to the rituals it practices, the sentiments or experience it evokes, the actions it recommends, and the institutional forms it develops.[20]

Lindbeck prefers the cultural-linguistic model for several reasons, all of which relate to the problem he finds with the other two models. His appreciation of and argument against the viability of propositional modes of doing theology are much too complex to summarize here. I think, however, it is fair to say that he believes that the pathway of propositionalism, which led to the ever more difficult argument with modern science over "proofs" of theism, while not dead (there are still a good many true Barthians around, for example), is increasingly difficult to sustain.[21] He appreciates the biblical roots such theologies emphasize, but believes that propositionalist ways of appropriating the Bible are based on outdated philosophical notions. The Bible is better seen as containing the grounding narrative of a religious community that seeks to structure its life according to the sacred truths contained in that narrative.

George Lindbeck's primary reasons for doubting the viability of experiential-expressivist approaches to doing the work of theology are two, both related to his understanding of the power of communal culture to shape human experience, including religious experience. The first has to do with the experiential-expressivist assumption of a common, universal core of experience that grounds and shapes the questions of religious experience. Lindbeck points to the pluralism of cultural contexts that create very diverse experiences for persons. "There can be no experiential core because, so the argument goes, the experiences that religions evoke and mold are as varied as the interpretive schemes they embody. Adherents of different religions do not diversely thematize the same experience; rather they have different experiences."[22]

As we might expect, Lindbeck's second reason has to do with the tendency of experiential-expressivist theologies to focus on the religious experience of the individual, as if religious experience begins inside the individual and then moves out in search of a community. For Lindbeck, the truth of the matter is the reverse. Persons do not pick and choose among various propositions about God or what is true about ultimate reality. They do not first recognize some internal religious need that is like that of others and then go in search of a community of such individuals. Rather, to become religious—no less than to become culturally or linguistically competent—is to internalize a set of skills by practice and training. One learns to feel, act, and think in conformity with a religious tradition that is, in its inner structure, far richer and more subtle than can be explicitly articulated. One's primary knowledge is not *about* the religion, nor *what* the religion teaches, but rather *how to be*.[23]

To be or become religious is therefore for Lindbeck through and through a communal experience. It is to have one's ways of feeling, thinking, and acting shaped by a community of faith and practice that orders one's life. That ordering, in ways both explicit and subtly implicit, embodies a tradition and its way of speaking about the world and life in the world. To belong to that community is to share in a life of ritual, prayer, and action that continually reminds the members of a community who they are and who they are to be in the world. To seek the *truth* as a member of such a community is to seek to *be true* to the primary narrative that structures the community's way of being in the world.

In a time of increased awareness of cultural pluralism with its accompanying threat of fragmentation, nihilistic relativism, and disunity, such an approach to the work of theology has great appeal. It acknowledges both cultural unity and cultural plurality. While recognizing the power of language and culture to shape individual lives, it nevertheless invites intercultural dialogue and the opening up of traditional ways of ordering life to new experience. For individuals buffeted by a plethora of often contradictory values and ways of thinking, feeling, and behaving, it offers an avenue of return to a grounding mythic narrative that tells them who they are in their deepest loyalty.[24]

A Cultural-Linguistic Model for Pastoral Care

The cultural-linguistic model of doing theology is the most fundamental model by which a community can care for individuals and families. It has the unique ability to provide people with a storied context of ultimate meaning for their lives. To the degree that this storied context maintains its connection with all the varied stories of individual, family, and community life in the world, it can provide a meaning-filled nesting place and thus provide the most elementary context of care.

When thus considered, the cultural-linguistic model provides a framework for maintaining a lively connection between the questions and problems that arise in the practice of pastoral care as well as in practical theology. Practical theology becomes the task of maintaining the connections between the varied stories of life and the grounding story of the Christian community. Pastoral care becomes the community of faith's living expression of that grounding story.

This way of formulating the relationship between practical theological work and the work of pastoral care moves well beyond what I described as the psychotherapeutic pastoral care model. You will remember that the psychotherapeutic model follows experiential-expressivist avenues of developing psychological or psychotherapeutic descriptions of people's needs and conflicts. Once the needs and conflicts have been described in psychological terms, the caregiver seeks to make what are often tenuous symbolic connections between those descriptions and the symbols of theology. Sometimes the symbolic connections are made explicit in the caring relationships; more often they are not.

The cultural-linguistic approach, by contrast, emphasizes the primary importance of interpretation and the language to be used in interpreting human situations and predicaments. For the Christian pastor or the Christian community as a whole, the primary language of care is the language of the Christian story and tradition. I will therefore speak of this model of pastoral care as a narrative hermeneutical model. Its structure emphasizes both the human penchant for structuring life according to stories, and the power of interpretations to shape life and express care.

We may schematize the narrative hermeneutical pastoral care model as in figure 3.

The Story of the	Pastoral	The Particularity of
Christian Community	Care	Life Stories
and Its Tradition		

Figure 3

Figure 3 locates pastoral care in the center of the dialogical space between the communal story of the Christian community and the

111

many life stories of people who are in some way related to the Christian community. That location is highly significant and is meant to indicate a number of important elements in the model.

First, locating pastoral care in the center of the dialogue between the Christian story and life stories suggests that its most fundamental caring purpose is to facilitate the process of connecting life stories to the Christian story and vice versa. I have already asserted that this is the most elementary form of care that the Christian community has to offer. Fostering and facilitating that dialogical connection is, therefore central to the work of pastoral care.

Second, the schema is intended to indicate that the dialogue between life stories and the Christian story involves a tension or dialectic. Even though, as Lindbeck has shown, the language, meanings, and even feelings persons use in experiencing their life stories are most often drawn from larger cultural stories, including the story of their religious community, life stories have a particularity of their own. The images and meanings attached to those stories have been given a particular cast by the life experiences of the individuals, families, and other groups involved. The fit between the particularity of life stories and the Christian story is never exact. They virtually always stand in some degree of tension with each other.

Pastoral care thus schematized always involves placing the caring minister somewhere between loyalty to and representation of the Christian story, on the one hand, and empathic attention to the particularity of life stories, on the other. Unlike pastoral care within a propositionalist model, the pastor in this model does not simply await the opportunity to proclaim the Christian truth that applies to the life story at hand. The pastor does not simply "prepare the way" for the truth about God to be proclaimed or the grace and mercy of God to manifest themselves. Rather, the pastor seeks to facilitate a serious, open dialogue between the two sides of the equation, a dialogue that will include sharing of feelings, stories of past experiences, mutual questioning, and search for authentic connections between the two poles. Such facilitation virtually always involves the pastor in a degree of tension.

As pastors experience this tension, they will at times symbolically locate themselves on the side of the dialectic identified with the Christian story and its tradition, speaking from that side of the dialectic to persons on the other end. This speaking and relational activity may indeed have some qualities akin to proclamation.

At other times the minister may be symbolically located on the side of people and their life stories, seeking to help people articulate their thoughts and feelings about their situations, including their questions and feelings toward the Christian story, its community, and its God. Here the minister's activity may partake of certain qualities of the experiential-expressivist mode of doing theological work. It may even involve a certain quality of pushing against or confronting the community, its tradition, and even God's own self. Thus pastoral work within the tension of dialogue always involves mobility, the ability to move from side to side.

Third, what has already been implied needs to be stated explicitly: the work of pastoral care involves responsibility for facilitating the maintenance and further development of the Christian community's story and its dialogue with its tradition, on the one hand, and for facilitating the growth and creative development of particular life stories, on the other. Pastoral care involves both the care of the Christian community *and* the care of persons: individually, in families, and in larger group relationships. Part 2 of this book will focus on the pastor's responsibility for the ongoing care of the congregation as a Christian community and its dialogue with and appropriation of the Christian tradition. Part 3 will focus on the care of life stories of individuals, families, and groups with similar life concerns.

The schema of figure 3 should be seen as a further development of the schema of figure 2 in chapter 1. Within the schema of figure 2 in chapter 1, pastoral care is likewise seen in fundamental ways as dialogical, taking place within the dialectical tensions that both play upon it and are the subject of its caring efforts. The two schemas should therefore be understood as complementary, both built on a cultural-linguistic model that also values certain aspects of propositionalist and experiential-expressivist models.

The Pastor As Interpretive Guide

In our earlier discussion of pastoral care's heritage, each era of pastoral care's history was seen as emphasizing one or another of the four pastoral functions that have commonly been designated healing, guiding, sustaining, and reconciling. The particular emphasis of a given era, as I interpreted it in that discussion, was seen as an outgrowth of what was going on in the church and the society at the time. Other modes of care may have been present but not prominent. In the recent past the most prominent mode of pastoral care has been that of guidance, most often understood in terms of the psychotherapeutic paradigm. Healing, sustaining, and reconciling, while present in such pastoral activities as grief ministry, care for the chronically ill, and family counseling, have largely been structured in the mode of guidance, most often understood in terms of the psychotherapeutic paradigm.[25]

I anticipate that in the coming decades of Western society's development the predominant mode of pastoral care will continue to be that of guidance, but the prevailing quality of guidance needs to be substantially altered in ways that take into account the broad cultural and societal problems I have described earlier in this chapter. While retaining some of the skills and sensitivities of the psychotherapeutic paradigm, guidance needs now to shift its focus in the direction of cultural-linguistic concerns. Likewise, the modes of pastoral healing, sustaining, and reconciling need now to become more clearly communal, giving greater attention to the fostering of inquiry and dialogue between the Christian community, its story, and people's life stories.

The role of pastoral leadership must more clearly and intentionally than in the recent past develop a quality of interpretive guidance. By interpretive guidance I mean not simply interpretation of the Christian tradition and its implications for communal, moral, individual, and societal life, important as that is for the role of pastoral leadership and relational practice. I mean also the role of interpreting the conflicts and pressures, the contradictions and pitfalls, the lures and tendencies toward fragmentation of contemporary life. In short, I mean the role of interpretive guidance as it relates to facilitating the dialogical process between life stories and the Christian story of how life is to be lived.[26]

PART II

Caring for the Community of
the Christian Story

The revised model of pastoral care proposed in the schema of figure 3 in chapter 4 asserts that <u>pastoral care takes place within the tension between the Christian community and its tradition, on the one hand, and the particularity of each contemporary human situation, on the other.</u> The schema suggests that each end of that equation is to be taken seriously. <u>Care in the Christian sense</u> of the word always <u>involves both care of the community</u> and <u>care of persons involved in any situation with which the pastor is confronted.</u> It involves the pastor both as leader of a community of faith and as symbolic representative of the Christian tradition in personal relationships. Part 2 of this book will deal primarily with the development of this model of pastoral care as interpretive guidance in relation to the leadership of a congregation of Christians.

Influenced by a dominant trend in Western culture in the twentieth century toward <u>specialization</u> of roles and practices, the pastoral leadership of a congregation has likewise tended toward a certain quality of specialization. Pastors have been taught to think of their ministry as a collection of specialized functions. This way of thinking about ministry divides the pastor's work into several functions: <u>preaching, teaching, administration, liturgical leadership,</u> and <u>pastoral care</u> and <u>counseling.</u> One of the results of this functional mode of thinking is that each of these functional roles has to a considerable extent become a specialization claiming dominance in the work of ministry. Functional thinking has encouraged pastors to perceive themselves primarily from within the roles and practices of their specialized functions. Pastors thus tend to choose one or another of these so-called functions as their specialization.

As a result, many pastors evidence a lack of coherence in their work, resulting in a fragmentation of purpose, confusion among often conflicting methods of operation in various functions, valuing of one function and neglect of another, and the like. Pastors need a foundational, organizing image of the whole of pastoral ministry that can give coherence to and inform all of the various functional roles that the pastor plays in the life of the congregation.

I propose that the conceptual image that best gives coherence to ordained ministry within the church is that of the pastor as interpretive guide within the life of the Christian community. That image embraces the care of the community of Christians in all its dimensions. Seen from within a functional understanding of ordained ministry, the function of interpretive guidance thus becomes in a certain sense the "master function" that informs all the various subfunctions of pastoral ministry in the life of the Christian community. It becomes the perspective from which all the functions of ministry—preaching, teaching, pastoral care, organizing and administering, and so on—are given coherence and unity of purpose.[1]

The two chapters of part 2 each take up an important aspect of caring for the community of the Christian story. Chapter 5 deals with the conceptualizing of the role of the minister as interpretive guide, particularly as that role relates to the caring leadership of a Christian community. Chapter 6 is concerned with the relationship between the Christian community and the surrounding cultural situation. Recognizing that Christians must live out their lives in numerous story-shaped activities and relationships, I will try to break open some of the implications of pluralism for the Christian community and its leadership.

Chapter 6 argues that in a fundamental sense the care for the community of believers as well as the care of individuals within or without the community is the work of the laity. The laity are not simply and primarily the recipients of the care of the ordained pastor, although the pastor's own care for the community and for individuals can and should provide all Christians with a symbolic model of care for one another and for the world. Care is thus seen as a primary metaphor that informs the ministry of the church, both lay and clerical. That metaphor symbolically connects the life of the community to the incarnate care of God for God's people and for the world as expressed in Jesus Christ, the One who cared supremely for the world.

CHAPTER 5

Pastoral Care As Interpretive Leadership

Some years ago I moved with my family to a community of twenty-five thousand people to become pastor of one of the churches of my denomination. We moved our household goods into the parsonage on a hot Thursday in June, and I conducted my first worship service the following Sunday. After greeting and being greeted by a good number of the members of my new congregation, we were just sitting down to a late lunch in our new home when the telephone rang. The person calling was the mother of one of the teenagers in the church.

"Has anyone talked with you about taking the kids to Summer Youth Institute this afternoon?" she asked.

"No, this is the first I've heard about that," I responded, somewhat nonplused by the question.

"Well, there are three of the youth going and I guess we just assumed that you would take them. Our last pastor always did."

As I quickly tried to formulate my response to what struck me as a very presumptuous request, several thoughts ran through my head. I remembered my first conversation with the pastoral relations committee of the church when my appointment as their pastor had just been finalized. My primary memory of that meeting was the question they had pressed me to answer: "What will be your program for our church?"

My response then had been to remind the committee members that it was really their church, not mine. "We will need to work out together what the program of the church we will try to become should be." The discussion that followed had not been an easy or comfortable one for me or, I sensed from the tone of several comments, the laypeople. I came away from that meeting with a clear realization that I would need in the coming months to clarify just what my pastoral leadership role was to be. Somehow, the presumptuous request now before me fell on my ears as an echo of the same tone of expectation about pastoral leadership that I had encountered in the meeting with the pastoral relations committee.

I also remembered vaguely my encounter with the mother on the phone after church that morning. She had been most fulsome in her greeting, a little too gushy, in a manner that seemed to reflect anxiety. I had made a mental note to make further inquiry about what was going on with this parishioner.

"I had not planned on going to the Youth Institute," I found myself saying to my caller. Her initial response was silence, an uncomfortable silence for me and, I assumed, an uncomfortable one for my caller as well. Then came the verbal response, spoken with anxious hostility: "But how will the kids get to Institute?"

"I guess the parents will need to get together and decide who will take them," I said.

"Well, all right then. I suppose that's what we'll have to do."

As the telephone conversation ended, I was struck with the awareness that I had taken a significant and perhaps risky step toward defining for my new congregation an important dimension of my pastoral role. I was not going to be the one who ran churchly errands or did things for them or their children that they could do for themselves. So what was I to be for and with the congregation? How were they as a congregation to experience my care?

The Multidimensional Nature of Pastoral Care

Our study of the history of pastoral care in earlier chapters has already confronted us with the complex dialectics of care in the church. Pastoral care involves not only the care of individuals and families, but also the care of the community itself. Pastoral care also entails the thoughtful reinterpretation of the tradition that shapes Christian identity as that tradition is brought into dialogical relationship with contemporary culture and its impact on the community of Christians as well as its individual members. I shared the story of my first encounters with members of a local church not in order to discourage readers from driving young parishioners to summer camp, but to illustrate how the issues contained in the quadrilateral schema (care of individuals, care of the community, care of the tradition, and care of the culture) quickly became relevant in my ministry in one local church.[1] Consider some of the issues the story illustrates.

First, the story suggests that the first question presented to the newly arrived pastor by the congregation will be one concerning both the content and quality of the prospective pastoral relationship. "Who will you be to and for us?" The ways in which that question will be asked will no doubt vary tremendously from one parish to another. The undisguised form of the question put to me by the parish relations committee is probably unusual, but the question will usually be asked in one way or another. It is significant that the form of the question has to do with leadership. What kind of leader will you be among us? Pastoral care in the parish begins with pastoral leadership. Setting the tone for that leadership will strongly affect every aspect of subsequent pastoral relationships.

Second, pastoral care in the parish is comprised of a complex set of relationships between the pastor and the congregation at multiple levels ranging from the congregation as a whole, to groups within the congregation, to families and individuals within the congregation. From the beginning of my first meeting with the pastoral relations committee, this representative group of laypeople was asking me who I was to be with them. Though there may have been members of that committee who had private and personal reasons for wanting to clarify that relationship, the first question concerned my relationship with the congregation as a whole. "What is your program going to be for our church?"

In an odd way the mother on the telephone was asking the same question. Who will you be here? What can we expect from you? Her decision to call me on the phone with her request rather than speak to me when we first met after morning worship perhaps suggests that at some level she knew that her question was loaded. The anxiety with which she spoke likewise indicates that she was asking for more than simple information. Her inquiry, at least as I heard it, seems to have been prompted by concerns at several levels. Her request most obviously related to the role I was to play with the church as a whole and with the youth ministry in particular.

At another level, the tone of her approach to me conveyed a vague, unstated disclosure of her own personal need for care. Reflection on that possibility alerts us to the likelihood that many, if not most requests for personal pastoral care will be made not in a direct manner, but in some disguised form. As a matter of fact, this may well be true of most requests for care at any level.

Third, this vignette of the beginning of my ministry reminds us that when we as pastors enter into ministry in a particular place, we become part of a story of life and ministry that has been going on for a long time before our arrival.[2]

Newly arrived pastors always come into the middle of the stories of a congregation and its individual members, not at the beginning of those stories. In a certain sense the new pastor's arrival on the scene comes as an interruption or an intrusion into whatever stories are being enacted in that place. Given that reality, one of the first requirements of successful pastoral care in a given place of ministry involves patient, curious, and respectful listening to the history of the place as related by different people. Some stories will be told by leaders of the congregation and some by people who are further from the center of the congregation's life. Friendly and respectful curiosity concerning these stories will do much to set a tone of care for the ensuing pastoral relationships.

Fourth, the story suggests that the pastoral response to requests and questions (especially the first requests and questions) from a congregation needs to be undergirded by and expressive of a clearly understood theology of the church and of ministry. Such a theology can provide a critical check both on the validity of requests made to the pastor and on the appropriateness or inappropriateness of a given pastoral response. A well-thought-out theology was crucially important in my response to the pastoral relations committee. "We will need to work out together what the program of the church we will try to become should be." This response implies several things. It clearly expresses a theology of the church that is nonauthoritarian, egalitarian, and democratic in its style of governance. It values the corporate nature of the church and expresses my desire to avoid if possible the pitfalls of clericalism that have repeatedly brought trouble to the church in the past. It expresses a valuing of a dialogical approach to determining congregational decisions and actions.

My response also assumes that there are no congregations that fully measure up to the standards of the biblical vision of what the Christian congregation should be. The church is always becoming the church, not simply celebrating and living out what the church has already become.[3]

Enabling the local congregation to value and appropriate its history is an important aspect of the pastor's care of the congregation. Just as important is the task of helping the congregation critically consider how it may more fully embody Christ's presence in the world.

Pastors enact their theological presuppositions to the extent that their manner of relating as well as their verbal responses to their congregants remains true to their theology of church and ministry. Pastoral theology is thus an enacted theology, an expression of what the pastor believes about the human condition, the Christian gospel, and the purpose of the church and its ministry as those beliefs are translated into caring pastoral response.

Viewed from the perspective of theology, the pastor's care of a congregation involves the pastor in leading the people in the construction and enactment of a "local theology."[4]

Theology will become real and relevant for members of a local congregation as it is related to the concrete realities of the people in the congregation. Tending the process of this contextualization of theology is an important aspect of the pastor's care of the congregation. By tending that process with care, the pastor expresses care for the Christian tradition and for the larger cultural circumstances that surround the local situation. Said another way, pastoral care of a congregation of God's people involves the construction of a particular, context-relevant theological awareness on the part of both pastor and people.

Dimensions of Congregational Life

To speak of pastoral care as involving the care of the congregation as a community that expresses its loyalty to the Christian tradition requires that we examine more closely what a congregation is and does. To provide caring leadership of a community of Christians, the pastor needs not only a clear vision of what a congregation should be, but also the capacity to think and act with clarity in relation to the realities of a given congregation. It is useful to think of the life of the congregation as having five dimensions.[5]

I will therefore speak of the congregation as (1) a community of language, (2) a community of memory, (3) a community of inquiry, (4) a community of mutual care, and (5) a community of mission. The caring pastor is one who gives leadership to the congregation's exercise of all five of these dimensions of its life.

A Community of Language

To say that a congregation is a community of language is to say that the Christian congregation cultivates the capacity of its members to think and talk in certain ways about a wide range of human activities and problems.

Communication makes possible the development of an identifiable Christian group. The Bible provides the language through which communication takes place in the church. Persons are identified with the church as they convey meanings to one another in the language of Christians. Meanings carried in language become a part of the mind and selfhood of persons as they speak and hear. The language of the Bible, as the language of communication to the church, makes possible a common life among Christians.[6]

James Gustafson asserts that for Christians there is a normative way of thinking and speaking meaningfully to one another that is rooted in an appropriation of biblical images and themes. To speak to one another utilizing the imagery of the Bible is to communicate in the native language of the Christian community. Biblical imagery is the mother tongue of Christian people, the language one learns to speak when one wants to say something important about life in the world. That does not, of course, mean that Christian talk is always Bible talk. But it does mean that within the Christian community the language of the Bible has been given a certain authority to which the members of that community are accountable.[7]

For that language to function normatively for Christian people it must not only be spoken freely and naturally, but it must constantly be reinterpreted in relation to whatever immediate human endeavor or problem prompts the community of Christians to want to speak in that vernacular. For Christian language to remain alive and relevant it must, in short, be cared for and cultivated. It is here that the pastor needs to function as interpretive guide. The pastor knows the Christian language and is fluent in the use of its images and themes; furthermore, the pastor seeks to sensitize the people to the nuanced significance of that language for their lives both as individuals and as a community.

To function as interpretive guide in relation to the church as a community of language the pastor needs not only to interpret the texts and stories of the Bible, but also to carefully guide the process of interpretation. The interpretive guide cultivates a dialogical relationship between biblical stories and the stories of people's lives today. Here the caring pastor functions as coach and facilitator. The good pastor is thus authoritative but not authoritarian. Rather than seeking to exercise the power of control over the thought and behavior of the people, she or he utilizes the power of the pastoral office to empower the people in their ability to make normative use of biblical themes and images in their lives and in the governance and activity of the church.

A Community of Memory

To comfortably and meaningfully speak the language of the Christian tradition, the community of Christians must remember that they are a people whose identity is shaped by the Bible. But being a community of memory means more than simply remembering how and when to speak the language. It also means remembering the stories that come down to us from the history of the people called Christians. It means the retelling of those stories and the celebration of events and symbolic acts that remind God's people of who they are. As James Gustafson writes:

Subjective understanding comes through remembering and reliving the past. Christians gain not only knowledge about the past, but in a sense participate in the past life of the Church. The self participates in the meaningful history of the Church, and comes to interpret and understand itself in the light of those meanings. The meaning of the past is internalized. The same past is internalized by many. In these processes the sense of common purpose and life grows, and the

123

identity of persons with the historical community is deepened. Continuity of an inner community, and a sense of inner unity, exist through common memory.[8]

Gustafson goes on to speak of the importance of Christians experiencing a continuity between their own life as Christians and the lives of Christian people of the past. To remember is to be reminded of who we are and who we desire to be. Nurturing that sense of continuity within members of the congregation is an important aspect of the pastor's care for the community.

Memory functions at multiple levels in people's lives, as does the pastor's work as nurturer of memory. Some memories can be held in common by members of the Christian community and thereby make possible the common life of Christians together. In the great celebrations of the church—Christmas, Easter, the Lord's Supper, even Sabbath worship itself—the gathered community of Christians is reminded of the life they hold in common not only with their fellow worshipers, but also with all the "fellowship of the saints" who came before them. The care-filled leadership of these celebrations is certainly one of the most important aspects of the pastor's care for the gathered community and for the tradition.

This public ministry of the pastor, important as it is, is not the only context in which the pastor functions as a nurturer of memory. In a sense the pastor wears the mantle of reminder wherever she or he goes in the daily round of varied personal contacts. In pastoral care circles this is often referred to as the "ministry of presence." As a symbolic figure, the pastor cannot escape being a reminder of whatever membership in the Christian community and ministry within it has come to mean to the individual.

Sometimes this can be a source of considerable discomfort to both the pastor and to the person receiving his or her ministry. I recall, for example, a pastoral care student who went to visit a woman who had just lost her young child to the ravages of leukemia. Introducing himself as one of the pastors in the hospital, he offered to pray with the distraught mother. Her response was immediate: "Your [expletive] prayers haven't done any good in the past. Why do you think they would help me now?" She then spit in the startled young man's face. Obviously his presence had not meant to this person what the young pastor intended. It did, however, give him the opportunity to convey to the woman the meaning of a caring and accepting relationship with a representative of the Christian community and its tradition. Startled by what the woman had said and done, he nevertheless made a courageous decision to stay with her and listen as she vented her pent-up rage and disappointment.

A Community of Inquiry

To be the pastoral leader of a Christian community means to engender in persons, both individually and as a community, a mood and habit of inquiry, most particularly inquiry into the ultimate meaning of their actions and the actions of others upon them. To care deeply for persons is to inquire with them, search with them, question with them about what the events of their lives mean at the deepest level. It also means to inquire with them into the ways in which their questions have been presented in the past and how those questions have been answered, most particularly with the people of the Bible.

To be a pastoral leader of a community of inquiry means to help people articulate their own questions and help them find answers to those questions. It means that the pastor eschews the temptation to provide for others quick and easy answers to their questions even when it may appear that an obvious answer exists. In this way the pastor seeks to nurture inquiry rather than end it by presenting an authoritative response.

It is here that the thoughtful pastor most often experiences the tension that was schematized in figure 3 in the preceding chapter. On the one hand, the pastor is called to be the chief representative of the Christian community and the theologian-in-residence of the community. As such, the pastor is expected to interpret human situations from the perspective the Christian tradition embodies. On the other hand, as I wrote in chapter 4, the caring pastor identifies with and takes seriously the particularity of whatever situation is at hand. She or he attempts to assist persons caught in any given situation, whether it be a situation of tragic illness or of interpersonal conflict, to articulate the questions that situation raises, and to press those questions against whatever the Christian tradition has to say about them. Here the pastor needs to cultivate the capacity to enter into and facilitate genuine dialogue between the two elements of the equation: the tradition and the situation. As interpretive guide, the pastor stands in the center of that dialogue while remaining open to the possibility of reinterpretation and new insight.

A Community of Mutual Care

A primary function of the Christian community is that of creating and maintaining a climate of relationship within which all members of the community are understood and cared for. To experience such a community is to overcome the loneliness that pervades contemporary culture.

The *Dictionary of Pastoral Care and Counseling* defines pastoral care of the congregation as "the ministry of oversight and nurture offered by a religious community to its members, including acts of discipline, support, comfort, and celebration."[9] To be a member of the Christian community thus means to give and receive a variety of forms of care. At times, one experiences one's membership in the community in some form of discipline. As noted in chapter 1, the forms of discipline exercised by Christian communities in ancient times have largely disappeared. Penance in the form of exclusion from the community of worshipers is unheard of in our time, for example. However, there are still ways in which the community of Christians exercises its social pressure on its members with regard to all manner of behaviors and attitudes. More often, however, active members of Christian communities experience their fellow Christians as sources of support, mutual encouragement, and comfort.

Life brings to some persons most of the time and to all persons some of the time situations that tax their own internal or material resources beyond their capacity to sustain hopeful, vital living. One cannot live entirely on one's own. If the truth were known, it is probably that fact about human nature that more than anything else entices people into the relationships of communities such as the church. All of us need and long for a set of sustaining relationships within which we can be open and assured of acceptance.

On the other hand, much of modern life tends toward alienation rather than mutual support. Competition rules much of the marketplace of human relationships. Prejudice, stereotyping, and indifference abound in human relationships, even among family members and coworkers, to say nothing of the Christian community itself. Countering these alienating tendencies in human relationships is an important aspect of the work of the church as a community.

The pastor nourishes and engenders a climate of mutual care in the community for which she or he seeks to provide interpretive leadership. By his or her manner of relating within the community, others are encouraged to create and participate in a community where everyone feels cared for and nourished. In addition, the pastor needs to recognize that she or he is not alone in providing pastoral care in the fellowship of the community. Guiding the process of care within the community should mean facilitating and empowering the members of the community in their capacity to care for one another. Organizing, offering training, and, where appropriate, supervising laypeople in their activities of mutual care are significant aspects of pastoral care leadership.

A Community of Mission

As a community that seeks to be faithful to its Lord, the church is called out of itself into the world around it. As H. Richard Niebuhr has said of the influence of biblical faith on Christians, the church "loses its character as Church when it concentrates on itself, worships itself and seeks to make love of the Church the first commandment."[10]

Niebuhr goes on to point out that to be faithful to the God of the church and to Christ, who is its head, the ultimate objective of the Christian community is to increase among *all* people the love of God and neighbor. Thus, important as is the mutual care of one another, that care is not enough to fulfill the Christian community's loyalty to its tradition.

As interpretive guide of the community of Christians, the pastor is thus called not only to nurture the process by which the community cares for its members, but also to nurture within the members of the community an awareness of the needs of all people in the world. Engaging in pastoral care as interpretive guide means much more than simply being a faithful chaplain to the congregation. It also means articulating the call of the gospel to be concerned for and actively involved in social ministries that care for the dispossessed, the homeless, and the victims of political and economic injustice everywhere.

Dieter Hessel reiterates what our study of the history of pastoral care in part 1 of this book demonstrated; namely, that any attempt to divide the work of ministry between pastoral care and social ministry is fundamentally false:

> Since God is radically social, all modes or dimensions of ministry are social in ways that encompass both personal growth and political responsibility. Congregations must develop the modes of ministry with intentionality and competence, so that ministry contributes to social transformation as well as human fulfillment, to health of community and country as well as human fulfillment, to health of community and country as well as congregational renewal, to local/global action as well as to church growth.[11]

The pastor is called to lead the Christian community to better care for one another *and* to care for the larger world of human need. In that ministry the pastor is both prophet and priest, and the mode of her or his ministry will most often be as interpretive guide to the people of the community, interpreting with them both the biblical vision of the Christian tradition and the situations that exist in the contemporary world.

At this point, it will be helpful to consider the pastoral care experience of an acquaintance of mine, in which virtually all the dimensions of pastoral care as interpretive guidance were evident. (In order to protect the confidentiality of those involved, I have altered some details of the incident.)

St. Matthew's Church is a congregation of 1,500 members located in an upper-middle-class suburb of a relatively large city where there is a major tertiary medical center. The church membership includes a sizable number of medical personnel, along with the number of business and professional people one would expect to find in a relatively affluent congregation. The congregation includes numerous retired persons living on fixed incomes, many families with young children, and a fair number of young and middle-aged singles. The diverse congregation includes a relatively balanced mixture of people with a so-called liberal religious and political mind-set and people of a more conservative persuasion.

The series of incidents that provide the focus of our attention here took place in connection with a three-week medical mission trip to Somalia organized by a small group of highly motivated doctors and nurses in the congregation and somewhat loosely sponsored by the congregational missions committee. The group making the trip included medical personnel as well as others who went along to provide support for other aspects of the mission. The associate pastor of the church accompanied the group to provide pastoral care for members of the mission and, as appropriate, for those receiving their care.

The instigators and unofficial leaders of the mission, many of whom were members of the mission committee, took firm charge of the arrangements and the selection of the participants. They made several informal reports of their activities to the committee, but did not ask for assistance in establishing the policies that would govern the mission. The missions committee remained somewhat passive in its stance toward the mission but was generally encouraging and supportive. The senior pastor was not consulted, perhaps because he was relatively new to the parish, having arrived after the initial planning had taken place.

It had been decided early in the planning by the project's instigators that the group going to Somalia would not include any married couples. Married persons could participate, but their spouses would need to remain at home. It was also decided that the mission group would meet intensively over a period of several months before departure in order that close relationships could develop and general policies for the mission be unanimously agreed upon. Prayer and Bible study were included in these preliminary meetings. In several announcements to the congregation, members of the church were invited to offer prayerful support of the mission; the lay administrative board of the church was not, however, asked to give its approval of the project.

The first incident for which the senior pastor was called upon to provide interpretive guidance involved a male and a female member of the mission group, along with their respective spouses. These two persons had become more and more romantically involved with each other prior to and during the time the group spent in Somalia. By the time the group returned home, this relationship had blossomed into a full-blown affair. Now both partners in the affair were considering divorcing their spouses in order that they could be free to marry each other. Neither wanted to leave the church and seemed, from reports made to the pastor by other members of the mission group, to expect that their newfound love relationship would be accepted by others in the congregation.

The affair first came to the senior pastor's attention when the associate pastor reported her suspicions about it upon her return. Not long after that, both of the spouses who had been left behind came to the pastor seeking pastoral care. The jilted husband expressed great anger toward both his wife and the other man, declaring that "there is not room enough in this church for both of us," and in a similar manner expressing a desire to "punish" his wife for her unfaithfulness. The forsaken wife also came to the pastor, asking for his help in restoring her marriage. She freely admitted her part in the demise of the marriage and talked about her preoccupation with the couple's two children and with the burden she and her husband shared in relation to her aging parents.

Not long after the pastor had the first of several conversations with the forsaken wife, the woman involved in the affair called the pastor asking if he would see her and her suitor together to discuss some of the implications of their relationship. When he saw them, somewhat to his surprise, they did not ask for his judgment or opinion concerning the relationship as such. Neither did they ask for his counsel concerning their relationship. Rather, they asked him about the effect their both seeking divorce from their spouses and subsequent marriage might have on their future leadership roles in the church. In reporting the incident to his peer group the pastor confessed his confusion at this point. He felt that the couple was asking for his care, but their request was made in such an ambiguous manner that he felt somewhat helpless to turn the conversation in a productive direction. He then became aware of his own negative feelings toward them and their relationship, mingled with a sincere desire to relate to them in a nonjudgmental manner.

A second incident requiring the senior pastor's involvement pertained to a young single woman in the mission group who was not yet a member of the congregation, although she had been participating in the young adult activities of the church for several months. She had recently completed training as a nurse in a distant city and had come to the community to work at the medical center. The daughter of missionary parents, she had been born in Vietnam but had spent most of her adolescence and adult life in the United States.

Greatly moved by the plight of the people of Somalia, this young woman returned from the mission trip with what she felt to be a clear call to go into full-time missionary work as a nurse in Somalia. She had talked informally with the pastor about her desire, but no plans had been made to present her to the lay board of the congregation and ask for the sponsorship of the church.

Not long after the return of the mission group, the chairperson of the missions committee called the pastor, saying that the missions committee would like to have a "commissioning service" for the young nurse at the close of morning worship the following Sunday. Feeling that a formal commissioning was premature since the congregation had not officially offered its sponsorship, to say nothing of formal action by the denomination, the pastor balked, saying that he could not do that without prior approval of the official bodies of the church.

Needless to say, the pastor's response was met with considerable anger on the part of the missions chairperson, who launched into a long diatribe about how the congregation was only interested in its own affairs and did not have an adequate concept of the mission of the church "out there in the world." The commissioning should be held in order to "draw St. Matthew's outside of itself into a larger understanding of missions."

Still uncomfortable with the irregular nature of the request and the lack of opportunity for elected representatives of the congregation to give or withhold their approval and blessing of the young nurse's plans, the pastor stood firm in his refusal to hold the commissioning service. He said that having such a service involving the entire congregation would be "like having a shotgun wedding! I would much prefer people to have the freedom to choose. Unless people have the right to say no, they cannot say yes. There has been no opening to say no prior to the service. It would be inappropriate to make promises prior to a chance to determine if this was appropriate for the church. Covenants are freely chosen acts of response. The congregation needs a chance to choose to make this covenant."

The pastor did agree to discuss the matter further with the missions chairperson and one or two others from the Somalia mission team over breakfast the following day. Prior to that meeting he spoke informally with both the nurse and her father, who, having retired, was now an active member of the congregation. In these conversations the pastor proposed that a private, informal "service of blessing and commissioning" be held prior to morning worship, to which anyone who knew the nurse and wanted to participate would be invited. Further, he proposed that he introduce her to the congregation at the close of morning worship. This compromise was acceptable to both the nurse and her father.

At the breakfast meeting with the small group from the missions committee the pastor met with considerable resistance to his proposed compromise. Again the issue seemed to turn on the question of how a big congregation like St. Matthew's was to be educated about their responsibility to care for people in far corners of the world rather than simply being self-centered. The missions committee chairperson used a metaphorical image of the church as a number of "little trains trying to move one big rock in the middle. Each little train must be allowed to do its own work." The pastor responded that the independent trains can work against one another as they try to move the rock (the church). He proposed an alternative metaphor of a "big ocean liner, where you turn the wheel and a long time later you see some results." There followed a long discussion concerning who had authority in the church, where that authority came from, and how it should be properly used.

The story of St. Matthew's Church continues. Like most stories of churches, its final chapter is yet to be written. We will leave the story at this point in order to reflect on what it has to tell us about the ways in which all the elements of congregational life very often come together at once in the life of any congregation. What does this particular story tell us about pastoral care as care of the congregation? Of the tradition that gives a congregation its identity? Of persons within the congregation and their care for one another? Of the care of the congregation for persons outside its own boundaries?

The first and most obvious lesson that the situation at St. Matthew's has to teach us is that very often the need for care at all levels is presented to the pastor at once. Rarely does the parish pastor have the luxury of caring for one individual at a time, or, on the other hand, simply caring for the congregation as a community. At various times during the course of the episode at St. Matthew's Church, the senior pastor had to consider at least three different responsibilities.

First, he had to consider his responsibility for the long-term care of the congregation in its pilgrimage toward becoming the people of God they were called to be. He could not act pastorally in this situation without first taking into account the long-term effects of his actions on the congregation. We see this most clearly in his decision regarding whether or not to hold the consecration service as requested by the missions chairperson. Here he saw not only an opportunity to educate his people concerning the importance of world missions, but also an occasion for making decisions about what the church was to sponsor or not sponsor. In this regard it is interesting that he exercised his authority as pastor to empower the congregation to act for themselves rather than assuming the power to act for them.

Reviewing the story of this incident we find ourselves empathizing with the pastor in his dilemma with regard to the missions committee and its chairperson. One can guess that in many respects his sympathies were with the mission faction and its leadership. The missions chairperson seems to speak much of the right language. He has heard the biblical call to God's people to "go into all the world." We can guess that the pastor probably shares much of the chairperson's impatience with the congregation's self-centeredness. Yet in this situation he quite apparently feels that he must stand against the other's position. His care for the congregation must take precedence. A closer look at the pastor's stance reveals the possibility that in refusing the chairperson's desire, the pastor may well be performing an indirect act of care for him as well. What is the chairperson to do with the pastor's refusal? Could it possibly be a time for the chairperson to reconsider the way in which he tends to insist on his own way? If so, we can see that, unpleasant as it is, he has been offered an act of care.

The pastor's care for the congregation is less clear in regard to the incident of the extramarital affair, no doubt because of the somewhat private nature of the problem presented. Here we can only reflectively question with the pastor how the two impending divorces and the remarriage will affect the congregation. Can the community contain such a violation and disruption of its standards with regard to marriage and family life? *Should* it contain such behavior? What about the care of the two marital partners whose covenants with their spouses have been violated? Here the problem of church discipline is raised in an interesting way. How are the pastor and the congregation to exercise discipline in this situation?[12]

Second, the pastor has to consider his responsibility for the careful interpretation and reinterpretation of the biblical and theological tradition that by his ordination he is called upon to keep in lively dialogical relationship with the events in the lives of his congregation.

If the pastor of St. Matthew's Church is to fulfill his function as theologian-in-residence for his congregation, he must be alert for opportunities to foster a reflective dialogical process between situations in the common life of the congregation and the images and themes that have shaped Christian identity in times past. We would expect that dialogue to be a mutually critical process rather than simply a proclamation of truths that have already been demonstrated. Where and when, we may ask, do opportunities arise in the series of incidents at St. Matthew's for the pastor to foster this kind of dialogue?

In that regard, several critical events in the story come to mind. I think, for example, of the conferences the pastor had with all four of the central characters involved in or directly affected by the extramarital affair. All four came to the pastor because they respect his office as pastoral theologian. The errant couple seem to be seeking the pastor's blessing on their relationship. Neither of them want to leave the church. Yet they wonder aloud about how their behavior will affect their future in the congregation. Does that not indirectly invite the pastor to help them think about what their behavior and the norms for Christian life have to say to each other? Their request for care seems clearly, albeit indirectly, to ask for talk about their situation in the language of Christian faith.

I think also of the tangled sequence of events involving the missions committee and the Somalian mission. Would not serious and sustained conversation about the meaning and purpose of the church's mission in the world and, perhaps even more, talk about the catalytic function of committed groups within the congregation be an important aspect of the pastor's care for the tradition and for the community of Christians? If so, how is the pastor to foster such conversation? Here the quality of *pastoral leadership* seems crucial.

Third, the pastor must consider his responsibility to fulfill the pastoral role with individuals and families in the congregation. The story of St. Matthew's Church demonstrates dramatically the way in which the care of the congregation and its tradition is virtually always intertwined with and complicated by the needs of various individuals for pastoral care directed to their particular need and expectation. The pastor of St. Matthew's could not simply deal with group and congregational issues as the story unfolded. In the midst of thinking and acting as pastoral leader and administrator of the church, he also had to respond to the unique needs of *particular* persons as well.

Balancing care of the individual with care for the larger community, such an ongoing challenge for the parish minister, is not as pressing a task for the clergyperson engaged in counseling or psychotherapy as a specialized ministry. In the latter case, ministers ordinarily have no acknowledged responsibility beyond that to the person being counseled in a private office. Not so with parish pastors. They quite frequently have to balance (and on occasion, juggle) their responsibility to individual parishioners and their responsibility to the larger congregation.

We have discussed how the pastor at St. Matthew's was confronted with his obligation to the first three nexus points of our quadrilateral schema: care for the community, care for the tradition, and care for individuals. I want now to consider the fourth point of the quadrilateral: care of the culture. The Christian community is not the only community to which its members belong. Rather, the Christian community and its tradition are set within a world of many communities. These multiple communities have a profound effect upon people, and they shape many of the human needs and problems that call for the care of pastors and churches. The next chapter will seek to address this complexity of modern life in multiple communities.

CHAPTER 6

The Christian Community in a World of Many Communities

"Howard" was no stranger to me. I had been his pastoral counselor for several years. Our relationship had been prompted by his general dissatisfaction with his work as an attorney, an increasingly troubled marriage, and his growing awareness that his drinking was beginning to interfere with his ability to cope with his job and his marriage. Over the years we had worked together I had seen him get his drinking problem well enough in hand that he had been "dry" for over a year, though he still had dreams (both while asleep and awake) that revealed a persistent wish to "get good and drunk, chunk it all, and go lie on the beach in Florida." Our work together had also resulted, quite without any direct suggestion from me, in his taking a more active role in his community of faith.

One day, Howard came to me to talk about his difficulties in prioritizing his commitments of his time and energy. As he put it, "I don't know when I should be faithful to what. All the worlds I live in keep wanting my full attention at the same time."

I immediately found myself strongly empathizing with Howard. I too had often found myself caught in a conflict of loyalties, as have, I would imagine, most people who read this book. But my lawyer counselee seemed more troubled about this human dilemma than what you and I ordinarily experience.

My help-seeking friend needed little prompting to relate the incident that had sparked his heightened awareness of his old problem of divided loyalties. As a corporate lawyer whose practice involved legal work for "big money" transactions between both large and small corporations, Howard was frequently involved in high-pressure, "we need this done by yesterday!" situations. On the weekend just before we met, Howard had been involved in one of those situations. The clients with whom he was working at the time had in a late-night Friday meeting finally come to an agreement in a complicated deal. When they finished, they asked the lawyers from each side to put the agreement into legal form and have it ready for them to sign first thing Monday morning. Now the work for Howard and the other attorneys began. Since it was the weekend, they agreed that they would all return to their home bases and draft contract proposals, then get together on the telephone Sunday morning to iron out differences. The senior attorney for the other side agreed to call Howard at his office sometime between nine and ten o'clock—an arrangement that, though he disliked working on Sunday, suited Howard since that would perhaps give him just enough time to finalize the document and maybe make it to church to be with his family for the eleven-o'clock worship service. Howard told me at this point in his telling the story that he realized now that his desire to be with his family at church was probably a vain wish. But, he reiterated, it was also a wish that he felt strongly about. Howard worked until nearly midnight Saturday (one of his usual days at home) and completed his draft of the contract. When he left home at eight-thirty the next morning, he promised his loyal but by this time frustrated wife that he would do his best to make it to church sometime close to eleven and spend the rest of the day with her and the children.

Ten o'clock came, and Howard's counterpart had not called. Eleven came, and still he waited. He fiddled with other work on his desk that had been held in abeyance while he had been preoccupied with this case. He spotted several other pressing matters that demanded his immediate attention. A virtual parade of his many obligations and relationships, not only in his legal vocation, but also in his private life, passed through his mind. He was worried about his marriage. It had been a shaky, strained relationship for some time. He thought about his oldest son, with whom he needed to spend more time. Young Howard, Jr., was not doing well in school and neither Howard nor the boy's mother approved of a recent intense relationship with a girl who young Howard's parents thought to be emotionally unstable.

As all this and more flooded its way through his mind, Howard found himself feeling frustrated and angry. Although his anger had been prompted by the silent telephone, his feeling focused not only on his tardy caller, but even more on the legal workaday world that had him trapped. This was by no means the first time that he had been caught in the midst of obligations and wishes that intersected. He knew that his wife would be furious with him if he did not keep his promise to her. He also knew that his work required that he not leave until the legal work on this case had been completed. He thought about the theology course he had taken some months ago in which he had argued that it was virtually impossible in the business world in which he lived most of the hours of his days to allow his Christian faith to exercise any priority. Besides, he knew that his hold on the faith as it had been represented by his church was very tenuous. He wasn't sure if the whole belief system wasn't so archaic and flawed as to have no bearing on the dilemmas that confronted him in his daily life.

It was nearly noon before the other attorney called, and the resolution of a number of differences in the wording of the contract took until almost two o'clock. When he finally arrived home in mid-afternoon, his wife would scarcely speak to him and his son had left to take his girlfriend to the movies. Tired and depressed, Howard retreated to his study and settled in to watch the rest of a football game on the television while he ate a sandwich. By midweek, when he came to see me for his regular counseling appointment, he had made several moves that had in a fragile way resolved the situation. By Monday he and his wife had managed to have a short conversation in which they mutually expressed their frustration with their lifestyle and Howard had apologized for allowing his work to intrude on their sacred time. Howard had also made the decision to bill the client who had set him up to have to spend his weekend on this case the full price for all the hours that he had spent working and waiting for the contract work to be completed. He took some grim satisfaction in knowing that "somebody had been made to pay!"

In a number of important ways, Howard's situation provides a prototype of the problems for pastoral care practice that I want to address in this chapter: the problems of offering guidance to communities of Christians and their individual members as they seek to keep and clarify their faith in a time marked by pluralism, relativism, and competitive cultural confusion.

Clearly, Howard's problems were at multiple, interrelated levels. Some aspects of his struggle to find integrity and balance in his life were undoubtedly grounded in a lifelong individual quest for authentic identity. The only son of an alcoholic father and an insecure, neurotically anxious mother, Howard had from an early age been profoundly insecure about his own selfhood, uncertain as to his abilities, and in need of a role model he had never had. Thus it may be said that the core of his uncertainty was relational. He rarely felt "at home" with others, and least of all his own immediate family and his closest business colleagues.

Yet Howard had many friends and acquaintances, most of whom would have described him as a very accomplished and talented person who had achieved success worthy of admiration or even envy. He was a good lawyer: hard-working, knowledgeable about the law, and creative in his ability to solve intricate legal problems. Thus it can also be said that Howard, albeit with much pain and anxious worry, had in many ways learned to adapt to a challenging life situation. He was also quite serious in his efforts to find meaning and coherence in his life. He had worked hard in his counseling relationship with me. After a number of setbacks, he had mastered his drinking problem enough that he had a growing confidence in his ability to remain sober.

Howard had enrolled in his church's intensive theological course for laypeople and actively engaged in searching discussions with his fellow class members as they sought together to relate their religious studies to the activities and problems of their daily lives. In short, he was a *serious* Christian, although one who admitted to equally serious doubts.

The pastor who keeps her or his caring eyes and ears alert to what is going on with members of the community of faith will see and hear many stories not unlike Howard's. Differing in detail, to be sure, these stories will be about personal, interpersonal, and relational problems of varying severity, intermixed with problems that are rooted in the practices of a time and place (i.e., cultural and societal problems). Furthermore, inextricably intertwined with these human dilemmas are themes of the human quest for meaning and that ingredient of life that we generally think of as religious faith.[1]

Pluralism, Relativism, and Keeping the Faith

In chapter 1, I introduced a quadrilateral schema for pastoral ministry, involving four dimensions of care: (1) care for the Christian tradition, (2) care for individuals and their families, (3) care for the community of Christians, and (4) care in relationship to the sociocultural situation in which the Christian community finds itself.[2]

Taking all four of these dimensions into consideration in formulating an approach to pastoral care practice seems at first to be a daunting, even disheartening task. How can the pastor possibly keep all these elements of care clearly enough in mind that they can be usefully applied to the concrete realities of a particular pastoral care problem?

Reflection on a story such as Howard's is instructive at this point. Like Howard, most pastors have difficulty holding all the forces that play on their lives in the kind of creative tension that nurtures authentic selfhood. To paraphrase Howard, "How are we to know when to be faithful to what?"

For Howard this dilemma was sharply focused in his divided loyalty to home and family, on the one hand, and the demands of his legal practice, on the other. This focus, however, was symptomatic of profound splits that cut across virtually every aspect of Howard's life. Divided loyalties was a condition that pervaded his character, making it difficult for him to feel satisfied with any area of his life's activity.

In order to understand Howard's situation deeply enough to offer him pastoral guidance, I needed to give attention to all four dimensions of the quadrilateral schema. To define his problem simply as one rooted in his childhood background and psychological development, important as it is to understand him from that perspective, would be to settle for a shallow understanding of Howard's situation. Furthermore, such an explanation would focus on his weaknesses rather than invoke his strengths.

The search Howard was undertaking in his counseling relationship with me, although it was not spoken of in these terms, contained all four of the elements of the quadrilateral. He certainly sought help in understanding himself as an individual. By the time of the interview described here, Howard had made considerable gains in his self-awareness and some significant gains in self-acceptance, although he still was often plagued by self-doubt. He also sought my help in understanding his relationships with the various communities to which he belonged. He was trying to understand his role in his marriage, as a parent, in the legal profession, and, significantly, in the church.

The limits on Howard's ability to act freely and creatively in his situation are not simply psychological; they are to a significant extent culturally systemic. They are endemic to the society in which his life is located. Our society has structured how the legal profession is to be practiced and assigned a high priority and value to work, relative to family responsibilities and leisure activities. Howard's problem reflects the relatively low priority his society has given to participation in a faith community.

Theological Reflection in Pastoral Practice

If pastoral care is to be truly *pastoral*, it must focus on more than individual and societal concerns. Pastoral care must focus serious attention on the norms that emanate from the biblical and theological tradition. How and when are these norms to guide the pastoral relationship and how do they offer guidance to help persons such as Howard understand the tradition as it relates to their decisions and actions?

It is at this point that both young, inexperienced pastors and pastoral care veterans may often find themselves caught between two horns of a dilemma. Shall I respond to an apparent invitation to share my pertinent biblical or theological wisdom and thus risk seeming to give authoritative or even authoritarian advice? Or shall I follow the admonitions of nondirective counseling and simply try to help the person clarify his or her own feelings, desires, and judgments about his or her possible courses of action? Should I be implicit or explicit in my representation of the faith tradition? Somewhere between those two extremes lies the ground, undergirded by empathy and trust, where pastor and parishioner can search together for solutions that consider the multiple facets of both the faith tradition that brings them together *and* the unique needs of the person who seeks help.

Larry Kent Graham has written cogently about this matter of the use of pastoral authority in his book *Care of Persons, Care of Worlds:*

The ministry of care is a particular context in which the suffering connected with symptomatic crises may be contained, their causes and meanings explored, and new patterns of relatedness fashioned. The ministry of care seeks to promote change. In general terms, change is understood as an effective increase of love, justice, and ecological partnership throughout the psychosystemic matrix. More particularly, the ministry of care seeks to promote a creative modification of the power arrangements in the existing structure of things. It attempts to reorder the values that are contributing to symptomatic behaviors. It identifies destructive outcomes. Thus, for the pastoral caretaker, symptomatic crises are an invitation to be a participant in changing the fundamental fabric of personal and social reality, and to reconstruct the environment.[3]

Pastors will find that people vary widely in the extent to which they are self-conscious in their efforts to govern their lives according to Christian norms, values, and meanings. Some, like Howard, will express these concerns quite openly and conscientiously. Some will appear to be obsessed with questions about the rightness or wrongness of their actions as judged by the way in which they have appropriated some interpretation of moral or religious norms. Others will appear to give little thought to such questions, rather making decisions and acting in a manner that seems quite unself-conscious. The care the pastor offers must be adapted to these differences, while at the same time remaining faithful to the role of the pastor as representative of the tradition of the church.

As figure 3 in chapter 4 depicts, pastoral care exists in the space between the story of the Christian community and the particular stories of individuals within the community.[4] In the one-to-one relationships of pastoral care, the amount and variety of talk about explicitly Christian matters will vary widely. At times and with some people, conversing about the norms that govern or should govern the behavior of the parishioner will be the focus of the relationship. At other times such explicit concern with religion and theological norms will be very much in the background. At no time should careful attention to these concerns be totally absent from the pastor's own reflections about the situation.

As I have emphasized throughout this book, the realities of life in the modern world require that all people, including pastors, muddle their way through life, making decisions and carrying on relationships while living with a complex web of story-constructed activities, communities of relationships, and value-laden ways of life. Our lives are structured not within one narrative, one story that shapes who we are or want to be, but many often congruent, but sometimes conflicting stories.

Howard strove to live up to the demands and values inherent in the ongoing story of the legal profession while yet attempting (and often failing) to fulfill the expectations inherent in the story of marital and family life he had inherited from his culture and his forebears, as well as the story of his own marriage. Just as Howard had to live within many stories, so it is with all of us.[5]

Here we encounter the pervasive pluralism that increasingly characterizes twentieth-century corporate and individual life. As the social psychologist Kenneth J. Gergen has said:

> The stage is set. We play out our lives largely within the languages of romanticism and modernism. These modes of understanding ourselves and others are built into the fabric of our daily relationships; without them daily life would be unlivable. Yet we are bombarded with ever-increasing intensity by the images and actions of others; our range of social participation is expanding exponentially. As we absorb the views, values, and visions of others, and live out the multiple plots in which we are enmeshed, we enter a postmodern consciousness. It is a world in which we no longer experience a secure sense of self, and in which doubt is increasingly placed on the very assumption of a bounded identity with palpable attributes.[6]

Although Gergen's book speaks primarily about what is most clearly seen in middle- and upper-class Western culture, in his judgments about the "saturation of the self" in contemporary life Gergen has identified a process that has profound implications for pastoral care by and within the Christian community. Again, we see Howard's situation as prototypical of a more pervasive problem.

As interpreter of both the Christian tradition and the contemporary situation, the pastor offers a broad range of guidance to individuals and families, as well as to the faith community as a whole. In sermons and stories, religious celebrations and crisis care, the pastor offers assistance to persons in their attempts to place all aspects of contemporary life within the meaning framework of Christian language and imagery.

In addition, the pastor helps guide the process of coordinating the demands of the various communities to which persons belong. Each community, with its unique story and its unique values, vies for the fidelity of its members. How does one adjudicate between the demands of the competing communities to which she or he belongs? Here is encountered the problem of relativism and the attraction of ideological monism—the desire for the simplicity of *one* way of seeing and experiencing the world versus the nihilism of existing in a world where all things have been made so relative as to lose all sense of what is normative. In contemporary pastoral practice, finding ways to assist persons to ground their lives in the Christian narrative while yet remaining open to and participating in other communities shaped by other ways of seeing the world becomes a major and sometimes overwhelming task.

The Pastor's Own Experience of Pluralism and Relativism

Many pastors experience divisions of loyalty similar to Howard's. Not only do pastors often feel caught between loyalty to family and loyalty to the demands of pastoral practice, they also live with a more or less constant set of tensions among various aspects of their ministry practice itself. Which of the various practices of ministry claims priority upon their time and talents? By what criteria are they to decide what is most important to do today? This week? This year?

I believe that we can extend the analogy between Howard's situation and that of the typical parish pastor. The extended analogy will be illuminating for our search for ways in which the quadrilateral schema for pastoral care can become operational in the ordinary, day-to-day practice of ministry in a time of pluralism and relativism.

Although there are numerous ways in which the dominant presence of pluralism and relativism in Western culture affects the caring ministry of the congregation and its pastoral leader, I will confine my discussion in this chapter to two ways that affect the work of pastoral care most directly. First, as pastors go about their work— visiting the sick, counseling individual parishioners, intervening in

145

marital and family conflicts, and the like—they will encounter a profusion of differing ways in which parishioners have appropriated the culture's changing methods of understanding and evaluating human behavior and relationships.

Some differences between parishioner's perceptions have their roots in conflicts of generational loyalties. Each passing generation tends to have its own dominant way of creating and coping with the way of life that characterizes its time. In everything from tastes in music and speech to modes of structuring relationships with intimates or strangers, each generation sets its cultural standards.[7] In very general, social-psychological terms, we may say that people in a given generation tend to resist the cultural practices of the following generation, while yet consciously or unconsciously, directly or indirectly, attempting to alter the values, practices, and ways of thinking of the preceding generation.

From a more individual-psychological perspective, we can see a multiplicity of ways in which a given individual may either resist, passively conform to, or enthusiastically endorse the emerging way of life of their own generation or even the succeeding generation. The popular notion that older people tend to be "conservative," while the young can be counted on to be "liberal" or even "radical" turns out to be nothing more than a cliché.[8]

Because pastors, like parishioners, are embedded in their cultural surroundings, they are as subject as anyone else to the influences of popular culture. Unless the pastor appropriates modes of critical thinking provided by theology and other disciplines, the pastor will consciously or unconsciously fall prey to popular cultural meanings and practices. That being the case, the pastor may find himself or herself the unwitting representative not of the theological tradition, but rather of the ebbs and flows of popular culture. Good pastoral care necessitates careful exercise of the pastor's interpretive skills. As we saw in our discussion of earlier historical epochs, a critical approach to pastoral interpretation, which respects *both* the authority of the faith community's tradition *and* the movement of the historical process, is esential for adequate pastoral interpretation.

This brings us directly to a second way in which the work of pastoral care confronts the impact of pluralism and relativism on the cultural situation of our time: namely, the pluralism of theories, both theological/ethical and social-scientific/psychotherapeutic, that vie for the pastor's loyalty and practical application to the ministry of care. I delved into important aspects of that problem in chapter 4, there emphasizing the pluralism of approaches to theological construction and interpretation.

In the day-to-day practice of pastoral care, however, theological pluralism is not the only way in which the pastor is confronted with the forces of pluralism and relativism. Since the rise of psychology and psychotherapeutic approaches to understanding human behavior and the helping relationship, pastors have been confronted with the need to select from a broad range of "secular" theories about human relationships and behavior that can be utilized in their pastoral work.

In the past several decades, during the heyday of the psychotherapeutic paradigm for pastoral care, a plethora of psychotherapeutic models for pastoral care practice—everything from Rogerian "nondirective" or "client-centered" counseling[9] to family systems theory[10]—have been brought forward as models for pastoral work.[11] Many of these adaptations of so-called secular methods for intervention into human problems may well be found to be, in the practical sense, useful to pastors who are searching for disciplined ways to help persons in need of pastoral guidance. Such adaptations can become problematic, however, in a number of ways, all of which involve confronting the problems of pluralism and relativism in contemporary society.

First, if the pastor makes decisions about which method to use in a given situation of need simply on a pragmatic basis, he or she may unwittingly become caught in the loose relativism to which contemporary Western culture is so prone. In the pulpit the pastor may indeed seek to uncover and combat just this kind of slippery relativism, while setting over against it the disciplined life of loyalty to the standards set by biblical or traditional Christian understanding. Simultaneously, in the privacy of the counseling room, there may be little evidence that these standards have been carefully and critically applied either in the choice of counseling methodology or in the manner in which a given method is practiced.

As a so-called generalist discipline that draws upon a wide variety of perspectives, disciplined ministry is not only *caught up* in the *problems* of cultural pluralism, it *depends* on the *richness* of pluralism for its lively variety of perspectives and methods of caring for people's needs.

Toward a Disciplined Ministry of Care in an Age of Pluralism

We have discussed the problems posed for pastors *and* parishioners by the prevailing relativistic pluralism of our time, and we have noted the rich variety of resources pluralism brings for understanding and potentially resolving human individual and communal conflicts. Yet one crucial question remains to be asked: How can the caring member of the Christian community, whether lay or ordained, be self-consciously governed by the norms embodied in the Christian tradition while yet participating in and making use of "secular" ways of understanding and working with human problems? Said another way, how can Christians in their life of care in the world be both faithful and worldly-wise?

In response, I offer a fourth schema for pastoral care:

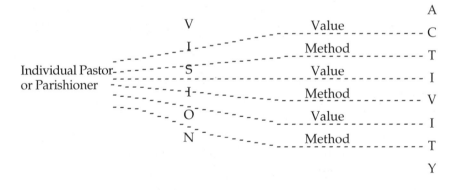

Figure 4

In this schema, which obviously needs to be utilized with imagination and flexibility, every human activity involves certain values and methods for getting things done or making things happen. These methods and values may differ widely from one activity to another. Usually, people exercise their values and methods for getting things done quite naturally, based on their preconceptions about the task at hand. Thus, without some grounding or over-arching vision, the many activities in which humans participate can become fragmented.

Within the schema depicted in figure 4, it is the vision provided by the primary narrative understanding of the world, the vision toward which the individual gives his or her ultimate loyalty, that alone gives life coherence and offers a means for making consistent decisions in the flow of life's varying experiences. For Christians, that vision emerges out of continuing participation in the life of a community of faith.

This does not mean that Christians are always thinking and speaking in the language of the church. They quite rightly think and speak the many languages of the varying activities of their lives. But the language of faith does provide them with a relatively constant check, a measuring stick by which they can make judgments about the methods and values expressed in any of their activities.[12]

A rather imperfect analogy has often occurred to me in thinking about this matter as it applies specifically to the pastor's use of non-Christian theories and methods of helping people resolve life problems. In certain ways it is like learning to speak a second language. The second language offers a new and different set of nuanced meanings that can be immensely illuminating of one's view of the world. The new language can greatly influence one's relationships and approaches to problems. Nevertheless, there will be times when one is moved to return to one's native language to find one's bearings.

The analogy is apparent. For the Christian pastor (and indeed for the committed layperson) the native language is Christian theological language. One's thinking and acting must meet the test of that way of thinking and behaving. The vision contained in that tradition provides the filter through which all other ways of speaking and acting must finally be tested and appropriated.

This chapter has only begun to plumb the depths of implications for pastoral ministry that the schema of figure 4 contains. Some of these implications will be apparent in the chapters of part 3. Remembering that each human situation that the pastor encounters will ask its own questions of the faith and practice of the people called Christians, readers may be assured that they will encounter in their practice ever new ways to put the schema to the test.

PART III

The Christian Story and the Stories of Individual and Family Life

Pastoral care in everyday life situations virtually always exists within some tension between the ongoing story of the Christian community and the particularity of life stories. We have already found this to be the case with the story of Howard in chapter 6. We saw how one's values and methods for making life decisions are influenced by one's commitment to the Christian community and its story-shaped vision of right behavior. Our actions are also influenced by the demands and commitments pressed upon us by the stories of other communities to which we belong, such as our families and business associates. The particularity of the individual's life situation is brought into tension with the priorities, ethical values, and behavioral norms embodied in the Christian community.

I now wish to turn the reader's attention to the particularity of individual life stories. My first purpose in part 3 is to examine some of the common pastoral care situations that present themselves at various stages of the human life cycle. The term *life cycle* has become commonplace in the twentieth century as a facet of the rise to dominance of psychological ways of thinking about the human situation. The psychoanalyst Erik Erikson was in large part responsible for the development and sophisticated explication of the concept. After introducing the idea that humans live out their earthly existence in a series of developmental stages in interaction with their social surroundings, Erikson went on to write numerous books that were highly influential in establishing the notion of life cycle stages among both psychological professionals and the general public.[1]

The life cycle concept provides a highly useful structure for the work of pastoral care. It helps the pastoral caregiver understand individuals, and it facilitates the pastoral task of gathering together persons with common problems in order that they may provide care for one another.[2]

My second purpose in part 3 is to introduce some of the "hot topics" that pastoral caregivers are encountering because of some of the radical changes occurring in Western society. They are topics that invite highly conflicting interpretations: child abuse, teenage crime, sexual harassment, women's rights, gay rights, and many others. These topics will be taken up as the human problems of various life stages present themselves for our consideration. I do not claim to have the "last word" on these topics: they all deserve more extended exploration than space in an introductory text allows. Yet they demand the attention of pastoral interpretive guides, and they need to be discussed and debated in congregations as God's people forge ahead in a difficult time.

CHAPTER 7

Care for the Stories of Life's Beginning

We begin our study of pastoral care in relation to the human life cycle by centering our attention on issues related to life's beginning. There is a certain inviting logic in doing that, although, as will quickly become apparent, the pastoral issues that emerge from life's early years are in large part issues that must be dealt with by and with adults, particularly parents. As Erik Erikson and others have shown, infants still in the preverbal years are already dealing with dilemmas that will pursue them into adult life. How they will come to terms with those issues will depend heavily on the caring environment provided by their parents.[1]

An Invitation to Remember

As we begin, I encourage you to pause briefly and allow your attention to follow any thoughts, images, and memories that occur to you as you think about the beginning of life.

Chances are that your first imagistic thoughts will be memories: memories perhaps of your own early childhood, or the childhood of one of your children. For many of you those memories will be pleasant, even sweetly sentimental. For others they may be painful, secret, harbored, concealed, perhaps never shared with another or shared only with one's closest friends. The fact is that if we think long enough, most of us have some of both kinds of memories.

After ruminating on these random memories for a while, think about the Christian community in relation to infancy and early childhood. Baptism? The acknowledgment in the church bulletin or by a rose on the lectern of a new birth in the community? Early experiences in Sunday school? As I write this, I find myself remembering a Sunday school class I attended as a five-year-old that met in a little room in the bell tower of the country church my father served as pastor. The class always ended when one of the men in the community came to ring the church bell to announce the beginning of worship. Sometimes he would let us help pull the rope to ring the bell!

Infant Baptism in the Christian Community

When those of us who belong to denominational communions that practice infant baptism think about infancy and the Christian church, we think immediately about the rite of baptism and its role in the community's care for the very young and their families. Baptism not only incorporates a young child into the family of God, it also extends support and encouragement to the parents, admonishing them to rear their child in an atmosphere of faith and love. The ritual of baptism likewise reminds the gathered community of its responsibility to surround the newly adopted child with faithful care and nurture in the Christian way of life. Just what that means will depend upon the quality of care that exists in that local community.

With what care should baptism be administered by the ordained pastor of a congregation? Is it enough simply for the pastor to take the child in her or his arms, fulfill the ritual of the Water and Word, and speak the name chosen by the parents before the gathering of the faithful?

Consider, for example, the possible benefits to be gained by routinely making a pastoral home visit with both parents present, either before or immediately after every baptism. This is an opportune time to offer support and discuss the responsibility of parenthood when the new parents are feeling the burden and almost inevitable ambivalence of parenthood. It is also a time when, in the informality of conversation, the joys, hopes, and desires of the parents for their child can be given the blessing of the congregation's ordained representative.

Several years ago, in one of my introductory pastoral care courses at the seminary, the class was discussing the opportunities for pastoral care at the time of baptism of young children. The time seemed right to set up a role play to provide some concreteness for what had become a rather abstract discussion. I asked for volunteers for the three roles of father, mother, and pastor. Several volunteered, and I rather randomly selected three participants. I set the situation as an early evening pastoral call, following up on a telephone request made by Mrs. Smith to have the couple's three-month-old infant baptized during Sunday worship in the near future. At the time of the telephone call, at the suggestion of the pastor, a time had been set for the pastor to visit. The three volunteers were told that they were to play their roles in whatever way seemed natural to them.[2]

I will not attempt to reproduce verbatim the three-way conversation that took place as the role play that followed. I vividly remember, however, the main themes of that conversation and the intensity of the emotions expressed. Early in the dialogue, Jim, the husband, expressed considerable ambivalence about having his daughter baptized at this time. Jim (as the student playing the role imagined him) had been raised a Baptist and, even though he had joined the United Methodist Church when he married Kathy, a lifelong Methodist, the baptism stirred some deep waters in him that spoke of disloyalty to his heritage. He somehow felt bypassed or manipulated by Kathy, who, after discussing the matter very briefly at breakfast one morning, had called the pastor to make the arrangements. Furthermore, the incident of the baptism was a reminder to him that he may have "given in" too quickly to his new wife's wishes about church membership at the time of their marriage. Observing, one wondered if that "giving in" hadn't become a pattern in the Smiths' marriage, a pattern that Jim secretly resented considerably.

In her role as Kathy, the female student tried her best to "be reasonable" with her husband, obviously not wanting the conversation to move in the direction of marital conflicts. "Let's just go ahead and talk about the baptism," she said rather forcefully.

By now the reader may be beginning to wonder what elements of this role play emanated simply from the imaginations of the participants and what elements had their origins in the real lives of the players. The young student playing the role of the pastor, as he confessed later in the discussion after the role play was over, was becoming confused as to how to proceed. He had entered the role play with a confident notion that the conversation should move fairly quickly into a straightforward discussion of the plans for the baptism and its significance for the Smiths' life as a Christian family.

But that was not to be. The longer I allowed the role play to proceed, the more it became apparent that the matter that my two role players needed to discuss was not the baptism of their child, but the power struggles in their imagined marriage. The problem was that this was not the agenda the pastoral role player wanted or intended to discuss. He kept trying in vain to bring the conversation back to the baptism, its meaning to the Smiths, and its significance for the congregation he served. The result was a developing stalemate. Thus he unwittingly was drawn into the couple's struggle over control.

There is much to be learned from a role play such as this one, not all of which is directly related to the topic of this chapter. Allow me to list briefly some of the possible lessons:

1. The most obvious thing to be learned from this role play is that the decision to have an infant baptized is a critical one for young couples. The birth of a child signals a new stage in a couple's marriage, particularly if this is the first child born to the marriage. With the birth of a child, what has been a couple now becomes a family. The request for baptism most often involves more than asking that the child be received as a preparatory member of a congregation; it is tacitly a request for the church's blessing on the new family.

2. The role play illustrates graphically that pastoral conversations often move in quite unpredictable directions, even when the subject of the conversation has been agreed on ahead of time. To be most helpful to those receiving the care, pastoral conversations need to be open-ended, so that underlying issues may be expressed and given response. Our role-play pastor got into difficulty when he overlooked this basic pastoral care principle. At the same time, however, as pastoral leader of the community of faith, the pastor does have the responsibility to educate parents concerning the meaning of the vows they are asked to take when they present their child for baptism.

3. The role-play conversation reveals that such a seemingly un-complicated occasion as the baptism of an infant may often bring to the fore conflicts in a marriage that have heretofore been hidden.

Had this been a real situation, the pastor would have been presented with a difficult choice fraught with significant ramifications. Had the pastor sensed the possibility of significant tension in the marriage and invited exploration of that possibility, he or she might have opened up a "can of worms," which might have led him to refer the Smiths for marital counseling.

The pastor in our role play decided to keep the conversation focused on the decision about whether or not to have their child baptized now, or to wait until Mr. Smith had resolved his mixed feelings about infant baptism. In effect, such a decision puts aside the issues of power and control that have emerged in the conversation. Had this been an actual situation, I suppose, the pastor would have tacitly decided that now was not the time to confront a possibly significant and potentially damaging rift in the marriage. Rather, the pastor would have decided to trust that another opportunity to pursue that conversation would present itself at a later time, but that for now the baptism discussion must take precedence.

It is not my intention to suggest that there is a wrong and a right way to respond in pastoral situations such as that confronted in the role play. There are, to be sure, general methodological principles that it is wise to follow. Certainly the pastor needs to be empathic, a good listener, and solidly present to the other. The pastor needs unabashedly to represent the tradition and office to which she or he has been called. But the options I have pointed to in this discussion of the role play are legitimate options. Furthermore, any option taken has its accompanying ramifications, so the choices of response need to be made with great care.

Human Problems at the Time of Birth

When we think of the event of the birth of a child, our common reaction is to wish to share in the parent's joy. Indeed, that is usually what is most appropriate and gratifying to the mother and father, though not always. There are a number of human problems associated with childbirth that may require skilled pastoral care and considerable supportive care from members of the community of faith.

1. The problem of the unwanted or ambivalently wanted child. I recall, for example, an occasion when a young seminarian making routine pastoral visits on a hospital obstetrics floor, after introducing himself as the unit chaplain, bubbled happily to a forty-year-old mother, "I hear you have a new little boy. Isn't that marvelous!" To which the mother replied angrily, "The hell it is. I've already got more kids than I can take care of and my husband ain't going to be any more help to me with this one than he is with the other six!"

This woman reminds us forcefully that not all children are welcomed into the world by their parents. She greeted her newborn not with joy, but with dread, anger, and despair over her life situation. If the truth were known, her outburst might well express at least one side of the ambivalence felt by many mothers—and fathers as well. The caring pastor will relate in such a way as to hear and respond to both sides of that ambivalence. If it is apparent that the mother or father is feeling isolated and despairing, it may be appropriate to facilitate caring lay support, perhaps from people who have faced similar situations in the past.

2. A second more and more common set of problems related to the event of birth is the problem of infertility. Although most obviously a physical problem, this problem appears at times to have cultural origins. As young people of the rising generation tend to postpone both marriage and the starting of a family until well into their thirties, many are discovering that they must seek medical assistance when, often after trying for several years, the desired pregnancy has not occurred. Infertility medical intervention, while sometimes successful, is most often very expensive and fraught with considerable risk to the emotional well-being of one or both of the marital partners.

I vividly recall my counseling with one couple in their late thirties who, after months of "scheduled" intercourse accompanied by many clinic visits, expensive medications for the wife, and fertility tests for the husband, declared the whole experience "dehumanizing." For them adoption became the only possible answer to their desire for parenthood. That, too, turned out to have its own difficulties, so that it was many months before the adoption of a three-week-old baby boy was finalized. They later attributed their ability to survive the ordeal to the support they received from a small group of friends and, not incidentally, regular weekly pastoral counseling sessions that enabled them to sort through their tangled feelings and keep communication open between them.

What this couple said about the essential support they received from close friends reminds us that one of the most helpful ministries a congregation can provide couples such as this is the provision of ample opportunities for giving and receiving of mutual support. In the small-town and rural congregation where most if not all congregants know one another, such mutually supportive interaction may occur spontaneously and without direction, though this is by no means always the case. In the urban situation more careful planning by lay ministry task forces is necessary.

Although the ministry of mutual support is a ministry of the laity, ordained pastors should, both by their attitude and by their preaching and teaching, acknowledge not only the commonality and shared pain of these reproductive problems, but also the acceptance and grace available to those who bring the pain of infertility into dialogical relationship with the Christian narrative, most particularly its way of speaking about human imperfection in the sight of God. Along the way, pastors may need opportunities to pursue their own questions concerning God's providence.

3. Some parents, after months of anticipation, are confronted with the reality that their child has been born with physical imperfections. The variety of these deformities is virtually endless—Down syndrome, spina bifida, a three-chambered heart, strabismus, clubfoot, and so on.

In such situations as these, the parental joy at having participated in the creation of a unique human being is inevitably tainted by disappointment and often by a gnawing sense of guilt. Did I cause this? The mother is, to be sure, more apt to blame herself than is the father, although he is not immune to feelings of guilt and shame.

During these times of confused emotions and trying to make sense of what has happened, it is even more difficult to share deeply harbored feelings of anger that this unwanted and unintended difficulty has been thrust upon the parental pair. It is not unusual for these angry feelings to be displaced upon the spouse. If given the right opportunity, parents in this situation may be able to sort out their tangled feelings toward one another; they may even be able to vent their anger at God, the one whom they ultimately hold responsible for the felt unfairness of what has befallen them.

The image of pastoral care as interpretive guidance becomes extremely valuable here. Parents facing the crisis of a birth anomaly need help from their pastor in placing this episode of their lives within the larger framework of meaning of God's movement in history.[3]

Is Pastoral Care Always Problem-Centered?

During the period of pastoral care's history in which the psychotherapeutic paradigm dominated, it became the fashion among many pastoral care practitioners to focus attention virtually always on the possible presence of a human problem in the other while engaging in a pastoral conversation. Although it is true that the pastor needs always to be alert for evidence of human pain, it is also important for pastors to be available to people as they desire to share their joys and accomplishments. Placing human joys within the context of Christian reflection is at least of equal importance as turning to Christian meanings and representatives of the Christian faith tradition for aid in times of trouble!

Problematic Societal Trends: Implications for Pastoral Care

As our quadrilateral schema for understanding the dimensions of care suggests, the societal trends present at a given time in history greatly influence for good or ill how life in that time and place will be experienced by individuals and families. Consideration of the issues and problems relative to life's beginning as we approach the end of the twentieth century must therefore attend to several recent trends in Western society. In many respects these trends may be related, but for purposes of analysis, let us consider them separately. These trends have greatly modified how vast numbers of children experience the early years of life: (1) the increase in the number of two-breadwinner families among households that include mother, father, and one or more children; (2) the enormous increase in the number of single parents, most often mothers, including many single-parent families headed by teenage mothers; (3) the apparent increase in the problem of child abuse, including both physical and sexual abuse.

1. *The Two-Breadwinner Family*

The years since World War II have brought vast changes in the commonly held ideal of the traditional family. Prior to World War II it was generally accepted, at least among the dominant middle class, that family living required a neat division of labor between marital partners. The husband and father's primary energies were to be directed toward making the family living by carrying on his occupation outside the home—being the "head of the household."

The wife and mother, on the other hand, was to be the "homemaker" or "housewife," whose main tasks were to support her husband in every way possible and to guide the development of the children, particularly their moral development, at least until they reached adolescence.

In times of stress, inside or outside the home, the couple tried to support each other as both labored arduously in their respective spheres to approximate the vision they shared of a normal, healthy family. They did so with varying success, but they shared a common set of beliefs about family life.

With the coming of World War II, that set of rules about roles began to change. When the majority of adult males in their twenties and thirties went off to war, their wives and sweethearts went to work in the burgeoning factories that produced the arms and other supplies needed to support the war effort. A popular song of that period was titled "Rosie the Riveter."

Thus began the shift toward two-breadwinner families, a shift that by the mid-1960s became solidified. Not only did many women decide that they liked the variety and freedom of having their own vocation outside the home, their own money, and their own commitments beyond the role of homemaker; but also the upwardly mobile standard of living and the creep of inflation began to necessitate two incomes.[4] Thus began a shift in family living patterns that by the 1990s had been realized both in the actuality of America's

---

patterning of gender roles in family life, and in the beliefs about what those roles *should* be.

More will need to be said in a later chapter about this radical cultural change with regard to gender roles. Here the significant question concerns what this shift has meant for children. For example, childcare is increasingly moving outside the home, with children's development often placed in the hands of strangers and near strangers. As late as 1985 only 14 percent of preschool children were cared for in an organized childcare facility. By 1990 half of all children of working parents were either being cared for in a center or in another home. In 1985, 25 percent of working mothers with children under five used a childcare facility as the primary form of care, compared to 13 percent in 1977. This transformation was unforeseen, unplanned, and is still poorly understood.[5]

These statistics, gathered by David A. Hamburg, president of the Carnegie Corporation of New York, are highly significant; and all indications are that the trend continues to escalate. Hamburg points out that not only is there a shortage of childcare workers in America, but also that in terms of wage scale and recognized qualifications for the job, childcare employees are at the bottom level:

> The crucial factor in quality of care is the nature and behavior of the caregiver. As the demand for child caregivers has surged, those trying to provide it have frantically sought to recruit more child care workers. Even with the best of intentions, this field has been characterized by low pay, low respect, minimal training, minimal supervision, and extremely variable quality.[6]

With these transformations taking place even in intact families, the caring ministries of the Christian community, which traditionally have strongly supported so-called family values, are confronted with a new and rapidly changing situation. The question, "What is happening to our children, even to our very young children?" becomes a compelling question that has implications for the caring ministry of the church at a number of levels.

For the pastor's own direct care of persons, a response to this question will entail not only the pastor's ability to listen sensitively to couples who are undergoing the stress of holding their busy lives together, but also the ability to fulfill the role of interpretive guide as couples confront the moral and spiritual dimensions of their intended or actualized actions. "Do we really need two incomes?" "How high a standard of living do we want or need to maintain in order to feel secure and comfortable?" "Is it fair and equitable to ask one of the partners in the marriage (traditionally the mother) to relinquish or postpone her or his career goals so as to ensure that the child has twenty-four-hour care from one of the parents?" "What is really best for our children?" On and on go the questions.

The pastor need not and cannot have ready and right answers to all these questions. Rather, caring pastors will attempt to make themselves available to persons as participants in psychological, moral, and spiritual inquiry, as they seek an acceptable path together.

Important as is this personal ministry of the pastor, it is not in itself an adequate means of confronting the problem of the care of young children. Since childcare is in many respects a cultural, communal problem, the response needs likewise to be a communal one. The church community needs to provide a forum where the dilemmas related to the welfare of young children can be openly discussed and those who are confronting the problem can find communal support. Here the dialogical relationship between the Christian tradition and the realities of contemporary life can be stimulated.

Further, the church's response may well include efforts at communal advocacy. For example, the church may encourage employers to provide such benefits as "flextime" and parental leave. Where appropriate, quasi-political individual or corporate action may be undertaken, though in America, with its long-standing tradition of separation of church and state, the church must take care to avoid the kind of ideological-political warfare that has occurred in the so-called Christian Right.

2. The Single-Parent Family

Alongside the felt need for two incomes to support family life and individual freedom lies another trend in most Western societies, including America: the increase in the number of families headed by a single parent, most often the mother.[7] The needs of these parents and their children are in many ways more complex and more pressing than are the needs of children both of whose parents are committed to professional employment outside the home.

To speak of single-parent families is to speak of a wide variety of situations, any one of which deserves careful consideration and analysis. Within that broad category are included families who have lost one parent through death or divorce, and mother-headed families in which there has never been a husband or father. It includes homes of resourceful, economically independent women who, because they have not yet been married and, at age thirty-five or so, sense their so-called biological clocks ticking away, decide to have a child out of wedlock. It includes homes of teenage mothers who become pregnant through casual sex and elect to have the child rather than abort the pregnancy. It includes both relatively affluent families and families caught in grinding poverty.

The pastor and the congregation who, with serious intent, decide to extend their care to any or all of these categories of single-parent families will quickly be forced to reconsider their images of what a family should be. In a book entitled *Lives on the Edge: Single Mothers and Their Children*, Valerie Polakow presents a history of the family that demonstrates the instability of the family over time and in differing cultures. Yet, at least in America and probably in Europe as well, what Polakow calls the "metanarratives" of the ideal of the family persist:

> The law of nature and the ideology of care; his and hers; the public space and the private domestic sphere; the stable enduring family with tender mother at center stage; she, the mainstay of civilization, the nestmaker, the bearer of the burden of the inner world. Have we yet separated the idea of family from patriarchy? For if women and children are still "formed to please," what landscape do incomplete mothers occupy—those who have transgressed the laws of nature and of public morality?[8]

In this paragraph Polakow points toward a major complication of the plight of single mothers in our society: that single parenthood is commonly judged to be faulty, incomplete, and therefore problematic. These attitudes, says Polakow, are based on the preservation of traditional patriarchal notions of what is and is not an adequate family structure.

There is a growing body of feminist literature on the family that tends to support the opinion that many efforts to be helpful with single-parent families are hampered by the presupposition that such families are necessarily flawed. Empowering single mothers to cope with the stresses and strains of family life is, say these feminist theorists, better accomplished by emphasizing their competence than by dwelling on their inadequacies.[9]

As I said in regard to two-income families, the needs of single parents and their children will vary greatly and require support and encouragement from members of the congregation as well as the pastor. Basic to a good program of intentional care will be the open acceptance of single parents and their children by members of the congregation, and also the provision of mutual support groups for single parents and the facilitation of relationships between such single working mothers and older persons who have confronted the stresses and strains of caring for young children earlier in their lives.

Here again a caring ministry of advocacy in the public sphere on behalf of the needs of single parents and their children may well be needed. For a congregation to undertake such advocacy, free and open discussion and education of members of congregations is important. Advocacy for changes in public policies that discriminate against women who are both wage earners and sole caregivers in families with small children is increasingly essential. However, as Valerie Polakow points out:

> Not much has shifted in our public sensibilities from the religious moralism of the eighteen hundreds pointing to the depravity of the undeserving poor, to contemporary conservative commentaries on the "politics of conduct" of the nonworking poor. Poverty is a private affair—its causes are rooted in failed individuals, failed families, and moral degeneration rather than in a failed public economy and a discriminatory public policy. It is an individual or underclass or ethnic problem in need of redress, not a structural one requiring a fundamental shift in our ways of seeing the politics of distribution.[10]

Here comes into view a striking example of the central importance of interpretive pastoral guidance in contemporary life. Polakow's judgment that "not much has shifted in our public sensibilities from the religious moralism of the eighteen hundreds" in all probability describes the attitudes of many members of Christian congregations today. To the extent that this is the case, care for single parents caught in the clutches of poverty and lack of understanding calls for congregational groups to reinterpret and reappropriate the biblical mandate to "care for the widow and the orphan."

3. *Child Abuse*

It is not possible to consider the need for care of young children today without giving attention to the problem of child abuse, a problem that has received increasing attention in the American media. Newspapers and television news programs daily contain stories of children being left alone for long periods of time, children being beaten and even killed by their parents, young children being sexually abused by older siblings, fathers, grandfathers, and trusted neighbors.

It is not clear whether the incidence of child abuse has actually increased or if there is simply increasing awareness and reporting of a problem that in the past has largely been kept hidden. Be that as it may, the abuse of children among us, often to be found in the least expected locations, is undeniable. It infests the homes of the poor and uneducated and the homes of the rich and powerful. As a pastor, one can almost assume that it is present in more than one family in the congregation.[11]

Child abuse typically takes one or more of three forms. First, there is abuse that is the result of the inability of parents to control aggression and hostility. Here the child often plays the role of scapegoat, the recipient of the frustrated rage and anger from relationships between the abusing parent and a spouse, supervisor at work, or someone else perceived to have power over the parent. In fact, as James Poling has pointed out in his book about the devastation brought upon children by sexual abuse, all child abuse is best seen as an abuse of power.[12]

Second, there is abuse of children in the form of punishment for some act or attitude deemed wrong by the parent or parents. In this case the parent carries out some form of physical punishment rationalized by the parent as being done for the child's welfare or to teach the child to be obedient. Whipping, spanking, slapping, or some other physical penalty is meted out to the child in order to foster the child's learning of proper behavior.

Physical punishment as a means of discipline has a long and painful history, linked in highly significant ways to the history of religion. "For many centuries the Book of Proverbs has provided parents, preachers and teachers with the basic aphorisms that have justified their commitment to corporal punishment of children," says Philip Greven, a historian of American religious consciousness and its connections to styles of rearing children.[13]

Although Greven is particularly harsh in his criticism of Protestant evangelicalism as fostering the punishing abuse of children, he indicts all religion since Old Testament times as authorizing physical punishment of children so much so that it has become a pattern of behavior embedded in Western culture. Greven summarizes his judgment that all forms of punishing abuse of children is in the end harmful:

> The past holds a powerful grip upon the future by shaping feelings, actions, and beliefs in the present. The pain and suffering experienced by children who have been physically punished resonate through time, first during the seemingly endless days and nights of childhood and adolescence, and later through the lives we lead as adults. The feelings generated by the pain caused by adults' assaults against children are mostly repressed, forgotten, and denied, but they actually never disappear. Everything remains recorded in our innermost beings, and the effects of punishment permeate our lives, our thought, our culture, and our world.[14]

The third and perhaps most destructive form of child abuse is unmistakably the abuse of children by turning them into sex objects for the illicit gratification of adult power needs disguised as sexuality. Accurate statistics on the amount of sexual abuse of children that actually occurs are impossible to determine, since it can be assumed that much, if not most, of such abuse is never reported. After reviewing a large number of studies done by others, James Poling, a pastoral counselor and theologian, says, "Experts estimate that 20 to 40 percent of all children experience some form of sexual violence before age eighteen."[15]

Rarely does the presence of a sexually abusive relationship in a family come directly to the attention of the parish pastor. Not only are the taboos against talking openly about sexual relationships powerful in enforcing silence, but also it is common for the abuser to threaten the victims with dire consequences of disclosure. However, the pastor and other adult sponsors of church youth and children's programs are in a good position to observe children who are troubled, including those who have been sexually abused. Rarely should pastors attempt to be the primary person to attempt to intervene in these situations. Rather, it is usually wise for the pastor to report suspicions of sexual abuse to the proper legal and social service agencies.

Merely reporting abuse is not, however, all that the sensitive pastor can do. Both the victim and the members of the victim's family will need gentle, understanding support and encouragement as they go through the crisis of coming to grips with the alteration in the relationship that disclosure inevitably brings about. Pastors who find themselves involved in these situations will need to come to terms with their own feelings toward the perpetrator in order to be able to encourage him or her to use whatever professional help is available.

As Poling asserts, the most important practical ministry of the church in relation to child sexual abuse as well as other forms of abuse may well be to become proactive in efforts to reorganize the society in ways that mitigate against the abuse of power. This is another example of the Christian community's responsibility to care for the society and culture that surrounds it.[16]

Our study of the care of life stories during the early years of human life has led us to consider some of the most important issues that call for the ministry of the church as it and the sociocultural situation that surrounds it move toward a new millennium. In the chapter that follows, we will turn our attention to a comparable set of issues, problems, and opportunities for ministry that occur as the stories of lives move through life's second decade, the period of adolescence.

CHAPTER 8

Growing Up, Letting Go, and Forming Covenantal Bonds

The responsibilities for confronting the issues that the pastor and Christian community must deal with in relation to childhood are fundamentally the domain of adults. The responsibility for issues of adolescence and young adulthood rapidly becomes primarily that of the youth themselves. Yet ease of transitions from childhood to adulthood are made easier or more difficult depending upon the qualities of the familial milieu.

Hence, this chapter includes the following sections: (1) a listing of the basic tasks of this transitional period in human living, together with comments on the skewing of these tasks by contemporary sociocultural processes; (2) a listing of the pastoral tasks of the ordained pastor and the Christian community evoked by the needs of adolescents undergoing the transitions of growing up, letting go, and forming communal bonds; and (3) a listing and brief explication of the public leadership tasks that face the Christian community and its leaders if some of the conditions that afflict the youth of America and other Western countries are to be confronted and the church's ministry is to be extended to the care of the culture.

The Basic Tasks of Adolescent Transition

1. Beginning the Resolution of Issues Embedded in Family History

I begin the work of this chapter with the story of one family, most particularly of two brothers in that family and their struggle to make the transitions that adolescence and young adulthood require. The story came to my attention through an autobiographical paper prepared by a student and is told through the interpretive eyes and ears of one of the brothers in the family, who was in his late thirties when the paper was written and is approximately one year older than his younger sibling. The two boys had the same father, but they had older siblings from their mother's previous marriage, who play little part in the story as presented in my student's paper. Their father had also been previously married, but nothing is known of the offspring of that marriage. We will call the younger brother Charles and the older brother Cedric. We will speak of the family as the Loring family.

The Lorings, an African American family, lived in the inner city of one of the large urban communities of the Midsouth. Poverty was all around them. By the time Cedric was nineteen months old and his brother only eight months old, "My father left the family and his responsibilities to it."[1] Mr. Loring, however, remained in the city and, as we shall see, had frequent contact with Charles, but only infrequent contact with Cedric. Mr. and Mrs. Loring had virtually no contact with each other, so that, practically speaking, Cedric and Charles grew to adulthood in a single-parent family.

Cedric speaks of the manner in which Charles's identification with his father and, concomitantly, Cedric's with his mother, took place. "Physically, my little brother looked just like my father and I resembled my mother. She never allowed us to forget that I got the better end of the deal. Mom could not lash out at Dad in her anger so she picked the next best target of opportunity. Charles was her 'scapegoat' and I was her 'savior.' " At another point, Cedric says, "It seems as if he was rewarded for rebellious behavior, while I was recognized for compliant behavior."

This highlights the determinative importance of the psychosocial milieu in setting the foundations and boundaries within which the individual's transitional process must take place. Later the individual may in important ways transcend her or his familial and social background. But in the beginning of adolescence and, most often, well into young adulthood, the task of coming to terms with what childhood means in *this* family in *this* social situation sets a cluster of problems for the budding adolescent.

For Cedric and Charles that meant coming to grips with a very difficult, albeit now very commonplace social and family situation. Not only were they surrounded by poverty and set in the context of a broken marriage, they were also coming of age within a social situation where drugs, violence, and alienation were rampant. Their needs for care were thus greatly exaggerated in a variety of ways.

Cedric speaks of the family situation as follows: "Charles desperately tried to seek the approval of my mother and when that didn't work he began a pattern of lashing out at me and my mother. I was not immune to anger. I needed and wanted my father's blessing and the fact that he was never there caused me to have deep-seated feelings against him. I believe that the biggest difference was that since so many people shared in my low opinion of my father, I never lacked someone to express my opinion. Nor can I remember anyone discouraging my verbal assaults against my father." He further says, "As far back as I remember, there has always been severe anger and profanity in our household. Problems were never resolved by negotiation. We lived by the creed, 'only the strongest survive.' It seemed as if my mother was always one of the combatants and she had to win."

What sort of solutions did the two boys find to making the transition from childhood to adulthood in their highly conflicted familial situation? Their highly differing solutions have their roots in their earliest experiences as young children, but begin to take shape out of the equally differing choices the two boys began to make as they entered adolescence. For Cedric the solution began when he discovered that not only did he perform well in school, but he also liked learning. Thus his teachers became some of his mentors, together with some leaders who encouraged him in the church his mother persuaded him to attend with her and an uncle he came to idolize.

For Charles, on the other hand, a very different solution began to take shape. "Charles' favorite group of people were the 'Type I hustlers.'" Both boys began to spend more and more time away from home. Their mother's remarriage to "a very abusing and frightening man" hastened the boys' departure from home. Not yet old enough to make it entirely on their own, they moved in with their father, who by this time had taken a job driving long-distance trucks. The boys, therefore, were mostly left to fend for themselves.

By the time they were young adults, the two brothers had moved in radically different directions. Cedric received a scholarship to go to college, graduated, and after spending some time in military service, went on to a seminary of his denomination. Meanwhile, Charles became more deeply involved in drug dealing and violence and as a result spent several years in prison.

From this example of the adolescent's task of resolving issues embedded in family history, it is important to highlight two observations. First, the kind of intense family conflict that formed the foundation for self-responsible life for Cedric and Charles occurs not only in African American families. Family conflict is no respecter of ethnicity. Indeed, as Don Browning has stated:

> It is now becoming clear that the feminization of kinship and poverty is not particularly good for children. This is where Thomas's [Aquinas] argument that the highly dependent human infant needs a definite father and mother rings true. Of course, this dependent human child and its parents need a variety of supportive human communities and networks as well. But this truth should not obscure the fact that these networks work best when they support fully involved mother-father partnership. A recently federally sponsored study for the National Center for Health Statistics shows that one in five children under age eighteen has a learning, emotional, behavioral, or developmental problem. By the time they are teenagers, one in four suffers from one or more of these problems. What is this study's explanation for these trends? These researchers hold that a leading factor is the continuing dissolution of the two-parent family.[2]

Second, the transitions from childhood to adolescence and young adulthood are greatly complicated by the continuing presence of racism in its many forms in Western society as well as in other societies of the world. African Americans, Latin Americans, Asian Americans, and people of other ethnic groups experience daily the debilitating struggle to cope with cultural and institutionalized racism and the resultant isolation. I recall one African American man who said to me, "It takes half my energy every day just to deal with the fact that I am black in a white society."[3] As Robert Woliver and Gail M. Woliver point out in their study of gifted adolescents in other emerging minorities:

> Being gifted brings about a sense of isolationism—after all, being in the top 2% of the population intellectually means having few people around who can communicate at one's level. Being an adolescent

brings its own brand of difficulty—and being Asian or Hawaiian and looking different from the dominant majority tends to exacerbate an already lonely situation. At a time when most adolescents enjoy being with and like others, the gifted Asian or Pacific Islander adolescent must forge a path that may lead away from loved ones.[4]

2. Solidifying a Sense of Sex and Gender Identity

In a significant sense, *the* central task of the teenage years has to do with the groping, anxious, uncertain exploratory response to the question, "Who am I, and who am I to be as I enter into the life of adulthood?" Use of the term *formulation* here would be, though accurate, inadequate. It implies a certain intellectual control and intentionality that the adolescent often does not experience. The adolescent's process of self-identification is more like a groping, exploratory search fraught with much anxiety, changes of direction, and uncertainty.

In *The World of Adolescence*, an important book that seeks to provide a multifaceted approach to understanding the transitions of adolescence over a period of several years and within the boundaries of a particular cultural situation, Beta Copley writes:

A dependent relationship with external parents will gradually diminish and end. Although an individual adolescent state of mind can recur at different ages, one can think in terms of broad chronological norms encompassing a psychosocial process which may often extend, in both directions, somewhat outside the actual teenage years. Early adolescence starts with the emotional responses to the bodily changes of puberty. It brings psychic energy to the surface in a sexual context, and ushers in the mental tasks and changes of the whole process. Major preoccupations at this time are likely to be around these bodily changes and concomitant confusions as to who one is in relation to this child-into-adult body. Soon there may be awareness of beginning to feel "out" of the family, but not yet "into" the heterosexual group life of adolescence, though groups of one's own sex may be prevalent. In the central years of this process life in the mixed peer group becomes predominant, and forms a background to the development of a personal and sexual identity. A working identity, in practice or in thought, also begins to take shape. Later stages see the lessening of the predominance of group life, frequently alongside the development of more established sexual coupling and the beginning of adult life.[5]

In an interesting and enlightening study of the differences between growing through adolescence in the United States and Japan, Merry White reports both on the high incidence of teenage sexual activity in both cultures and on the differences in cultural meanings in active adolescent sex. In both countries adolescents are increasingly sexually active. In the United States, for example, 72 percent of high school students have engaged in sexual intercourse. Twenty percent report four or more partners.

The meanings attached to sexual activity are, however, somewhat different in the two countries. In America the struggle over whether or not to engage in active sex most often has a moral meaning. (Should I do it or not?) In Japan, on the other hand, the struggle has to do with keeping one's sexual activity private and out of view of the social world. It is considered "natural" activity, but it is not to be exposed to others.[6]

Any consideration of the emerging problems of sexual and gender formation within Western culture must take into consideration the impact of the increasing legitimization of gay and lesbian lifestyles. On the one hand, what is frequently called "coming out of the closet" of homosexuality in our society has brought with it increasing freedom for homosexual persons to participate in virtually all aspects of the society's activity while openly living a gay or lesbian sexual lifestyle. On the other hand, this shift in sociocultural mores and practices has brought with it a whole new set of problems for the maturing youth of the society. Recognition of latent homosexual tendencies comes much earlier to even the preadolescent boy or girl. Meanwhile, peer pressures and parental sanctions against any sexual experimentation are often in conflict and can cause great confusion for both homosexuals and heterosexuals as they enter midadolescence.[7]

Here, a concept first proposed by the psychoanalyst Erik Erikson is instructive. Erikson, reflecting on his own adolescence and that of the great founder of Protestantism, Martin Luther, proposed an adolescent "moratorium"—a time within adolescence during which the young person is free to explore without having to make premature and lasting commitments. Adolescence, said Erikson, should be a time when young persons try out roles, explore their worlds, and make tentative moves toward finding out who they are and want to be. Whether or not this includes sexual experimentation will depend on the peer pressures prompted by the cultural situation of the time and place. It also involves a degree of choice on the part of each person.[8]

3. The Search for Intimacy

Another, perhaps most crucial task of late adolescence, is the search for a long-term commitment to a marital partner or other companion with whom one can express one's need for intimacy and care for the needs of the other. For most young persons this task requires years of experimentation, characterized by short-term or long-term commitments.

As is the case with many other social practices in American culture, however, the age at which long-term commitments are being made has been advancing. At the same time, people are becoming sexually active and making premarital, tentative commitments at younger and younger ages. Not only is it common for teenagers to make deep and intimate though temporary connections with another as early as fifteen or sixteen—this resulting often in teenage pregnancy—but it is likewise common for persons to postpone a lasting commitment in marriage until they are in their late twenties or even their early or later thirties. Furthermore, second or even third marriages undertaken in young adulthood are no longer unusual, a social practice sometimes referred to as "serial monogamy." Thus the whole matter of what might be called "cultural scheduling" of lasting intimacy with another has become very slippery indeed. If one looks carefully at gay and lesbian communities, one finds similar confusion about commitment, now greatly complicated by the devastation of AIDS, particularly among homosexual men.

4. The Search for Community

In chapter 6 of this book I spoke of the reality that the social world in our time is made up of not one or two, but many communities within which the individual must with integrity establish a balanced set of commitments. The story of Howard, the busy, overly committed lawyer, with which I began that chapter, illustrates both the importance of and the conflicts that can accompany efforts to establish and maintain these communal commitments.

The story of Cedric and Charles further illustrates the importance of choices made by adolescents regarding how they search for supportive communities and where they find them. For Cedric, the search turned toward church and school, both directions supported strongly by his mother as well as by the larger society. For Charles, the search that drew him into drugs, criminal activity, and separation from his mother and brother seems on examination to be both a search within his father's world and a growing commitment to a community that lived by a code of violence, exploitation, and abuse. The story of the two boys' adolescent efforts to locate themselves within some community illustrates the dynamics that lie beneath these choices.

Finding communities of support through late adolescence and into adulthood also demands for most persons that they locate themselves within the world of vocations: the workaday world of making a living and expressing one's talents in ways that are valued by the social world surrounding the young person. Here, perhaps more than in any other dimension of the transitional tasks of adolescence, the radical differences between the child of affluence and the child of poverty come strikingly into view. The vocational options for a child growing up in a middle-class or upper-class home are remarkably more varied and potentially financially remunerative than are the work options for the lower class and working poor. Here we see clearly the exceptional nature of the accomplishments of persons like Cedric, as well as the importance of providing good educational opportunities for the poor.

Historians tell us there is a long and tortuous history of obstacles encountered by lower-class adolescents in finding their way into the world of making a living. Speaking of this process during the past two centuries , Quentin J. Schultze and his associates report:

> The demands of ordinary life and making one's way were severe. In seventeenth-century America, most unprivileged adolescents were either apprenticed or indentured to other families. At the height of the American Industrial Revolution in the late nineteenth century,

and early in the twentieth century in England, the average workweek for working class urban children, who often began working at age nine or ten, was well over sixty hours. Working conditions were both unhealthy and dangerous. Life on the farms proved little better, with intense seasonal labor and year-round morning and evening chores.[9]

Lower-class youth in the late twentieth century are rarely indentured, but they are quite often confined in their choices to working on the lowest rungs of the economic ladder. Opportunities for promotion and advancement in lifestyle are limited and becoming more so as large corporations "downsize" and workers are frequently required to work at two jobs in order to support themselves and their families. One side effect is that these working-class people are often robbed of any sense of community in their work situations. Jobs change; fellow employees change; there is little opportunity to establish communal working relationships over time. Having said that, however, I am reminded of my observation of a group of African American cooks and maids in a hospital where I was a patient. It was abundantly clear to me that these people had developed a genuine sense of community and enjoyment of one another as they did very ordinary work, which I conjectured kept them well confined to the working class.

The Work of the Congregation
in Relation to Adolescents

Insofar as the mission and ministry of the church is concerned, the caring ministry for and with adolescents is fundamentally and primarily the responsibility of the Christian community. As I shall say later, the ordained pastor has significant responsibility to give leadership to that ministry, but it is the community itself that will or will not respond appropriately to the issues that must be dealt with by teenagers.

The first issue that faces virtually all congregations in this regard is the provision of safe and supportive space within which any of the issues discussed in the previous section can be encountered in a supportive atmosphere. Recall the contrast between the ambiance within which Cedric made his way through a difficult transitional process and that which surrounded his brother Charles. A central difference was the atmosphere he encountered in the church.

In his paper, Cedric said it this way:

> You begin with two avenues of pastoral care that have always been prevalent in the African American community. The most dominant is the proclamation of the word through teaching, singing, and preaching. The second notion is not as easy to label. I choose to call it "village pastoral care." The concept that the whole of the village is responsible for each member in the village. The way it could be modified today might be to say that the whole of the church is responsible for every member of the church's community. I am defining membership in that community very loosely.

After grounding his discussion of the importance of the proclamation of the word, Cedric goes on to say, "I am convinced that being baptized and going to church at age ten did much to turn my life around. The church gave me a place where I belonged and the preaching provided me with moral boundaries that I always tried to stay within."[10]

Concerning Charles, Cedric says, "Whenever I asked Charles why he hung out with his group, he stated they respected him and they understood him. Conversely, whenever I speak to present-day teenage perpetrators of violence they use the same reasoning. They commit these acts so their peers who care about and understand them will give them their juice and respect."

How is the Christian community to respond to young people's needs for a nurturing community, both within their own membership and outside? This is a question to which the church needs to devote more time and effort than it presently does. For Cedric, the problem solving took a positive turn on the bases of his response to this mother's cajoling and his own developing interests. However, the confluence of those two forces and the result in Cedric's life were, to say the least, unusual. Yet the provision of safe and nurturing space is crucial for all young people. Where was Charles to find that space? To be sure, his difficulties involved numerous bad choices. But does that provide a sufficient answer? I think not.

The Christian educator Charles Foster identifies "flaws in church education" that contribute to a lack of vision for the church's educational and missional efforts:

> If we are to create a new vision for church education relevant to our present circumstances, we must be specific about the flaws in the structures and strategies of our current educational practice. As I have struggled over the years to understand changes taking place in church education, clues to five flaws in its goals and structures have become increasingly clear. They include: (1) the loss of communal memory in congregational life; (2) the irrelevance of our teaching about the Bible for contemporary life; (3) the subversion of educational goals; (4) the cultural captivity of church education; and (5) the collapse of the church's educational strategy.[11]

Foster's comments have numerous implications for disciplined inquiry into the congregation's responsibility to exercise a significant caring impact upon the problems encountered by adolescents. Perhaps most significant is what he has to say about the cultural captivity of the churches: The story of the cultural captivity of the church's education is often painful. The residue of nineteenth-century teachings about human relations persist to this day in the racism, sexism, ageism, classism, and other "isms" diminishing God's intentions for all people.[12]

Foster's arguments about the deficiencies in church education could well be applied in similar ways to the recent periods of pastoral care practice. Pastoral care has focused primarily on the work of the ordained on behalf of individual parishioners, thus ignoring the importance of the care of the congregation itself. Furthermore, pastoral care has tended to be held in captivity by the commonsense values of the culture. As I have said elsewhere, the return of the Christian community to its proper place in the fostering of a Christian vision of life together in the world involves efforts to alter the "common sense of the people."[13]

Roy SteinhoffSmith, writing in a critical essay designed to further the project I undertook in *Widening the Horizons* and *Prophetic Pastoral Practice*, reflects on the manner in which prophetic church members who, in the service of a different understanding of love or care, seek to serve marginal people by reclassifying them solely as recipients or objects of care.

Recognition of this tendency to classify people as either active care-givers or passive care-recipients illuminates the difficulty socially active congregations often have with suffering members. Characteristically, such members often complain that such congregations do not care well for them. "Prophetic" pastors are "too busy" to visit hospitalized parishioners. Committed church members may take communion and tapes of the Sunday morning worship to home-bound members, but they do not do much else to help them. . . .

The problem with such members is that they do not fit fully into the category of members, they are expected to fulfill the role of activist servant of the suffering and oppressed. But their affliction identifies them as in need of service. . . . [T]hey are caught between the categories and so tend to be neglected.[14]

Although SteinhoffSmith is speaking here primarily about the church's ministry with adults, his comments as well as Foster's have numerous implications for the ministry of the congregation with teenagers and young people. They suggest the need for the following: (1) the provision of a hospitable place, a "home away from home," where a teen can find peers and set limits for oneself, as was the case with Cedric; (2) the provision of a place to appropriate the deepest meanings and memories of the Christian tradition in ways that make those meanings and memories relevant to the contemporary cultural situation facing young people in our time; (3) the provision of a racially and ethnically inclusive space that invites the expansion of the young person's world and combats the ambivalence of violence within which many young persons must live today; (4) the provision of inquiring space where the young person can find peers and make decisions concerning who she or he is to be and to what values he or she is to declare fidelity.

Tasks of the Ordained Pastor Involved
in the Care of Young People

1. Leadership of the Church Community

Here we encounter once again the reality that pastoral care in the parish begins with pastoral leadership. Although it is the community's responsibility to provide the hospitality and nurture of its young that is needed if they are to make the transitions of adolescence successfully, that will rarely happen unless the pastor gives high priority to fostering the community's sense of responsibility. What may be called the atmosphere or style of a congregation will generally emanate from the pastor's and lay leaders' style. Fostering a certain ambiance is both an intentional and a subtly unconscious relational process.

Pastors, to be sure, differ greatly in their natural abilities to foster open, supportive, and encouraging relationships across generational lines. In very general terms it may be said that pastors tend to identify with their own generation and most easily lead people their age into fellowship with one another. The capacity to identify with youth who may be struggling with a very different cultural situation is a gift that some pastors seem to have, and others do not have. Having children of one's own or having had children in the recent past who are going or have been through these changes is likewise a clarifying reminder of the needs of youth.

At the same time, as the late James Hopewell's careful study of congregations disclosed, each congregation will have its own unique character that sets certain markers and boundaries for the pastor's work as leader.[15] Some congregations pride themselves on being on the "cutting edge" of understanding the problems that grasp a society in a particular time and therefore the problems of young persons who must find their way into adulthood in a society that is itself in transition.[16] On the other hand, some suburban and rural churches, in both attitudes and programs, tend to express fears concerning the exposure of young people to the rapidly changing world around them; therefore they seek to "protect" the values they consider traditional and worthy.

The first and primary task of the pastor as leader is to become aware of her or his strengths and weaknesses in being responsive and open to the needs of young people. The second, equally important task is carefully to consider the interpersonal and social climate of the congregational ethos. Once the pastor has accomplished these two tasks, other tasks, both relational and programmatic, will begin to clarify themselves.[17]

2. *Articulating the Christian Tradition*

A sad but true reality in Christian churches today is that there are fewer and fewer people who possess deep, accurate, and abiding understanding of the wisdom of our tradition. In place of this deep understanding is quite often found fragmentary knowledge and even what might well be called folk religion.[18]

This problem has arisen partly because the church has failed its young people in helping them learn and appropriate the wisdom of the tradition of the church in their daily lives. This failure has gone on during much of the middle to late twentieth century. In a real sense, the church is now reaping the rewards of this failure in that we can no longer count on most parents to actively embody and teach their children the basic stories and themes of the tradition to which they say they belong.

It is therefore a major task of the ordained pastor to articulate the Christian tradition as it encounters the problems of the present. In that task, the ordained pastor needs to be joined by a cadre of dedicated laypersons who, though not paid in full-time church ministry, are dedicated to what the Christian educator Richard Osmer calls the "teaching office":

> The teaching office never merely repeats the past in the present. It uses the inherited tradition as a way of formulating normative statements of faith and moral guidelines for today's church. The tradition is preserved by extending it into the present. This brings us to the second task of the teaching office, the ongoing reinterpretation of the church's normative beliefs and practices in the face of the shifting cultural and historical contexts.[19]

Osmer's definition of the teaching office leads directly into consideration of the third set of tasks for the ordained pastor who cares for children and youth.

3. *Leadership in Social Advocacy for Youth*

The story of Cedric and Charles is representative of the sociocultural ethos within which young people must grow to maturity in contemporary North American society. Cedric and Charles grew up in a world of unfaithfulness, family and community violence, and the threat of a meaningless, even destructive life. Yet for Cedric, the church provided an environment and a set of purposes for his life that enabled him to overcome what surrounded him. As for Charles, it may be said that for a variety of reasons, including the inclinations of Charles himself, the church failed to provide an environment that could rescue him from a life of crime and violence.

It is the ordained pastor's task to lead the members of the community, individually and collectively, to engage these problems—problems too great for any single congregation to resolve by itself. The evidence of these problems may be found both within and surrounding the congregation. As interpretive guide within the congregation, the ordained pastor has both a public and a private ministry of prophetic pastoral guidance. Guided fundamentally by the principle of the primacy of care for all persons, the pastor must lead the congregation in a process of inquiry and action. Such a process asserts the tradition's primacy in determining goals of Christian action and evaluating strategies for confronting these problems appropriately and effectively.[20]

Nowhere is the pastor's public leadership of the congregation more relevant than in fostering or even provoking discussion of the peculiar needs and problems of young people in contemporary society. This will inevitably create tension within the congregation and between members of the congregation and the ordained pastor. That very tension can enliven the process of congregational dialogue with its young people and with the society around it.[21]

Once again, I am arguing for a drastic revision of the assumed limits of pastoral care as having to do with the pastor's caring work with individuals and families. To care for young people negotiating the rough waters of adolescent transitions means more than simply counseling with them. It means mobilizing the church as a community to engage the social conditions that surround and confront youth in a time of growing crisis in our society.[22]

4. Guiding, Mentoring, and Mediating

Though it is necessary to widen the conventional horizons of pastoral care beyond care to individuals, an important and often neglected set of tasks of the ordained pastor has to do with direct and personal ministry to individual adolescents and their parents. In general, the first task of adolescence is to initiate the process of leaving home and coming to terms with one's familial background. In this process, most young people need a variety of transitional parental figures whom they can trust and in whom they may find model figures that help them differentiate themselves from their parents. Recall that Cedric found these figures in his pastors, certain of his teachers, and an uncle.

A primary obstacle to the fulfillment of this role by contemporary pastors, most particularly those in larger churches, is availability. The teenager cannot learn to trust or identify with a pastor whom she or he sees only in the pulpit on Sunday. The teenager needs contact with the pastor in informal settings. The teenager needs to talk with the pastor, confide in the pastor, and ask "what the pastor really thinks" about the issues uppermost in the young person's experience at the moment; and the pastor needs to hear "what the young person really thinks" about these matters.

Many pastors are inclined to give these contacts with the young in their congregations a low priority. In my own experience as a teacher of both young would-be pastors and older pastors seeking advanced degrees, I have found that the great majority of stories about ministry with young people have come from youth ministers. Senior pastors tend not to bring these stories for peer group analysis, although they may be aware that families in their churches are facing these problems. Unless the parents or the young person seeks out the pastor directly, the problems that are virtually unavoidable in the process of growing up very often go unattended or are left to lay youth advisors to handle as best they can.

Another important aspect of the ordained pastor's direct ministry with families is that of acting as the mediator between the generations.

> Sometimes the positive feelings and ties that bind people together are covered over by negative feelings, accusations, and counteraccusations. This is frequently the case when teenagers run away from home, for example.
>
> In situations of this kind the pastor will often find himself or herself drawn into the position of go-between, to whom people on either side of the gap can talk while they are yet unable to communicate with

each other. This is, of course, a difficult position to be in. One must be careful not to be drawn toward inappropriate collaboration with one side or the other. . . . But the position of go-between, if it is temporary, is a potentially useful role of reconciliation.[23]

Inherent in this quotation is the understanding of pastoral care ministry as frequently focused on crisis situations. In this chapter we have seen that the dimensions of caring crisis ministry to youth involves both pastor and congregation at many levels, both individual and social. What began as a brief analysis of one story of two African American youths as they found their way into adulthood opened before us a broad and puzzling range of critical issues confronting Western society and Christian congregations and their pastors in a period of transition. As we end our consideration of adolescence, we anticipate that what has opened before us here will reappear in our consideration of later life-cycle periods, though with particular angles of vision provided by adulthood and old age.

CHAPTER 9

Stories of the Adult Years: Gender Differences, Generative Commitments, and Failed Relationships

It was Erik Erikson who first designated the adult years as the years of generativity. By generativity Erikson meant not only the desire and responsibility to generate and nurture one's offspring as the next generation; he also meant the human urge to create and make better whatever one has engendered by way of projects, skills, and contributions to the common good of human life. Describing each life-cycle stage in dialectical terms, Erikson points to stagnation as the dark possibility that always stands in tension with generativity.

Although Erikson speaks of generativity in virtually all of his writings, perhaps his fullest explication of the term is in *Insight and Responsibility*. There he places his pioneering work concerning the stages of the human life cycle within a structure of the formation of what he terms virtues, a fundamentally ethical construct.

The most immediate connection between the *basic virtues* and the *essentials of an organized human community* is that adults are organized (among other reasons) for the purpose of deriving from the collectivity and from its traditions a fund of reassurance and a set of methods which enable them to meet the needs of the next generation in relative independence of the vicissitudes of individual fate. Trustworthy motherliness, thus, needs a trustworthy "universe," and the religion of women can be observed to have a different quality from that of men. The womanly verification of faith lies less in a logic that permits action without guilt than in what the woman can do with faith itself, namely, give hope and establish trust in new humans.[1]

Erikson goes on to assert that what he calls the virtue of adulthood for both men and women is that of *care*, the necessary consequence of generativity: "Care is the widening concern for what has been generated by love, necessity, or accident; it overcomes the ambivalence adhering to irreversible obligation."[2]

Although in this passage Erikson seems to be speaking largely in individualistic terms, the whole of his psychology has far-reaching social implications. Erikson's assertion that care is the virtue of adulthood is compatible with the controlling place I have given to the concept of care in this book. The one conception I would add—a notion that Erikson acknowledges in other writings—is that our current understanding of care comes to us out of a long tradition of human thought.[3] In the Christian community, our conception of care has been shaped by the long history of Judeo-Christian thought and activity.

Readers will remember that part 3 of this volume is constructed according to a double set of organizing principles: first, a consideration of common needs and issues of four periods of the human life cycle; and second, a brief but penetrating look at certain current life-cycle related dilemmas that present peculiar difficulties for the ministries of the Christian community. To seek to fulfill this two-pronged task in relation to adulthood is a daunting task. Not only is adulthood the longest period of the cycle of life, extending from early in the twenties until sometime in the middle to late sixties or early seventies, but it is the time of life during which persons experience in peculiar and diverse ways the burdens of commitments and responsibilities. Here Erikson's aforementioned perspective becomes most pertinent.

Our attention will be concentrated on three overlapping areas that are universal among adults and in our time peculiarly problematic and difficult: gender differences, generative difficulties, and failed relationships. To be an adult in the West today is to encounter in singular ways one or another of these problematic situations; and for many, it means to encounter all three.

Sexuality, Gender Differences, and Pastoral Care

If generativity is the prime virtue of the adult years, then it closely follows that adulthood presents to all persons the task of finding comfortable ways to express their sexuality and "fit" as nearly as possible into the cultural images of male and female. At its most basic level, this search is in fundamental ways within biological parameters. The sexual apparatus of women and men is different. Nevertheless, just how those biological differences are to be accounted for and organized behaviorally is subject to a wide variety of cultural, social, and individual standards. Those standards are themselves most often set in the midst of conflicts among parental expectations, peer group pressures, and larger cultural patterns that are now undergoing radical modification. The working out of one's sexuality and gender identity likewise takes place within a socioeconomic structure that grants certain rewards for being of a particular sex (usually male) and often metes out subtle penalties for being of another sex (usually female).

A homosexual identity, whether by choice, developmental vicissitudes, or biology (most often a combination of the three), often carries with it particular penalties and disadvantages. In many communities, some of them faith communities, gays and lesbians are scorned and deemed inadmissible.[4] On the other hand, the "coming out" of the gay and lesbian community has meant for many gays and lesbians a partial end to the loneliness and shame that in earlier times virtually always accompanied homosexuality.[5]

Regardless of their sexual orientation, men and women living in the latter decades of the twentieth century must live within the societal and cultural structures that define who men and women are supposed to be and how they are to relate to one another with greater or lesser degrees of discomfort or outright conflict. Even with regard to heterosexual relationships, clearly the society and its culture are in the midst of a radical, even revolutionary transition. How women and men are to be shepherded through this time of change becomes a highly significant question for pastoral care.

A Case Study: The Haringtons

The case of Tom and Ruth Harington (not their real names) is representative of common marital conflicts that have at their core differences in sexuality and sex roles. Tom and Ruth, now in their midthirties, have in the course of their six-year marriage begotten two children, now four and two. In many ways their relationship with each other and with their children has been rather conventional yet strongly affectionate. They have followed the patterns of sex roles inherited from their parents and culture with the exception that, like most of her generational cohorts, Ruth has worked outside the home. With the birth of their second child, Ruth (with Tom's support) quit her job to become a full-time mother and house-keeper—a decision she made with very ambivalent feelings but great determination.

For a time, all seemed to be going well. Tom was succeeding in his work, earning an adequate income for the family. Ruth enjoyed her children. But during the past two years the relationship has become strained, their communication about their similarities and differences and the problems of rearing two active children less open and mutually helpful.

The Haringtons have lived on the fringe of a Christian congregation, attending only occasionally, though Ruth in particular has often expressed a desire for more involvement, as a result of which she hopes she and her husband would receive more support for their essentially generative struggles. Their involvement has been hampered considerably by Tom's work; his job requires that he travel extensively, often out of the country, so he is often away from home over the traditional family weekend. This heavy travel schedule has left Ruth with the primary responsibility for the children and for the common household tasks—a responsibility she has become more and more resentful of having to carry by herself. Tom tries to "help out" when he is at home, but he usually comes home tired and ready to relax.

Lately, the conflicts have increased to the point at which Ruth can no longer go on without help. She turned to a pastoral counseling center simply because the name of the center included the word "pastoral," and she was raised in the church. Having met her on my walks around the neighborhood, I supported her in her decision to seek help. As it happened, I knew the pastoral counselor she had seen on her first visit and could recommend him to her as a competent and caring professional.

A problem arose when Tom was at first reluctant to go for counseling. He expressed anxiety about what might happen to his job if his superiors found out that he was seeking help for marital problems. "I think we can work it out ourselves if you will just settle down," he told Ruth. At this point in the process an outside occurrence intervened in the form of a job offer in a distant city near where

Tom and Ruth had grown up—a job that would not require heavy travel. The pay, however, would be considerably less than his current salary. After much agonizing thought and discussion with Ruth and their pastoral counselor, Tom accepted the new job, they sold their house, and the Haringtons were off to Detroit to seek to rebuild their lives.

What do we see here concerning the transitions in our society in relation to sex roles and the opportunities and difficulties involved for pastoral care practice? First, we see, first dimly and then more and more apparently, the dominating presence of traditional patriarchal understandings of gender roles. The Haringtons, even though they were in most respects committed to the new egalitarianism in marriage, still were entangled painfully in the structures of patriarchy that continue to dominate their cultural context.[6] Their gender roles were conventional. The burdens of family and children were carried primarily by Ruth. Tom lived in fear of displeasing the authorities of his company (presumably primarily male). The children saw little of their father, though he tried to make up for his absence by a degree of activity (mostly play) with them when he was at home.

For the pastor and his or her congregation, caring for families like the Haringtons seems at first to be a relatively simple task. To reach such families, the church must develop out-of-the-ordinary, proactive methods of seeking out people like the Haringtons in the church's vicinity and inviting their participation in the supportive activities of the church. Most churches at some time provide discussion groups, special events, and worship experiences that are meant to respond to the high number of couples who are going through similar, difficult transitions. Here the congregation can engage in its pastoral role: the care of one another in a time of both interpersonal and cultural transition.

Of course, such congregational caring activity is not confined to young couples like the Haringtons. Many older couples, particularly those who are interested in changing cultural practices, can profit from mutual exploration of these issues, as well as from intergenerational dialogue with their younger peers.

The pastor has a role in providing leadership that facilitates these activities. As in other things, some members of the congregation will take their attitudinal signal toward changes in gender roles from the pastor. For these people the pastor can play an important role in "showing the way ahead." For others, pastoral leadership will arouse resistance and argument about new cultural directions. Even for these people, the pastor's leadership, if offered in a truly pastoral manner, can help change what needs to be changed and preserve what needs to be preserved.[7]

Important as is the communal caring activity of the congregation with families like the Haringtons, we need to remember that it was not to the local congregation that Ruth Harington first turned when her distress became more than she could bear. Rather, she turned to a pastoral counseling center, where she surmised that she could receive expert help. As John Patton reminds us, the pastoral counseling center is a ministry of the church—a particularly important ministry with those who have for one reason or another become disconnected from the fellowship of a local congregation.[8]

What, then, is the ministry of the parish pastor, beyond leadership of the congregation? At one level, the pastor's ministry involves the development of intimately confidential relationships with individuals and families so that she or he is privy to the inner climate of congregants' lives. Good pastoral care makes possible trust, openness, and honesty in relationships, and a spirit of inquiry concerning how life within the framework of the Christian story is to be lived, often in difficult or problematic situations. It invites open sharing of concerns about one's generativity and one's struggles to find new paths to follow with regard to sex and gender relationships.

At another level, the ministry of the parish pastor involves immediate availability and wise counsel in times of crisis between marital partners or boyfriends and girlfriends, and during intense moments of anguish concerning a parishioner's sexual identity or that of another with whom a parishioner has a close relationship. Here the pastor needs to learn to not be surprised at anything.[9]

The pastor needs to be open to talking about the most intimate subjects in a nonjudgmental fashion, while yet maintaining a stance of seeking for the best, most ethical, most creative solution to whatever critical situation is at hand.

A Case Study: The Lassiters

The Lassiters, Carl and Charlotte, are substantially older than the Haringtons, and have been married for over thirty years. Carl is a dentist with a modest practice that, while bringing an above average income to the family, seems never quite adequate to Carl. Charlotte, a professional in the field of secondary education, has worked outside the home for many years. She has done this partly by choice and partly to supplement Carl's income as the family has grown to three children—two sons and a daughter. She had worked to support herself for several years before her marriage, quit working when the babies came, and began again when the school expenses began to mount, with college costs for all three children.[10]

The Lassiters were referred to me for marital counseling by their pastor. He said that the Lassiters "were good folks, but seemed to be having trouble lately." According to the marital history they shared with me on their first visit, their marriage had always "had its stresses and strains," but had generally been satisfactory to both of them. They spoke of having an enjoyable sexual relationship during the first ten years or so of their marriage, but confided that Charlotte had in recent years become restless about the infrequency of intercourse and about Carl's passivity with regard to sex as well as other aspects of their life together.

Carl's lassitude was, as is often the case, in marked contrast to the remarkable vigor and liveliness that characterized Charlotte's style of personhood. Not only did she work hard in her job and perform most of the household duties, she also was a joiner who thoroughly enjoyed being involved in all kinds of volunteer activities in her church and elsewhere. Carl meanwhile tagged along with her when necessary and pursued his own private interests, which consisted primarily of weekly rounds of golf and long evenings by himself in the den watching television or reading.

Two clusters of events began to more and more radically upset the already precarious balance that the Lassiters had been able to maintain through their children's early years. The first events were directly related to the Lassiters' old struggle with finances and desires. The children were now reaching college age, and it became apparent that Charlotte's ambitions for her children were in serious conflict with Carl's abiding fear not only that he could not provide enough for the family, but also that he would find his energy completely depleted. Arguments ensued over money—arguments that Charlotte, with her greater energy, usually won. In the end, the children all went to expensive private universities, and one son went on to law school, all at the parents' expense. Providing the very best for their children provided the tie that held the Lassiters' marriage together.

At the heart of the rising conflicts over the years of this transition in the Lassiter family was undoubtedly a struggle over power. Could Carl exercise enough power to resist Charlotte's ambitions and their children's seemingly bottomless desires? Could Charlotte exercise enough power to control what she perceived to be Carl's "stinginess"?

The other set of events that served to exacerbate the Lassiters' sex role conflicts and power struggles came about through Charlotte's deepening involvement in the feminist movement. She was one who read widely and, of course, read a great deal of the popular feminist literature of the seventies and eighties. She also began attending feminist gatherings and soon joined a feminist support group. Being at heart a passive person, Carl did not openly object to Charlotte's feminist efforts either within the home or outside in the community. In fact he verbally supported her, though it was apparent in the counseling relationship that he harbored more resentment and resistance than he could express.[11]

In counseling it became more and more apparent that the Lassiters were moving toward the necessity of making a decision. Would they give up on a difficult marriage now that the children were grown, or would they accept that they were very different people and learn to better adapt to their differences? At one point, when Charlotte was particularly angry about Carl's lack of sexual interest, she almost came to the point of telling him that she wanted a divorce or else she would seek to satisfy her sexual needs elsewhere. She could make her own way financially and find male companionship with other men. At that point Carl became quite depressed, but held his ground, saying that he could not be someone other than who he was. After months of vacillation on Charlotte's part and with increasingly honest and open efforts to respond to Charlotte's needs on Carl's part, they made a decision to stay together. The decision involved the admission on both parts that there were more sources of satisfaction in the marriage than there were reasons to separate. Charlotte became more accepting of Carl's personhood; she even learned to play golf, and Carl learned to wash dishes and clean house. Carl participated more actively in sex and with Charlotte and in community activities. The marriage, though still painful at times, survived.

The story illustrates well the critical transitions often involved in the middle years that have at their core both differences in personhood and rediscovery of personal and relational needs that have in part been set aside during the active years of procreation. The glue that held the Lassiters together during the early years of their marriage was the task of raising children. Raising children meant different things to Charlotte from what it meant to Carl. Nevertheless, the needs of the children and the enjoyment of their company provided a cushion against the inherent conflicts in the parents' relationship.[12]

Generative Commitments and Pastoral Care

The case of Carl and Charlotte Lassiter provides a useful transition into a broader range of generative issues in midlife that have to do with maintaining fidelity to meanings and relationships that give definition and purpose to lives over a period of decades. The primary tasks and therefore the principal sources of conflict and difficulty during the middle years of life have to do with keeping one's commitments over the long years of adulthood. Without commitment, adult life can degenerate into chaotic relationships, an insecure sense of self, and confusion concerning values and purposes for living. Middle life is a long haul that demands making and keeping commitments. Helping people maintain their commitments thus becomes a pivotal task for the ministry of pastoral care.

I will consider pastoral care in relation to the making and maintaining of commitments under three intertwining subtopics: commitments in regard to parenting and other forms of generativity, commitments to faith, and commitments of occupation and vocation. These three subtopics are not easily separated, nor should they be. Nevertheless, it seems useful to consider them one at a time.

The first two of these subtopics are well illustrated in the following story reported to me by a pastor in a suburban community. The story recorded here is drawn from the pastor's own written report of the incident provided at my request after he had told me about it in a more or less casual conversation.

A Case Study: Al Browning

Al Browning's fifteen-year-old son had been in a Twelve-Step drug and alcohol treatment program for nine months. In a previous conversation initiated by Al with me as his pastor, Al stated his disappointment with the involvement of the church in its failure to address drug and alcohol abuse among teenagers. Al also indicated his desire to be part of a community and a church which passed along information among parents of alleged drug use among their children.

Al's attitude toward uncorroborated information from the community had changed because of his son's drug usage. Formerly he saw such information as gossip. Now he believed that this information belonged in the hands of parents. He said, "There must have been ten to fifteen people who came to me after my son was in treatment saying that they had heard about his drug use but did not think it appropriate to share hearsay. If they had come to me when he was still using, the first four or five times I know I would not have believed. But then I might have started looking in his room and checking out his stories."

I remember feeling defensive and uncomfortable in response to the accusations Al made about the church. He had been supportive and generous to me, he insisted, so where was I when he needed me and his church? I must confess that I work out of a quid pro quo mentality. Give to those who have given. Earn respect. Relationships are based on good works, not gifts. Al's disappointment with me caused me to reconsider the basis of my ministry decisions. I reminded myself to become more involved when next he called.

Al Browning did call, on a very busy Friday as I was leaving at noon for an appointment to plan a funeral. He had information from a reliable source of two seventh-grade boys who were experimenting with marijuana. I knew the parents, one couple fairly well and the other as just slightly more than acquaintances. The boys were classmates of both Al's child and my son. Mr. and Mrs. Browning wanted to protect their son from involvement in any information sharing. Could I pass the information along? Would I? Al was confident the information of marijuana use was accurate and needed to be shared with the parents.

I trusted Al enough that I could share the information confidently. Yet I felt anxious. Could I deal with my anxious feelings? Where were those anxious feelings coming from? Surely part of the cause was that this was a new situation with no precedents for me in my role as pastor. Nevertheless I knew that the parents would trust me and take me seriously. And this was my son's class! I was sure he did not have a clue about participating in drugs. He is obedient and straight, someone who tries hard to please. I recognize in myself the need to please, to be obedient and straight.

Could I share the information? How could I not? I was obligated to Al. I was guilty by his implications for not acting in his son's drug usage, never mind that it had little to do with me. It was then that I remembered my own experimentation with drugs when I was in college.

In his account of the situation the pastor went on to speak at some length of his ambivalent conflict over what to do and his own obligation to his family versus his commitment to be a good pastor to his congregation. He talked to several people whom he trusted, the most important of whom was his wife, though he had to struggle with the question as to whether or not to involve her in the problem. "She might inhibit me. Even if this did deal with *their* family and *their* child, I was acting to protect and secure against encroaching problems such as drugs." (Here, of course, we see the power of traditional sex role stereotypes even in a pastor who conscientiously works to overcome them in his ministry.)

Much to his surprise, the pastor found his spouse being supportive, yet confrontational in her response to his dilemma. She reminded him of his tendency to be self-righteous. (Thank God our child is not like other children!) She also raised the question as to why he felt he had to take all the responsibility for the care of these families himself? Why not bring Al into the situation so that the parents who did not yet know of their son's drug experimentation could experience care from a member of the congregation?

The pastor's account of the case continues:

So I woke Al up on Sunday morning and asked him if he would join me. I didn't want to say it this straight. It is against my nature to ask directly. . . . But against my reactive self, I asked straight up; I asked him to be there. He did not hesitate to say yes. [The pastor tried to explain why Al's presence was needed, but he was quickly cut off. "If you want me to be there, that's all I need."]

In meeting with the parents separately, both parents doubted the information about their children. The names of the other child or other family were not given by Al or me. Al made it clear that it was not nearly so important where the information came from or even the accuracy of the information as that the information belonged with the parents. Al shared his story of his own son and his personal denial of his son's drug use. Out of his pain and his struggle, he spoke of picking the battles he would now fight with his son. . . . He spoke of the therapy sessions when the counselors had advocated parents telling the youth that they loved them and giving them hugs. Al confessed he could not remember when he had spoken of love and given a hug to his son. Al said his parental approach with his son, when Al suspected the son might be involved in drugs, was to yell at him and suggest that his son could not be so stupid as to use drugs. Al now realized that this caused his son to have lower self-esteem and contributed to driving him to drug usage. Al offered himself, his wife, and his son to speak with parents or youth about drug usage and alcohol abuse. Al said his wife had more good instincts about raising a son in this culture than he did.

The pastor goes on to say that one of the most important lessons for him in this situation was that he did not have to carry the full load of ministry himself. "Instead of being the righteous bearer of the information, I became the convener of the meeting, introducing people who did not know each other. I occasionally asked questions, clarified comments and stayed out of the way of Al's powerful witness. With a surprising emotion within, I acknowledged that I was going to go home to my child and tell him I loved him."

This case is instructive both for the participants and for pastoral care ministry in general in four important ways. First, the pastor's participation in the case and his reflection on that participation raised several new questions for him concerning how he was to fulfill his vocation as a pastoral minister and as a father. Perhaps even more important, it confronted him with the differences between his declared faith (nonjudgmental acceptance, grace, and individual freedom before God) and his "faith in action" (salvation by works, self-righteousness, manipulation to express his own authority). His encounter with the problems of ministry in this situation quite apparently had been very useful to him in keeping both his sense of vocation and his faith alive and in lively relationship to the concrete situations of his pastoral care.

The pastor also, and not incidentally, learned something about how his faith in action affected his relationship with his son. He began to realize that he wanted to let his son see more of the soft, tender, caring side of himself and perhaps less of the strong, righteous leader of his church and the family. Showing physical affection toward his son took on enhanced meaning for him. Also, not incidentally, he learned that his wife brought a soft, wise, and knowledgeable perspective to his work.

A second way in which this case is instructive is that Al, the father who played the lead role in the ministry to the two other sets of parents, had quite obviously, through his experience with his son's involvement in drugs, learned to reevaluate the way he had balanced his obligations to his work and his responsibility to his family. He had gained a new and enlarged sense of vocation, which included not only what he did to make a living for his family, but also his role as husband and father. His new sense of vocation had taken hold of him in ways that caused him to want to be involved in ministry to others with similar problems.

The matter of how men in America are to meet the changing demands on their energies and commitments is a lively one. In an important study entitled *No Man's Land: Men's Changing Commitments to Family and Work*, Kathleen Gerson categorizes the various ways males in our society are moving to deal with deeply penetrating cultural changes. She speaks of those who turn ever more stubbornly toward breadwinning as their primary mode of being; those who turn toward autonomy, even if necessary at the expense of avoiding marital and family relationships; and those who turn toward family involvement, even if it becomes at times expensive in relation to job responsibilities:

> Upholding standards of justice and sharing in personal commitments is neither a punishment nor an unmitigated loss to men. We have seen that men have much to gain from more equal relationships with women and more caring connections to children. Economic and social changes may require men to relinquish some long-standing privileges, but they also offer men a chance to claim new rights and

surrender old burdens. No longer held solely responsible for the economic health of their families, men can look forward to sharing the obligations of breadwinning and enjoying the pleasures of care. Moreover, if men become more involved in the care of their children, they gain the moral authority to fight for personal rights inside and outside of marriage. Not only do involved fathers have a greater claim to parental rights in the event of divorce, but they are also less likely to abandon their children. If marriage becomes more just and equal, then so can divorce. On the other hand, if men want parental rights, they must earn them the way women do—by being responsible, caring, sharing parents who meet their children's needs in myriad ways every day.[13]

Another important longitudinal study extending over four decades by the research psychologist and ethicist John Snarey underlines the moral significance of choices made on both the personal and societal levels:

Father-child relationships, like mother-child relationships, have moral significance. By this I mean that fathers directly experience the moral claims of their children and are personally obligated to their children. Erikson's psychoethical model suggests to me that our society is now providing men with unprecedented opportunities for parental generativity. However, parents in our society frequently find that their primary obligations—breadwinning and childbearing—are in conflict. Fathers as well as mothers face numerous practical moral dilemmas because they cannot do all the things they ought to do. Conflicts in moral obligations are inevitable, of course, but they seem to be unnecessarily intensified for parents in our society at the present time.[14]

A third way in which the case is instructive is that all participants in the case learned something about the meaning of being the church, though they might not have been able to articulate it in theological terms. Viewing the situation from outside, we quickly see that it is representative in significant ways of what the church is meant to be. As Evelyn Eaton Whitehead and James D. Whitehead suggest in their book *Christian Life Patterns:*

Religious generativity is expressed most centrally, perhaps, in service to the communities in which one lives. *Diakonia* is the New Testament term for such adult service or ministry. *Diakonia*, as the action of believing adults, is action for others, action expressive of one's individual talents and gifts, and action in accord with the vision or dream of Christianity. . . . This theology of ministry is grounded in Paul's understanding of the community as composed of adults with a variety of gifts, whose mutual care results both in individual growth and in the development of the community of faith (1 Cor. 12).[15]

By inviting Al to participate with him in the ministry of the church with the other two couples whose children were in danger of becoming involved in drug abuse, the pastor communicated to all participants this primary meaning of the church as the community of mutual care and service. What allowed this experience of the church to happen was the decision not to deal with the situation in the complete privacy of a pastor-parishioner relationship. Deciding when to involve the church in mutual ministry is undoubtedly one of the most difficult but important decisions the pastoral caregiver must make.

Fourth, as observers of the case we can learn that the expression of faith that really counts in life is faith expressed in attitude and action rather than faith expressed as proposition and argument. The Christian tradition must, to be sure, sustain and communicate a framework of ultimate meaning and moral boundaries. The ideas the tradition hands down to us concerning God's relationship to human beings and right relationships among human beings must be tended. I have earlier referred to this activity as the "care of the tradition." But in the nitty-gritty of everyday life, it is the translation of those meanings and boundaries into actions and relationships that really differentiates a Christian individual or community from one that simply wears that cloak as a covering while living fundamentally out of a different story of the truth of things.

Failed Relationships and Pastoral Care

The middle years of life are often years marked not only by achievement and success, but also by failure. Relationships begun in exuberant promise crash or end in stagnant alienation. Commitments made with the best of intentions turn sour and are either abandoned or diminished. Shared desires for a future joined in mutual anticipation become separated; and alienation, acknowledged or denied, begins to dominate the atmosphere of relationships. This is the human condition; relationships are prone to failure.

As we reflect on the cases of the Lassiters and the Haringtons, we are reminded just how close the participants came to abject failure in both cases. We are also reminded that it was the recognition of past failures and the coming to grips with them that proved salutary to both couples; by recognizing the dangerous directions their relationships were taking, they were able to alter their course.

A significant aspect of the pastor's caring ministry with adults in the generative years is, as a consequence of the inevitable presence of failure, assisting individuals, institutions, and even larger social entities to recognize and counter the presence of relational failure with the good news of the gospel. Just how that is done will vary widely from case to case, but the task, theologically designated that of redemption and reconciliation, remains constant as a central aspect of the pastor's mission. To function as the interpretive guide for the people of God requires the ability to assist people to confront their failures.

Failure in adult life takes place at many levels, both personal and social. It is now common knowledge that nearly half of the marriages in America end in failure. It has become popular in some circles to speak of "serial marriage," a term that expresses the expectation that fewer and fewer American couples will follow through with the traditional marriage vow, "Till death do us part." The term evidences an altered perception of marriage as a lifelong relationship— a commitment.

At a related level, expressive of the effects of marital failure, are the failures of adults to properly care for the next generation. As Don Browning has said:

> There is a thunderous debate in our society over whether the family is simply changing or actually in decline. The facts that follow and the horizon of values I have just set forth lead me to affirm that the family is both changing and declining. The word "crisis," however, is the best metaphor to comprehend both of these dynamics. Of special importance for describing this crisis is the present-day situation of children and youth.[16]

Browning goes on to speak of the 10 percent decline in the marriage rate since 1975 and the approximately 1.5 million abortions that occur in the United States each year. Furthermore, out of wedlock births have increased from 5 percent in 1960 to 30 percent (68 percent in the black community) in 1992. Poverty, says Browning, has become increasingly feminized.[17]

We cannot speak of failure in families without also mentioning the increasingly difficult time many families are having in inculcating in their children the values that the parents have taken for granted as offering the proper structure for right relationships. Here I must speak carefully, because I do not want to say that all the values by which adults learned to organize their lives are true and therefore not subject to modification. Despite what some political figures are saying in the 1990s, not all of the values that gave structure to nineteenth-century America were good and humane. Many of them proved to be oppressive and stultifying of individual freedom and creativity. Nonetheless, life requires setting limits on behavior and making commitments to ideals. Many families are having difficulty in following through with this task in our time. For many, commitment has become "old-fashioned."

At another personal and relational level, the communities of our society are filled with situations of failure among kinfolk, failed relationships between aging parents and their younger children, conflicts between neighbors, and outright animosity between persons of differing ethnic origins. Everywhere we look we can see the evidence of this relational failure. So much is that the case that the word "harassment" has become a commonplace expression—one that was rarely heard as recently as thirty years ago.

In cases of failed relationships, the pastor is most often approached by one who feels injured in a relationship. The injured person usually expects support and often agreement with an accusation against someone, even though that request is usually made so as to disguise the hurt and anger. Here the pastoral caregiver must strive to remain disinterested, not seduced into taking sides, yet caring and encouraging.

Relational failure is not confined to the interpersonal level. Our society is torn apart by societal failure. Employees are no longer as loyal to their employers as they once were. Corporations make decisions that affect the lives of many of their employees seemingly without regard to any values save that of the so-called bottom line. In writing of this level of relational failure, Richard Sennett had this to say:

> Shame has taken the place of violence as a *routine* form of punishment in Western societies. The reason is simple and perverse. The shame an autonomous person can arouse in subordinates is an implicit control. Rather than the employer explicitly saying "You are dirt" or "Look how much better I am," all he needs to do is his job—exercise his skill or deploy his calm and indifference. His powers are fixed in his position, they are static attributes, qualities of what he is. It is not so much abrupt moments of humiliation as month after month of disregarding his employees, of not taking them seriously, which establishes his domination. The feelings he has about them, they about him, need never be stated. The grinding down of his employees' sense of self-worth is not part of his discourse with them; it is a silent erosion of their sense of self-worth which will wear them down. This, rather than open abuse, is how he bends them to his will. When shame is silent, implicit, it becomes a patent tool of bringing people to heel.[18]

Just what Christian communities and their pastors can do to counter this massive breakdown of the expression of care and mutual respect among our citizens and their corporate entities is at best questionable. The realities of late-twentieth-century life do, however remind us in fresh and vigorous ways of the meaning and power of such ancient metaphors as the remnant, corporate witness, and sacrifice of self-interest for the sake of the poor and the stranger. Drawing from these metaphors will provide the interpretive strengths that can empower the church in its caring ministry to the complex realities of the adult world.

CHAPTER 10

Final Chapters in Life Stories: The Community of Faith and the Care of Older Persons

Two vignettes set the stage for this chapter. The first lasted only a few minutes. It took place on Park Avenue in New York City as my wife and I were riding on a bus going to the Metropolitan Museum of Art. An old man with a cane in one hand and his other hand on the shoulder of a younger man, whom I imagined to be his son, hobbled off the bus in front of St. Patrick's Cathedral, looked straight at me through the window of the bus and said bitterly, "Getting old is nothing but hell!" That image has stuck in my mind ever since, and I think of it more and more often as I get older.

The second vignette has as its central character a woman with whom I worked many years ago at the Boys Industrial School in Topeka, Kansas. Her name was Leita. When we worked together she was a psychologist and I the chaplain of the institution. The last time my wife and I visited her was three months ago at the home she shared with her second husband, Ed. Leita was eighty-six when we visited. We had a most enjoyable visit, as has always been the case over the years whenever we have been together. She shared with me that she was "in process of placing her things with persons she knew would care for them" and gave me a book that had belonged to a mutual friend and coworker of ours years ago who died early in life of pancreatic cancer.

I shall never forget the moment when she put her hands on both my shoulders and, smiling with her characteristic warmth, gazing at me with all the intensity of the man on Park Avenue, but with profound joy, said, "Charles, every day is Thanksgiving Day!" Not long before this writing I learned the sad news: Leita had died of a massive heart attack.

"Getting old is nothing but hell!" "Every day is Thanksgiving Day!" Here are diametrically opposite, yet equally authentic expressions of what it means to grow old. I would hazard a guess that anyone who has lived into their seventies, as have I, or on into their eighties or nineties, has in a unique way experienced something similar to both expressions. That is to say that growing old is a time when life is both infinitely precious and at times excruciatingly, angrily painful, so that one wants to cry out to friend or stranger that moving toward the end of life is unfair and humiliating.

My Own Aging Process

Having already disclosed that I am in my early seventies, I want now to speak briefly of my own experience of the last five years as offering a paradigm of sorts by which the stresses and strains, the joys and sorrows, the anxieties and expectations of the later years of life may be understood. Since this chapter is not meant to be fully autobiographical, I will not speak of all that has happened and is happening to me, but simply report a few highlights that in paradigmatic ways open before my readers what it is like to get old.

I remember clearly that while in my sixties, I often spoke to my friends and colleagues of "looking forward to my seventies." I imagined I would not only be able to play more golf, I would also have more time to work in my yard, spend time at our cabin in North Georgia, and write this book, which I had already begun, at a much more leisurely pace. I knew that illness could interrupt those plans, but I really did not think much about that. I was relatively healthy. I exercised regularly and ate moderately. In fact, I had recently lost twenty pounds in order to keep my borderline diabetes under control.

It did not quite work out as I had imagined, although as of this writing I am close to being back on the schedule I had earlier anticipated. During the past three years I have been hospitalized several times for a variety of ailments including radiculopathy, a malfunction of the autoimmune system that caused me to lose control of my left leg, resulting in several nasty falls and some time with a walker. While in the hospital for that, I contracted a staphylococcal infection that attacked a heart valve and my kidneys. More hospitalization! During 1994, I had radiation treatment for prostate cancer, and was hospitalized for a heart seizure that, according to my physicians, was triggered by the stresses of the previous year and the use of a prescribed antidepressant that sometimes can precipitate such attacks.

According to most writers about advanced aging, elderhood can be divided roughly into three stages: young old age, middle old age, and frail old age.[1] The first stage begins sometime in the middle to late sixties and continues until approximately age seventy-three. Stage two extends from age seventy-three until eighty or eighty-one. Stage three, frail old age, includes anyone over eighty or eighty-one. These stages are not, to be sure, universal. Individuals and differing social contexts can create greater or lesser modifications.

My own jolting reminders of my physical limitations set for me a new and at times disturbing agenda of issues involving my acceptance of the inevitable diminishment of my powers, and my coming to terms with death at some unknown point in *my* future. I had to begin to think and feel my way through to concretely realizing and accepting my own demise. During this time, my wife and I found and purchased a plot in the oldest part of a cemetery near our home. Near that plot is a grave marker for one who was undoubtedly a black slave who, according to the marker, "was black, but had a white soul." One of my dearest colleagues is also buried nearby. Thus we made a simple decision that in an odd, symbolic way marked our mutual acceptance of what is inevitable in our future and allied ourselves both with what we had believed in and with important persons in our past who are now "on the other side" of death.

Having made practical steps toward accepting my own mortality, I had to think seriously about setting an agenda regarding what I wanted to accomplish in the days (months? years?) I had left to me. More and more I began to enjoy each day, a day at a time. At the end of a day I would say to myself, "That was a pretty good day," or "I got through that day okay, I want tomorrow to be a better day!" I began to feel less pressure to accomplish more and more, while at the same time, I deeply wanted to finish the tasks I had set before me.

Now that I had begun to adjust my attitude toward aging to one of acceptance and optimism, I had to begin the process of allowing my children to take care of me in little ways, as I had once taken care of them. The residual effects from the radiculopathy meant that I could no longer trust myself to climb high on a ladder, and I am no longer physically strong enough to do everything I once was able to do. Yet I keep working at anything I feel safe and strong enough to do. That seems crucially important to me, though the compromises I now must make are still very difficult.[2]

A Loosely Constructed Typology of Styles of Aging

As I have thought about my own aging and read the literature about the subject coming from sociologists, social psychologists, pastoral care specialists, and others, I have formulated a loosely constructed typology of styles of aging, some of it coming directly from the literature, much of it, however, emerging from my own thought on the topic. Consider the following as a somewhat rough-hewn typology of the ways persons manage the process of growing older after age seventy.

1. Aging in the Style of Continuity

Many people, by desire or necessity, seek to make their years of retirement continuous with their years of adult generative activity. My writing of this book is a good example of what I mean. These people seem to feel that it is important to "have something to do," and the activity that most suggests itself is usually something that resembles what one has done earlier in life. If one has always been a housewife and gardener (as my wife has), then it seems natural to continue that, even though the emotions that drive the activity may have changed considerably.

Two radically different examples come to mind. The first is an old teacher of mine, who lived into his mideighties. All his adult life, he was a clinical pastoral education supervisor and chaplain, then a college and seminary teacher. In his later years, he expended his considerable energy teaching in a college for seniors, and now and then he even taught undergraduates. He and his wife had always enjoyed traveling, and they continued to travel frequently, as their strength allowed, until his recent death.

The second example comes from the sociologist Joan Weibel-Orlando's essay "Grandparenting Styles: Native American Perspectives":

> One Sioux woman applied for and received foster home accreditation. During the first two years of her return to reservation life she harbored seven different, nonrelated children in her home for periods of four to eighteen months. At one time she had four foster children living with her at the same time.
>
> "Well, I got to missing my grandchildren so much. And none of my kids would let me have one of their kids to take care of so I decided I had to do something. And there's so much need out here . . . you know . . . with all the drinking, and wife abuse, and neglect of the children and all that . . . so I felt I could provide a good home for these pitiful Sioux kids whose families couldn't take care of them. So I applied for the foster parent license. I was scared that maybe they would say I was too old at sixty-five. But, you know, within a week after I got my license I got a call from them. And they had not one, but two kids for me to take" (Sioux woman, sixty-seven, Pine Ridge, South Dakota).[3]

2. Aging in the Style of Radical Change of Vocation or Location

Some people seek to assimilate the events of retirement by means of planned change, rather than continuity. A couple may decide to sell the house they have lived in for years and move to the mountains or the beach. The assembly-line worker may decide to devote most of his or her time to fishing or becoming a folk artist or running an antique shop. I have two clergy acquaintances who retired within the past few years. One of them is now selling real estate; the other is executive secretary of a charitable foundation. Not a few retirees buy recreation vehicles and travel for a year or more before settling in some location at a distance from where they have lived in their adult years. All these forms of change have about them the air of control of one's aging process by action to bring about change.

3. Aging in the Style of Withdrawal

For many, the time of retirement is experienced as a time to withdraw from the activities that filled their adult years. For many of these persons the result is a gradual or more rapid closing in of the boundaries of their lives so that they either become "couch potatoes" or confine their activity to brief visits with friends and neighbors, children and other relatives. The pace of life becomes slower and slower as the years go by.

Two incidents in my own recent experience come to mind here. The first took place the first Sunday I attended my church after my retirement was announced. The family sitting in the pew in front of me included a grandfather who appeared to be in his middle to late seventies, his son and his wife, their young son about twelve, and a grown daughter and her husband. As we were passing the peace, the grandfather congratulated me on my retirement and then, with a touch of anguish on his face said, "I hope you have something to do. It's pretty difficult with nothing to occupy your mind!"

The second encounter with withdrawal that sticks in my mind is somewhat different. It occurred at the time of one of my sons' marriage at the ripe old age of forty. The grandparents of the bride were both in their mideighties. Of Polish extraction, Grandfather K. had been all his life a conductor on freight trains for a major railroad. He now gets around with difficulty by the use of a cane; his disability was caused near the end of his working life, he told me, by his stepping off a caboose too soon . His foot got caught on the step and he was dragged twenty or thirty feet before the train came to a halt.

He told this story in good humor, but went on to say that he had been retired for twenty years and had spent most of that time watching television or visiting with his friends. I also met Mrs. K., a bright, vivacious woman who spoke of spending her time keeping her house clean and cooking for her husband. The K. family were quite obviously in many ways withdrawn from the larger world of human activity, but were still very much alive and lively.

4. Heroic Aging

Now and then I observe or read about people who are clearly examples of what I can only call heroic aging. They are the people who not only demonstrate their ability to cope with the exigencies of aging, but use that period of the life cycle to overcome lifelong disabilities and share themselves with others in unusual and creative ways. Seemingly untroubled by the anxieties and losses of aging, these people have elected to turn their energies outward in ways that are helpful to others.

My first example of heroic aging came to me by way of a short article by Marilyn Washburn, M.D., who is both a primary care physician at Atlanta's public hospital and a Presbyterian minister. The article is entitled "Seeing Jesus at Grady Hospital." The central character of the article is Mrs. C. Dr. Washburn writes:

> Mrs. C. became my teacher of ethics and pastoral care early in my career, and has continued in that role for over a decade. I ordered a "routine" screening test for syphilis on her admission to the hospital. When the results were positive, I was surprised and distressed; she and her husband were devoted to one another, and I dreaded having to tell her something that I dreaded might destroy their happiness. I arranged for a private time and place, and hesitatingly began. After a few sentences, she interrupted me, and asked me to sit down. She gently reproached me for ordering any test without her knowledge, and quite simply told me her story: she had been raped as a teenager and had been positive ever since. She went on to talk about how that experience had shaped her life, how it had affected her marriage, how she had been treated, and how she wished she had been cared for by medical professionals. Throughout her life, God has been her companion, and she talked about her faith with joy and assurance. She asked me if I had any questions, and answered them straightforwardly. I learned so much from that half-hour. Her gentleness and honesty and patience brought us both into the presence of the Teacher we share, and we left as colleagues in ministry.

Dr. Washburn goes on to report that Mrs. C. has always been ashamed of the idea that she was "sort of mentally retarded," that she had grown up in an institution in another state, and that she couldn't "read or figure." Nevertheless, her name was mentioned often by new patients, especially elderly folk. "They would tell me Mrs. C. had arranged for their transportation, come with them to show them the bus route, helped with their prescriptions, done their shopping, and brought them their meals."

The happy ending to this story came when Mrs. C. conspired with Dr. Washburn's colleagues to insist that she attend Mrs. C.'s church on Christmas Eve. Dr. Washburn had questioned the truth of Mrs.

C.'s retardation and found that she had perfectly normal intelligence. During the service, Mrs. C. stood behind the lectern and, with confidence, grace, and pride, read the account of Jesus' birth from the Gospels.[4]

My second example of heroic aging is, like Mrs. C., one of America's poor. His name is Roland, and he has been, according to Jay Sokolovsky and Carl Cohen, authors of an essay entitled "Uncle Ed, Super Runner, and the Fry Cook: Old Men on the Street in the 1980's," living on the streets of the Bowery in New York City for many years. After describing Roland's life on the streets, the authors write:

> Roland is no ordinary bum. He has the money, and, more importantly, the connections to get a room in a cheap hotel. Many years ago when he was still drinking he slept with 400 other men in a dormitory-style flophouse, resting on cloth-covered planks of wood. Periodically he would lose most of his accumulated money by either going on month-long binges or being robbed in his hotel. Now a decade later he will relate with a slight shudder how he left the flop, began living in an abandoned building uptown, and simply decided that life on the street as a drunk was too dangerous. He ceremoniously broke his remaining bottles of wine and just sat in his room for a week of hell until the tremors of withdrawal had gone away. Since this time the streets had been his home. . . .
>
> . . . Roland is a super runner in that he has graduated from the "get a bottle and keep the change from the ten" level to working only for social workers, priests, and nuns. He is now an amazingly fit and energetic sixty-four year old. . . . Each weekday at noon he becomes the delivery unit of the Bowery's main "Meals on Wheels" program. Up and down the steps of flophouses he can be seen effortlessly hefting a cart laden with prepared lunches from a local soup kitchen. Moving in a fluid half-run through each building, he deposits a meal, shouts "How ya doin," and accepts the quarter tip he receives in each of the forty-odd rooms he will visit. He is constantly ferreting out hotel bound and homeless old men who need food and clothing and bringing them together with the Bowery's social service resources. He will not buy a bottle for you, but he will get your prescription filled.[5]

Not all heroic aging persons are poor. Some are or have been middle class or even financially privileged. What they have in common is that they find meaning in their aging through service to others without preoccupied concern for themselves. Perhaps the most famous contemporary American example of such a person is the former President Jimmy Carter. Not only has he devoted great energy to developing the Carter Presidential Center with its social, medical, and political programs designed to benefit a wide range of the peoples of the world, not only does he continue his work as a politician peacemaker, he also spends a significant time each year with a hammer in his hand working for Habitat for Humanity.

5. *Tragic Aging*

Unfortunately, not all persons are able to experience aging with some semblance of dignity and self-respect. For some the whole process can be degrading, even tragic. I think of a woman I met at Grady Memorial Hospital whose name I do not remember. We will call her Ms. James. I met her after she was brought by ambulance to the hospital suffering from congestive heart failure and a variety of other ailments. As I remember, she was in her late seventies or early eighties.

In talking with Ms. James and her nurses I learned that Ms. James had literally for years been confined to her little one-room tenement apartment, her only contact with the outside world provided by a taxi driver who had somehow befriended her. She apparently had no family to care for her. By the time she came to the hospital, she had been bedfast for months on end. She had a little electric hot plate within reach of her bed and a water bucket nearby that was filled each day by the cab driver. He also emptied her bed pan and brought her what food she could afford on her small Social Security check.

When the cab driver finally decided that he could no longer provide what Ms. James needed, he called for the Grady ambulance. The nurses reported that the paramedics had to cut her body away from a dirty sheet that had probably been on the bed for months. It took weeks to begin to get rid of the bed sores that covered her back and legs. Her heart condition barely improved, and she died without leaving the hospital. The only thing dignified about her death was that she died clean and lying on clean sheets, surrounded by nurses who cared for her.

Not all of the tragedy of aging comes because of being left utterly alone. Sometimes it comes for what appear to be opposite reasons—the tragedy of having to be cared for by adult children who have their own lives to live and their own children to care for. *Duty Bound: Elder Abuse and Family Care*, by Suzanne K. Steinmetz, is filled with stories of families whose lives have been rendered disorganized and tragically painful by the presence of an aging parent in the home. Steinmetz reports that many of these families become abusive even though they are not fundamentally violent or uncaring. Sometimes the aged parents seek to take charge of the household of their adult children. Sometimes their needs are so great that the family is prevented from having a normal life of its own. An extreme example is the aging parent who has Alzheimer's disease. Irrational and sometimes dangerous behavior can be the result, as can the abuse of the elderly out of frustration—situations tragic for everyone concerned.[6]

Pastoral and Congregational Care of the Aging

Having briefly sketched the stages and styles of aging, I want to attend to the other half of the problem, namely, the tasks of care of the aging by pastor and people in the Christian community.

Stage One: The Care of the Young Old

The young old are those who at first faintly and then more insistently are confronted with the reality that they are becoming "senior citizens" in the truest sense. They can no longer deny the realities of aging. Their health problems often increase; their physical powers begin to diminish; and they begin to realize that the surrounding culture regards them with a radically different attitude. They may still at times feel young, but they are constantly reminded that they are old.

This growing awareness not only sets an agenda for the aging person; it also defines an agenda for those who are to provide care for the elderly. One or more of the following demands the attention of pastor and congregation:

1. The aging person's need for assistance in making decisions about the styles of aging. All too often these choices are made by default. People simply find themselves moving in one direction or another. Often, of course, the choice is forced. Few options seem available. At this crucial juncture in the aging process, sensitive pastoral care by the ordained leader and an enfolding community is critical. Aging persons need to discuss with pastor and friends such questions as, "Should we stay in our present home, where we feel comfortable, or should we venture out to start over in a new place?" "Should one or both of us plan to keep on working, albeit perhaps at a reduced pace?" "How much activity in the community (the church and the larger community) should we continue?" "How much more time do we want to spend in leisure activities?"

Although I have mentioned only a few, many such questions become urgent for the aging person. Often these are considered to be very private decisions that do not invite sharing. Yet open discussion of them can be remarkably helpful. Such discussions offer the aging person the chance to hear expressions of support and encouragement. It is often through simple conversation with others that one can clarify one's thinking about one's aging. The benefits, of course, go both ways; hearing someone share his or her struggles with the issues of aging encourages the listener to come to terms with his or her own aging process.

It is just at this point that the care of aging persons within the congregation becomes the task of the whole church rather than simply being the work of the pastor or of groups for aging persons within the church community. The church should provide opportunities for intergenerational discussion and sharing of ideas, hopes, and fears. Very often during such discussions, participants from differing generations uncover feelings of a common destiny. Informal sharing among friends of one's own generation is helpful, but such sharing needs to be supplemented by more formal occasions of sharing and discussion.

In his book *Ministry with Older Persons*, the pastoral theologian Arthur Becker reminds us, "Elders are more likely than younger people to be blocked by factors such as fear of making a mistake or fear of appearing foolish." He quotes from a study done some years ago by a psychologist on age changes in learning and memory. The study's findings indicated that elders became more nervous in learning situations, and consequently performed more poorly than their younger counterparts on learning exercises. When the elders were given a mild sedative, however, performance differences were minimized. Based on these results, Becker concluded that "we learn better when we are free from anxiety and worry."[7]

If delicately offered, conversation between pastor and aging parishioner or parishioner friends can, I believe, overcome much of the anxiety experienced by the young old as they are newly confronted with their changing status. Nothing is more reassuring than loving relationships offered and received in an atmosphere of mutual care.

2. The aging person's need for assistance in making decisions about reappropriating his or her faith tradition. Later in *Ministry with Older Persons*, Arthur Becker refers to John Bennett, until his retirement the president of Union Theological Seminary and professor of social ethics. Bennett described the process of retirement as "a time of *disengagement and reengagement*. . . . Reengagement can be a reentry into the warp and woof of creative responsibility, of continuing participation in God's creative activity in the world."[8]

From another source, Erik Erikson (writing while in his nineties), Joan M. Erikson, and Helen Q. Kivnick's *Vital Involvement in Old Age*, we learn that the ongoing human community needs the wisdom of elders to undergird its ongoing life of meaning and faith:

> From the past, from myth and legend, from anthropologists and historians, we learn that the elderly of society were the transmitters of tradition, the guardians of ancestral values, and the providers of continuity. . . . Their life histories provided the warp on which the lively threads of the ongoing community were in the process of being woven. This interconnectedness of the social fabric, which stressed the interdependence of all age groups, tended to establish a harmonious wholeness. . . . Perhaps what we need today is this "clear insight" into how the elders in our present society can become more integral coworkers in community life.[9]

The early years of aging are thus also a time for a different level of thinking and conversation about virtually every aspect of the faith tradition, including what the tradition has to offer us with regard to the meaning of mortality and death. Unless some unforeseen tragedy or loss has temporarily or for the longer term interrupted our experience, early in life we are inclined to take for granted that the future stretches out endlessly ahead of us. Later in life, however, we must begin to place our own aging and coming death within some faith frame of reference that places our future in God's hands and undergirds our efforts to decide how we will spend the time we have left to us.[10]

Stage Two: The Care of the Middle Old

The aging boundaries vary extremely from person to person in this stage. Some people are able to continue the activities and interests of the young old well beyond their eightieth birthday. Others, because of serious health problems or emotional and spiritual conflicts and inclinations, are more apt to accelerate the aging process and join the frail elderly group long before age eighty. It should be remembered that this is not simply a matter of individual proclivities. Family, communal, and even societal circumstances play important roles in escalating the movement toward enfeebled old age.

Freda A. Gardner, in a short essay entitled "Another Look at the Elderly," writes of this participation of societal and cultural forces in sharpening the impact of signals of aging that those in the middle group can no longer deny:

There should be no need to rehearse the lengths we go to in our culture to remove the specter of death from our daily lives. From cosmetic wizardry in the preparation of a dead body for viewing to the technological wonderland that surrounds the act of dying in a modern hospital, we hold death at arms' length. . . .

If we live with a deep, pervasive, primitive fear of death, we also live with another message that we know at a deep level because it has been taught us in so many ways. Be independent. Independence is first a goal and then a plumb line by which we measure maturity. We are rewarded from our earliest years for what we accomplish on our own. The initiative and courage that created a new nation are still primary values in the institutions of that nation.[11]

217

While the young old have had to begin to come to terms with the inevitability of death and the encroachment of dependence, for the middle old these issues must be faced daily. The middle old therefore must find ways to incorporate these issues into their self-understanding. For many, a new and difficult basis of self-worth must be painfully, frustratingly developed. Unless the aging person accomplishes that task successfully, despair will threaten to engulf the person.

A component of the despair that threatens the middle old may be their growing sense of their apparent uselessness to society and, in some cases, even to their own families. "What can I do that is worth doing or makes any contribution to the ongoing processes of life?" "Am I now simply to be placed on the shelf?" "Am I to be increasingly abandoned to nothingness, except the television?" All these questions can eat away at a person's sense of integrity and purpose in life.

In writing about the need to renew and retain integrity in a time of increasing loss of powers, the social psychologists Evelyn E. Whitehead and James D. Whitehead comment:

> In periods of reflection and in prayer we can come to sense the extent to which illusions and masks make up our lives. Times of crisis or ecstasy challenge us to lay these aside, to accept ourselves as we really are and to confront life as it is. This is the invitation to authenticity—to give up all that is superficial in order that we may find our truest self, to die to the things of this world in order that we might live to the things of God. In those moments—however fleeting—when we experience such authenticity, we come to sense the power of integrity. Mature age is the season of this power. The older person is brought by choices within and forces without to that point of growth at which integrity ripens. As I grow old, I am challenged to lay aside the illusions I have needed in my youth. They may have served me once—even well—but they serve me no longer. I am asked to lay aside, as well, many of the fragile advantages that have contributed to my sense of worth.[12]

As with the young old, the issues that confront the middle old provide an agenda of possibilities and ministry challenges for the pastor and the Christian community. Although imaginative ministry and differing situations will determine how particular responses to the middle old will take place, several possibilities invite consideration:

1. The provision of certain institutional arrangements designed to allow the middle old to continue their participation in the church and the larger world of human relationships. This may include everything from the provision of hearing aids and large print bulletins during Sunday worship for those who are now handicapped by visual or hearing problems to the organization of transportation services for older persons not only to church activities, but also to the grocery store, the pharmacy, and the doctor's office. It may also include activities particularly designed for the middle old—activities such as bus trips to a resort or a conference that is focused on issues of aging, health, or the reaffirmation of faith.

Regarding the matter of reaffirming faith, it is perhaps better to provide opportunities to reaffirm faith meanings of those symbols and stories that have been meaningful to the aging person in the past, rather than at this late stage in life attempt to radically alter what has become familiar and reassuring. I say this last with some hesitation, even ambivalence, because it goes against the grain of considerable research that indicates that the middle old are almost as capable of mastering new information and altering their ideas about life as are their younger cohorts.

It may well be that for many of the middle old who retain great curiosity about the world around them and new expressions of the faith, the congregation and its pastor need to provide more, not less, opportunities for contemplation of such prominent issues for the church as feminist theologies and the implications of what science now has to tell us about the world in which we live.

2. A vital part of ministry with the middle old involves assisting them in finding ways to continue their participation in the activities of the world around them. Many aging persons, of course, will find ways of doing this on their own. I think of two quite elderly women of my acquaintance who have successfully done this. Ms. L., a woman in her early eighties, lived in the home she had shared with her husband for many years after their children were grown. Her husband died several years ago, and realizing that her own years were limited, she sold her house and moved into a multilevel facility for the elderly operated by her denomination. She still has her own

car and regularly provides transportation for her disabled friends. I have often observed her making notes on her church bulletin on Sunday. Curious about what her notes could be about, I peeped and saw that she was noting the names of people who were in the hospital or who had new grandchildren, even those who had provided flowers for the altar that Sunday, in order that she could phone them or pay a visit during the coming week. In short, Mrs. L. is still a very active member of her community, though within the limits set by her advanced age.

The second person I think of is considerably more disabled than Ms. L. Unable any longer to drive or even to walk without assistance, she still uses her telephone to involve herself in the life of her church and in other volunteer activities. For example, every year she goes over her calling list seeking volunteers to host the Christmas open house at a local arts center. She also stays very involved in politics, and regularly writes or telephones her representatives in Congress and the state legislature.

For those without the creative initiative to so involve themselves, the congregation should create ways in which the middle old can continue active involvement. Invitations to serve on committees, make telephone calls to shut-ins, and assist with the stewardship activities of the church are only a few among the many ways in which persons in this age group can be invited to remain active.

3. As with the young old, the pastor will now and again have opportunity to provide a direct ministry with the middle old that is best termed "counseling." Questions about the changing situations of a person's life, interpretations of recent or impending events, decisions about whether to move into a retirement home, or move in with an adult child—any of these or other questions and issues can be brought into a helpful conversation with a trusted pastor friend.[13]

Stage Three: The Care of the Frail Elderly

In the final section of this chapter we are considering the problems and issues of ministry on behalf of those persons whose lives have extended beyond what most of us would consider to be the time of a "good death." They are the ones who, rather than suffering an untimely death too young in life, now must suffer the untimeliness of death at too old an age.

I cannot write about this stage of aging without first sharing with my readers the stories of two of my older sisters, one of whom died several years ago at the age of ninety and the other now living alone halfway across the country from me in her tiny condominium. She is eighty-seven, and the last time I talked with her on the telephone she for the first time spoke of her fear that her "mind was slipping." Fortunately, she has two sons living nearby who look in on her regularly. One of these sisters mothered me during my infancy when my mother suffered a long illness; the other, now dead, inspired me to get an education while she raised as a single mother a son somewhat younger than I who became a Rhodes scholar and a graduate of Princeton University.

I well remember my last conversation with the older of these two sisters. She was by then in a nursing home receiving around the clock nursing care and unable to walk even to the bathroom or the dining room a short distance down the hall from her room. "It's not just that I should not have to live like this!" she exclaimed. "Why wasn't the world created so that we could die when it is time? What kind of life is this?" I had no answers for her; I could only listen and agree with her.

In an essay entitled "The Elderly in Modern Japan: Elite, Victims, or Plural Players?" Christie W. Kiefera writes:

> As the human life-span has a definite upper limit somewhere around a hundred years, the closer one approaches that limit the less secure one is, as measured in the likelihood of dying. All old people share to various degrees an insecurity of life. When I speak of the "security" of the aged, then I mean something other than sheer survival. I mean the security of values, the assurance that what remains of life, including the manner and circumstances of one's death, will be *meaningful*— just, decent, comprehensible, or at least acceptable. The absence of this assurance, in my experience, leads to greater anxiety in the old than the threat of death itself. When I ask old people in America *or* Japan what they fear most, the answer is usually the same, a long, helpless hopeless illness. It has various names: stroke, cancer, senility, or just *hen na kako* (the ugly decline).[14]

One of the most graphic documentations of such a death I have ever seen was given to me by one of my students. It is titled simply *Gramp. A Man Ages and Dies*. It is a set of pictures with commentary that tell the story of an old man's gradual decline into senility and death while being cared for by his family. Leafing through this pictorial record, which spares no modesty or illusion about the pain and frustration to both the dying man and his family, provided me with the nearest thing I have experienced to having such a set of events go on in my own home with one of my loved ones.[15]

Ministry to the frail elderly should be thought of as going on at three levels: the communal provision of trustworthy institutions to care for these persons who can no longer survive outside an institution; the provision of a network of both ordained and lay contacts with the aging person that reminds them that they are not forgotten; and the provision of support and, where necessary, counseling, for the family members charged with their direct care or decisions about their care.

Fortunately, the long tradition among both Roman Catholic and Protestant denominations of providing hospital care has in our time been widely extended to include the care of both the middle old and the frail elderly. In fact, some of the best care facilities for the elderly are organized as ministries of denominations. That means, however, that the denomination sponsoring such a facility must work diligently to assure that only the best care is provided. Surveys have shown a shocking degree of neglect in some eldercare facilities, including tying patients into wheelchairs, failure to keep patients clean, and other extreme forms of negligence. Care of the frail elderly therefore involves careful monitoring of the quality of these institutional expressions of the church's ministry.

Care of the frail elderly must always include care for the caregivers. Often themselves past sixty-five, caregivers need not only considerable support in carrying out their roles, but often information that will help them make the decisions they must now make on behalf of their loved ones. As Carole Cox writes in her book *The Frail Elderly: Problems, Needs, and Community Responses*:

> The support needs of caregivers cannot be restricted to just direct interventions through instrumental assistance. Knowing that individuals are available who will listen to worries and concerns and

understand the problems that they face provides caregivers with needed reassurance. Having these types of bonds may protect caregivers from the associated burdens of their roles, while lack of such relationships has been found to be associated with depression. . . . Supportive relationships also serve to reinforce caregiver self-image and the belief that the stressful situation is manageable. Unfortunately, caregivers often feel that others do not truly understand their concerns or problems.[16]

The pastor is in a peculiar position to have access to family members of the frail elderly, comparable to that of knowledgeable health care professionals. Likewise, the lay members of congregations to which caregivers belong are in a good position to offer support and encouragement.

Care of the frail elderly also must include various ways of reminding the elderly themselves of their continuing value and worthiness of care. For many, their greatest fear is not of death itself—that fear has long since been dealt with in some way—but the fear of abandonment. To be dying and utterly left alone is indeed a fate worse than death. Yet both pastors and laity are often baffled as to how to communicate a sense of continuing care that can be felt and understood by the frail, often sickly person, who is frequently even unable to speak.

I recall an experience my wife and I had years ago when we visited parishioners at a nursing home. One parishioner was Margaret, then past ninety and quite obviously dying. Our ministry to her was greatly complicated by her profound deafness. When I was finally able to communicate to her who we were, she, in a weak but commanding voice, requested that we sing for her. So we began, using a gospel tune we thought she would know, "The Old Rugged Cross." "Louder! Louder," she cried. So we sang as loud as we could while the nurses stood around and laughed at our efforts. As awkward as it may have seemed for my wife and me and the nurses, this was apparently a most satisfying experience for Margaret! The gospel hymns were familiar, her associations seemed to be reassuring, and the result was that she seemed to feel connected to her church. Needless to say, we in a strange way felt connected to her. Together we had experienced the church in its care for the frail elderly.

Some Pastoral Theological Afterthoughts

Although the primary purpose and concomitant structure of this chapter has been concerned with the pastoral *care* of the aging, rather than pastoral *theology* as such, I end the work of the chapter with a few brief reflections about the difficult theological problems that the time near the end of life presents. These problems in reality confront all of theology; they are the issues of life itself as life is related to faith in God. But *pastoral* theology has a particular contribution to make to the ongoing search for truth about God and the relationship of human beings to God.

Pastoral theology always begins with human experience and tries to put that experience into some framework of meaning. It does not simply impose a set of meanings constructed apart from human experience on whatever experience is under consideration; it begins with an attempt to understand the experience at hand. The reader will, I believe, find that this mode of reflection has been operative throughout this chapter, as it was in earlier chapters. Although there is not space to discuss fully the pastoral theological implications of aging and the anticipation of death, I will here briefly point to three of the more important issues that demand pastoral theological thinking.

1. The human experiential problem of finitude, with its pain and inevitable disappointments. As the stranger who spoke to me on Park Avenue expressed so poignantly and angrily, to grow old is both tormenting and inescapable. Theologically speaking, this raises for one and all the profound need to make peace with finitude. There are no easy answers to the human problems inherent in coming to the limits of mortality. To assist persons in their lonely search for *their* answers is undoubtedly the most important pastoral theological task for both pastor and Christian community.

Despite the pain of facing our mortality, aging can for some provide a time for new and potentially rewarding experiences of devoted and loving expressions of faith. Here I would again point to my friend Leita, whom I introduced at the beginning of this chapter. Leita was truly a woman of faith and love. She had worked most of her life in faithful service to disadvantaged children and adolescents. As she grew older, she knew she was approaching the time of her death. For her that was not an angry, disappointing time, but a time to share lovingly what she still had, with a certain faith in God's care for her and her loved ones.

2. The anguished questions, "Why wasn't the world created so that we could die when it is time? What kind of life is this?" At age ninety, my dying sister knew she was dying and couldn't understand why her death was being delayed beyond its appropriate time. As I had to admit, I couldn't understand it either. For both of us the problem of theodicy was painfully real. Any answer is hidden within the mystery of God, a mystery that at times seems to be more cruel than loving.

There are countless others who raise the same questions. In relation to aging, one of the more distressing examples of unexplained suffering is that of the victim of Alzheimer's disease. Alzheimer's seems a patently unfair way in which to die, many times prematurely. When confronted with this disease, the pastor and congregation can only be as supportive as possible to both victim and loved ones. Meanwhile, pastoral theological thinking must ask the hardest questions about God and God's justice.

3. The juxtaposition of aging as an experience unique to each individual, on the one hand, and a communal experience, shaped by the culture and the community, on the other hand.

In an increasingly multicultural society, pastoral theological thinking needs to ask about the differences among the many and various ways aging and death are experienced in various ethnic, religious, and geographical cultures. We can no longer take for granted that aging and death as they have been experienced in North America or the rest of the Western world provide the standard or correct pattern for structuring aging and death. Indeed, we in the West have much to learn from other cultures. We also need to seek forgiveness for the deprivation and oppression we have imposed on the peoples of other parts of the world, including the exploitation of those peoples that has brought to many of them an early death.

In much more provincial terms, pastoral theological thinking needs to carefully examine the abilities or inabilities of our communities to respond to the aging in caring, faithful, and helpful ways. Aging and death are indeed individual, unique experiences, but the care of those individuals is the responsibility of the community. Pastoral theological thinking has much to contribute to theology and the church at that point.

CHAPTER 11

Pastoral Care and the Fragility of Life

As we come to the final chapter of this book and look back on the work of earlier chapters, we inevitably become aware of the manner in which life ebbs and flows, now moving with vigor and creativity toward some purpose that we find meaningful, now caught in the throes of conflict, pain, defeat, and even violence and death. The knowledge of life's unpredictability, its sudden twists and turns, is common among us, though we tend to ignore that reality as we make our plans and count our achievements. However, the truth is that life is very fragile; it can come apart at the seams at any moment.

Awareness of Life's Fragility

We are most intimately aware of life's fragility in relation to individual and family life. The newspaper tells the story of a happy family of four on vacation with dreams of play in the sand, sailing, and hours of leisure and new experiences. As if out of the blue, a drunken driver hits their car head-on, killing all but the father, who is left alone in a sea of grief and bewilderment to put his life back together. Or we watch as our neighbor, a young woman in her twenties, struggles to make a life for herself while her mother slowly dies of Alzheimer's disease. Then the word comes that she herself has been diagnosed with life-threatening cancer. Such stories as these are numerous in the ministry of any pastor. Such is our awareness of life's fragility. Pastoral care as crisis ministry is by and large what is understood as ministry in life's fragile situations.[1]

The truth is, of course, that human life and all of creation are very fragile at every level. There is nowhere we humans can turn within life as we know it for stability, certainty, and assurance that our life, individual or communal, will remain as we have planned it. Life moves in time and therefore is constantly in a state of flux. That reality itself makes for a fragile, unstable existence for all human-kind.

Exploring the Dimensions of Life's Fragility

It is the purpose of this chapter to explore briefly some of the dimensions of life's fragility and to inquire into the implications they have for the work of pastoral care. In a more basic sense, we will also be exploring aspects of the work of suffering and the tensions that the fluctuations of life's ever moving, swiftly changing processes inevitably bring. To do the work of this chapter, I return to the structure for the care of God's people and for the world that I originally proposed in chapter 1.

In chapter 1, I developed a triangular set of tensions out of which a general theory of care in the Christian community over time can be governed. I then modified that structure into a quadrilateral schema for analyzing any situation that calls for pastoral care. The four nexus points of the quadrilateral are (1) care of the tradition, (2) care of the culture, (3) care of individuals, and (4) care of the community.

Our Tradition's Understanding of Ultimate Truth

How does care of the tradition relate to the fragility of life? How is the Christian tradition being represented by the tradition's people? Is it (and we know that there is not simply *a* tradition, but rather a *host* of traditions, all with the same central characters) being adhered to rigidly as if it were inflexible, never-changing truth? Or is it being represented with faithfulness that is humble, knowing that our perception of the tradition may be proved inadequate at any time?

The Complex Forces of Culture

Our culture highlights the fragility of life in unique ways. Here we become keenly aware of the two-way pull between care and the cultural processes and powers. Christian care is always set within a culture; it cannot be otherwise. Here H. Richard Niebuhr's classic study *Christ and Culture* stands alone as an analysis of ways various Christian groups have sought to reconcile Christian theology and an examination of a particular cultural situation.[2] After acknowledging that the problems of defining Christ and of defining culture are difficult and enduring problems, Niebuhr sets forth five ways that various Christian groups have responded to the problem: Christ against culture, Christ of culture, Christ above culture, Christ and culture in paradox, and finally, Christ the transformer of culture.

For pastoral practice by and within the Christian community, the command to care as articulated by Christ means to seek to transform the culture within which the pain that calls forth care is experienced. At times the forces arrayed against our efforts to bring about transformation seem overwhelming. The structures of corporate American business life seem to act without reference to the day-to-day needs of families or individuals who depend on those corporate entities for their livelihood.[3] More and more insurance companies are making American health care decisions, so powerful have the so-called health maintenance organizations become.

Corporate mergers and buyouts result in downsizing of companies, so that persons who had always believed that "I would work for this company for the rest of my working life" are finding themselves among the nation's unemployed. While on vacation recently I talked with a man who had been employed as an expert in the field of computer technology. Downsizing left him with a generous separation bonus, but no job. He shared with me that he did not know if he would ever go back into the field in which he had worked so hard. "I might just buy me a small motel and be on my own."

Individuals, Families, and Communities

Epidemic corporate downsizing demonstrates clearly the fragility of life on a cultural level. This and many other cultural factors make us all the more aware of the fragility of individual, familial, and communal life.

At first glance the nexuses of care for the individual and care for the community seem easily defined. Everyone knows what it means to be an individual or a family of individuals in this society. But is that really the case as we approach the end of the twentieth century? The family made up of wife and husband and children, though still the ideal held before us as a cultural norm, is now actually numerically in the minority. Families are more often made up of a single mother and one or more children, a single father and his teenage son or daughter, or even a small group of people—unrelated as blood kin—who have agreed to make a life together. The so-called norm for family life is now practiced only by a minority of our citizens.

Something similar is the case at whatever level the term "Christian community" may be applied (local church, a church judicatory, a particular denominational connection, or the church at large). The use of the term "Christian community" is slippery in many ways. It seems to mean many different things to different people. To some it means a tight-knit group of people who are all devoted to the same mode of worship or the same set of moral and spiritual attitudes. To others it simply means a loose fellowship of generally kindred spirits who enjoy being together. "My church" can simply mean the church that I inherited from my parents. Being a Baptist or a Presbyterian may have little to do with doctrines or beliefs. Rather, a denomination may be a social community inherited from one's ancestors.

This lack of clarity along denominational lines among Protestants is a twentieth-century development. At the turn from the nineteenth to the twentieth centuries this was not the case. Denominational differences were strongly felt and often subject to argument and conflict even among adherents of what are commonly called the mainline denominations. Furthermore, this blurring of denominational lines is not, to be sure, universal. Many Episcopalians are as devoted to their particular denomination as are devotees of the Church of God or devout Roman Catholics. But the trend toward ambiguity and even indifference about denominational identity is widespread in the United States. Elsewhere, in Canada and Australia for example, denominations have merged to form "united" churches.

The sociologist Robert Wuthnow, in a study that seeks to predict trends in the churches in the twenty-first century, points out other directions that he sees developing. He writes, "To ask about the future of the identity 'Christian,' . . . is to raise questions not so much about individuals as about social institutions. . . . [E]ven in an age of voluntarism, it is the institution that confers the identity 'Christian' on the individual."[4] Wuthnow goes on to say that this identity-granting function is all the more important because so many of the other traditional functions of the church have eroded or been taken over by other societal institutions.

> In many cases, it seems, churches no longer confer much of anything else, other than identity. They do not certify people as being wise. That capacity has fallen largely to the colleges and universities, to science, and to professional associations. Even when a distinction is drawn between wisdom and knowledge, the wise are seldom any longer theologians and clergy. The expressivist orientation in modern culture attaches wisdom to the artist and the activist.[5]

Wuthnow turns to speaking in greater detail about the challenges facing the church as a "community of memory." Without its memories, the church becomes like any other institution in contemporary society. But its memories are kept alive primarily by a particular local church. A person who does not currently have a strong attachment to a local church may nurture memories of a church that was important to him or her in the past. Denominations as such will have less and less meaning to the laity and more and more become the responsibility of the clergy, thus risking an increasing degree of anticlericalism in their parishioners.[6]

One of the important motivations that keeps the local church alive is its support role in the lives of many people. Currently, to say that the church is a natural source of support is to acknowledge the importance of more or less formally structured small groups. According to Wuthnow's studies, 29 percent of the American public said they were "currently involved in a small group that meets regularly and provides support or caring for those who participate in it."[7]

The American family is in a state of crisis. Children are being molested or otherwise abused by their parents. Parents are heavily burdened by childcare responsibilities while both parents are in the workforce seeking to maintain or improve their standard of living. Parental ambitions for themselves and their children among the middle and upper classes become burdensome to both parents and children.

Among the lower classes and those living at or below the poverty line, the struggle is not so much to realize high ambitions as it is simply to sustain a level of life that is acceptable to them. That does not mean that the poor have no ambition. Many of them do, to the extent that they will sacrifice their own well-being in order to support their children's ambitions (which they themselves have planted).

Television, with its strange mixture of the good, the bad, and the ugly, has been a very dubious teacher and voice of culture for our citizens. On the one hand, it brings into countless homes programs that express the best of what we in the West have developed over centuries: the symphonies of Beethoven and Brahms, the operas of Puccini and Wagner, and on occasion the poetry of Shakespeare and Robert Frost. On the other hand, television has been denounced by both religious and secular leaders as a propagator of violence and sexual promiscuity. Some of us seem to be glued to it nearly all of our waking hours. Others use it only to catch up on the news or the weather, and perhaps to watch an occasional sporting event.

The pastoral theologian Donald Capps is undoubtedly correct when he speaks of our age as an age of narcissism and individual human depletion.[8] The common expression of this sense of being depleted, while yet focused strongly on the fulfillment of individual needs, is that of being "caught in the rat race." Thousands of American citizens feel compelled to run faster and faster in order to keep up with life's demands, or else they feel depleted and unable to keep up with the pace setters. The result is a tendency to focus on the self, as if to ask constantly, "How am I doing?"

Capps, to be sure, is not the first to point to narcissism as a primary dynamic for the individual living in Western culture. As Capps acknowledges, the social critic Christopher Lasch first coined the phrase in his acerbic critique of Western culture that appeared some fourteen years prior to that of Capps.[9] Lasch was highly critical of the way in which the professionals in the field of childcare had invaded the homes of America, subtly undermining the authority of parents and setting themselves up as the "experts" on family life. The result, said Lasch, was a host of American parents who did not trust their own judgments: a state that can easily lead to frustration resulting in violence.

Clearly, the quadrilateral structure we have been working with is held together only in an exceedingly fragile way. There are pulls and tugs in all directions. The balance among faith, culture, community, and individual well-being is maintained only very tenuously. The nexus points cannot be separated except for purposes of analysis, and they are all contained within a dynamic, interactive process.

Pain and Care: Two Angles of Vision on Life's Fragility

Writing about what seems at first a very different theme, that of the permutations of human pain at every level of life, Elaine Scarry takes upon herself the task of examining the human situations and occurrences that evoke care. In her discussion of human pain, she writes of "the difficulty of expressing physical pain; . . . the political and perceptual complications that arise as a result of this difficulty; and . . . the nature of both material and verbal expressibility or, more simply, the nature of human creation." She continues:

> It might be best to picture these three subjects as three concentric circles; for when we enter into the innermost space of the first, we quickly discover that we are (whether or not this is what we intended) already standing within the wider circumference of the second, and no sooner do we make that discovery than we learn we have all along been standing in the midst of the third. To be at the center of any one of them is to be, simultaneously, at the center of all three.[10]

Taking a similar perspective on the four nexus points of the quadrilateral structure of care, we quickly discover that we cannot stand only in one corner of the schema. All four nexuses are present in any event at the same time. As Scarry suggests, they are like concentric circles, the outermost of which is that circle by which we attempt to understand all of creation. We can speak of them only as dimensions of one great circle that is from one standpoint a circle of pain and fragile holding on to life, and from another perspective a circle of care that holds life's fragile vitality together. Were it not for the pain and fragility of life, there would be less need for care. Were it not for care, the pain of a fragile life would for most of us become unbearable. So pain and care are forever linked, as are individual, community, tradition, culture, and ultimate meaning.

The Work of Pastoral Care

Having completed a rather cursory and perhaps somewhat abstract analysis of life as inexplicably fragile, we need now to turn to reflections on the dimensions of pastoral care that arise in response to situations that reveal life's fragility. In this section I will attempt to explicate with illustrations four levels of the work of pastoral care that roughly correspond to the four nexus points of the quadrilateral schema of care. Thus, in schematic form we will be looking together at the work of pastoral care in relation to all the dimensions of life's fragility. For want of a better way to speak of them, I shall call them the levels of pastoral care.

Level 1: Crisis Ministry with Individuals and Families

I have already spoken of the level of crisis ministry to and with those who are profoundly experiencing the fragility of their own personal lives. The variety of personal crises is endless. Things happen to persons and families that are quite beyond prediction or control. The daily newspaper tells that tale. Again and again I have said to my wife or she to me, "That's unbelievable!" And then it happened to me.

I have worked hard all my life, as has my wife, Mary. We raised six fine children, now all functioning well as adults. I have managed to achieve some recognition in my work, largely through my writing. In the midst of writing my fifth book, I retired from active teaching, having reached the mandatory-retirement age of seventy. Then my life began to come apart—though not entirely, thanks to the grace of God and my family's faithfulness. Within four years I suffered the many illnesses I enumerated earlier. I have enumerated these infirmities of my later years not to boast of my aches and pains, but to give a very personal and graphic illustration of just how fragile our life is. We truly do not know what tomorrow will bring.

From whom did I receive care?

That is a difficult question to answer, not because I had nobody to minister to me, but because I had so many! Some of the people who ministered to me were clergy; many were not. When I was in the hospital, several of my colleagues at the seminary dropped by to see me. So did my primary care physician, a genuinely caring man who, I surmised, had turned my care over to others with some reluctance.

Frankly speaking, I do not remember what any of them said, except for my closest friend, whom I sent for during one particularly critical period. I remember one of the university administrators who came and stood by my bed with a warm and gentle nurse in the middle of one night when I was undergoing the agony of disorientation. There were other nurses, some outwardly gruff and matter-of-fact, others deliberately warm and encouraging. During my hospitalization with a critical staph infection, the best care I received was from an orderly, who ably did his job, but also talked and shared with me his hopes and ambitions.

Some of the care I received was certainly systemic. I stayed in well-organized hospitals, where the personnel followed stated procedures closely. With some of this organization I was pleased. It gave a certain structure to my recovery: I could count on my caregivers to treat me in ways that had been given careful planning and attention. With some I felt more dissatisfied, as if I were just one more patient who was to receive this procedure or that. (The charts—oh, the charts!)

I cannot say enough about the care I received from my family. From one of my sons spending the night with me in the hospital when I needed it to their putting aside their own responsibilities to come to the hospital to meet with my physicians, they were present with me through the whole experience, seeking only to support me, assure me of their love and concern, and generally affirm their solidarity with me and with one another.

The care I received from that cluster of ultimate meaning is more difficult than any of the others to define with any precision. Having taught pastoral theology for most of my working life, I had an abundance of theoretical ideas and questions about just how and whether God is active in times of personal crisis. Intellectually, I must admit to sometimes being somewhat agnostic about that. I could never quite convince myself that God acted to save some and not others from the pains of life and the agonies of death and grief. The problem of theodicy was very real for me.

All that is as it has been for a number of years in my head. Yet in the deepest recesses of my emotional life, something else was happening. During the recurring crises I found myself singing over and over to myself an old hymn I had not sung for years: "Be not dismayed, whate'r betide. God will take care of you." Old memories of sitting beside my mother as a boy in church edged back into my consciousness. I remembered a host of people who represented to me the simple literal faith of Christians who had not read all those books on theology: Aunt Hattie Evans, Grandpa Henry, my sister Doris, who cared for me when I was an infant and my mother was ill. I found myself longing for a faith like theirs, though I knew I could not discard the intellectual faith I had learned. Being a Christian once again became a dilemma as well as a central aspect of my life.

Level 2: Maintaining Communities of Memory

Communities, like persons and families, come in all varieties. There are lodges, community action organizations, labor unions, baseball teams . . . and churches. Among these, churches have a special significance because they are, in the words of Robert Wuthnow, "sacred places."

> Frederick Baptist was not so much an idea or a set of beliefs as a place. People drove there on Sunday mornings and evenings, parked on the sanded roads that ran along two sides of the red brick building, climbed the eleven steps leading to the front door, hung their coats in the vestibule, and went into the sanctuary. Inside, the church was like a second home. Nameplates at the bottoms of the stained glass windows reminded people of the departed. People sat in familiar pews. Downstairs was where classes and Vacation Bible School and church suppers were held. Up front, behind the pulpit, was the baptistry—which everyone had helped paint at one time or another.[11]

All of us who have been members of any church have similar memories. Such memories tell us who we are. Even if we have long since left a particular congregation, or even a denomination, our memories lie deep in our consciousness, and like the old hymns that flooded my memory when I was ill, they tie us to a community that, as we say, "lies deep in our bones." Christian communities thus extend over time, at least they do in those nascent ways that, while scarcely identifiable, are nevertheless quite real.

But the cultural circumstances in the West enter the equation and alter that idyllic situation. We live in a mobile culture, where little remains the same, except perhaps in those small enclave communities where people have lived in their ancestral homes for years and everyone knows everyone else. But fewer and fewer of us live in such environments. More of us live in cities, and furthermore, we do not stay in the same cities. We migrate, or we have our homes in one city and work in another. I have a friend on my street whose company merged with a larger one. The only job available to her was in Philadelphia. So she commutes every week between home in Atlanta and work in Philadelphia. She is not alone. All over America people are having to go where the jobs are; corporate mergers and downsizing make it essential.

Even in what has come to be known as the "health care industry," the effects of the corporate culture are readily apparent. The care of the sick has become technologized, thus saving lives of many persons who would otherwise have died prematurely. But in the process something is lost. In a thoughtful article in *New York Times Magazine*, Michael Norman, quoting from Thomas R. Cole's *The Journey of Life: A Cultural History of Aging in America*, says that in the past two hundred years the social and biomedical sciences have thought of old age as only "an engineering problem to be solved or at least ameliorated." But by reducing old age to a "problem," science has impoverished it. "Science has robbed old age of the rich symbolism and purpose it had for most of our history," continues Norman. "In other words, old age no longer stands for anything. It is empty, purposeless, without meaning." And, as Cole's book argues, as "spiritual animals we need meaning . . . no less than we need sustenance and health."[12]

And what of the poor? Seldom do they commute to Chicago or Detroit, but they do migrate, and even more of them must hold down two or even three jobs to make ends meet. Where are they to find community? In their churches, if they can get to them without jobs interfering. Often they find it in one or another of their workplaces.

Level 3: Building Christian and Other Forms of Community

I have already spoken of pastoral leadership in chapter 9, but reflection on the complex cultural situation in which we in the church find ourselves prompts a closer look at what is indeed a complicated problem. To imagine that the leadership of the church should even think of taking responsibility for leadership of the larger cultural situation is, to say the least, mind-boggling. Though many of the leaders of the corporate world are also members of churches, they tend not to look to the church for answers to their questions. Pragmatism based on purposes defined by the corporate culture itself rules most such decisions—which is not to say that there is not an occasional decision maker who stands against that tide and considers the care of persons as decisions are made.

How, then, is the pastor to give leadership that reaches beyond the congregation itself and seeks to penetrate those great issues that lie beyond the immediate purview of the congregation or its denomination? As has been the case earlier, I can only be suggestive in responding to that question. I turn for help with that problem to the scholar of church and society, Dieter T. Hessel. Hessel is firm in his critique of mainline Protestant churches with regard to the leadership they have given in these matters:

> Though the mainline churches have been talking poor and picturing themselves as marginalized, many local churches are better equipped than they realize to respond in theology and practice to this societal crisis. Local churches in the United States have enough *money* and talented *members* to give social form to the gospel *message*. The message, of course, has definite social meaning. Insofar as churches "know" covenant law, the prophets, Jesus' teaching, and the shalom vision, they can discern their mission to be compassionately righteous communities working globally for justice, peace, and integrity of creation.[13]

From that rich statement in Hessel's introduction to his book *Social Ministry*, we can glean a number of important suggestions for the work of pastors and churches. Pastors of churches need to confront their people with the quality and extent of their resources. This traditionally has been considered the realm of stewardship rather than pastoral care, but if we take seriously the understanding of *care* as the central metaphor of life in the Christian community, the stewardship of the community's resources becomes central to the caring task. Sometimes this has to do with material resources, information about which has traditionally been kept private. Often it has rather to do with resources in leadership, knowledge of community and cultural problems, and feasible solutions to community problems.

But it is not enough simply to recruit the resources of a community. The community's human and material resources need to be directed toward goals that conform with the values of the Judeo-Christian tradition: justice, compassion for the poor and disinherited, peace, and the tending of God's creation. How to mobilize a congregation or significant numbers within it toward true commitment to those ancient truths from the tradition becomes the prophetic challenge for pastoral caregivers.

At this point, such programs as Habitat for Humanity and the various programs that emphasize the proper care of the environment become highly valuable as vehicles for involving persons in activities that concretely express care for others and for the world. I know of an African American church and a white church that joined together to build a house. Young people from across the South go annually into the hills and coves of Appalachia to work with the rural poor.

One of the most imaginative and unusual projects I know of, which undoubtedly has been duplicated elsewhere, took place between members of an Episcopal Cathedral in the Northeast and a little mission in Bolivia. The minister of pastoral care recruited persons to participate in the project from among the affluent members of the congregation as well as the youth and those with only modest means to participate. Money was raised from church members and corporations represented in the congregation. For several years now a mission has gone high up into the Bolivian mountains for a week or more of service in a primitive mission hospital. One nurse made the decision to remain for a year.

Level 4: Pastoral Leadership in Theological Reflection

The above reflections on the leadership of the church in relation to sociocultural and environmental problems brings us full circle around the quadrilateral theory of care. One cannot think in Christian ministry terms about any of these problems without returning again and again for theological grounding. I am reminded again of Paul Tillich's insight into what he called the *Spiritual Presence*. For Tillich, all created life is fundamentally ambiguous. Thus also is God, who is simply a *Presence* acting within all things. We can only talk about that *Presence* in terms of a force that works within all things. But it is not a force like other forces, but a *Presence* within all other forces and actions in the world.[14] Thus the theology of pastoral care is grounded in a mystery, the force of which broods over all that we have considered in this book. It is the mystery of the *care of God*, that care within which all human cares, both the pains of life and the human efforts to care for them, are contained.

NOTES

Preface

1. William James, *The Varieties of Religious Experience* (New York and London: Longmans and Green, 1902); Edwin D. Starbuck, *The Psychology of Religion* (London: W. Scott, 1914); James H. Leuba, *A Psychological Study of Religion: Its Origin, Function, and Future* (New York: Macmillan, 1912); and George Albert Coe, *What Is Christian Education?* (New York and London: Charles Scribner's Sons, 1929).

2. Anton T. Boisen, *The Exploration of the Inner World* (New York: Willett, Clark and Co., 1936).

3. See Richard Cabot and Russell Dicks, *The Art of Ministering to the Sick* (New York: Macmillan, 1936).

4. Paul E. Johnson, *The Psychology of Pastoral Care* (Nashville: Abingdon Press, 1953), Wayne E. Oates, *The Christian Pastor* (Philadelphia: Westminster, 1946), and Carroll A. Wise, *Pastoral Counseling: Its Theory and Practice* (New York: Harper, 1951) are the principal examples of this literature.

5. For two somewhat different explications of the psychotherapeutic paradigm, see Howard Clinebell, *Basic Types of Pastoral Counseling* (Nashville: Abingdon Press, 1966); or Carroll A. Wise, *Pastoral Psychotherapy* (New York: Jason Aronson, 1980).

6. Seward Hiltner, *Preface to Pastoral Theology* (Nashville: Abingdon Press, 1958).

7. Wayne E. Oates, *Protestant Pastoral Counseling* (Philadelphia: Westminster Press, 1962); Carroll A. Wise, *The Meaning of Pastoral Care* (New York: Harper & Row, 1966); and Edward E. Thornton, *Theology and Pastoral Counseling* (Englewood Cliffs, N.J.: Prentice-Hall, 1964).

8. Charles V. Gerkin, *Crisis Experience in Modern Life: Theory and Theology for Pastoral Care* (Nashville: Abingdon Press, 1979); *The Living Human Document: Revisioning Pastoral Counseling in a Hermeneutical Mode* (Nashville: Abingdon Press, 1984); *Widening the Horizons: Pastoral Responses to a Fragmented Society* (Philadelphia: Westminster Press, 1986); and *Prophetic Pastoral Practice: A Christian Vision of Life Together* (Nashville: Abingdon Press, 1991).

1. Earlier Chapters in an Old Story

1. John T. McNeill, *A History of the Cure of Souls* (New York: Harper and Bros., 1951), 2.

2. William A. Clebsch and Charles R. Jaekle, *Pastoral Care in Historical Perspective* (Englewood Cliffs, N.J.: Prentice-Hall, 1964). See also Seward Hiltner, *Preface to Pastoral Theology* (Nashville: Abingdon Press, 1958), 64.

3. See, for example, Don S. Browning, *The Moral Context of Pastoral Care* (Philadelphia: Westminster Press, 1976), for a text emphasizing the prophetic aspects of pastoral care; and Elaine Ramshaw, *Ritual and Pastoral Care* (Philadelphia: Fortress Press, 1987), for an exposition of pastoral care and ritual practice in the church.

4. For a carefully documented selection of texts from such early church fathers as Origen, Ignatius, Cyprian, Chrysostom, and others who made use of the shepherding metaphor, see Thomas C. Oden, *Becoming a Minister* (New York: Crossroad, 1987), chap. 2.

5. See, for example, Seward Hiltner, *The Christian Shepherd: Some Aspects of Pastoral Care* (Nashville: Abingdon Press, 1959). See also his *Preface to Pastoral Theology* (Nashville: Abingdon Press, 1958), 64-69. Although Hiltner's analysis of the shepherding focuses primarily on the "tender and solicitous care" of individuals, another interpretation of the shepherd image as presented in Psalm 23 and as modeled in the ministry of Jesus might well include aspects of ministry embodied in all three of the Israelite role models: the prophet, the priest, and the wise guide.

6. See notes 1 and 2 above. Although these two histories present slightly different periodizations of pastoral care history, they are sufficiently similar as not to conflict significantly. They likewise have in common a primary focus on the care of individuals and, to a lesser extent, families in their interpretations of pastoral care history. However, if read carefully, one can detect in these histories both the presence of changing patterns of care for the identifying Christian tradition and of concern for maintaining the organizational and meaning boundaries of the living community of Christians.

7. Clebsch and Jaekle, 17.

8. McNeill, 90.

9. Clebsch and Jaekle, 95. See also McNeill, 91-92.

10. John Chrysostom, *On the Priesthood*, chap. 2, sect. 4, p. 58, quoted in Oden, 50.

11. Clebsch and Jaekle, 19.

12. Ibid., 123.

13. Ibid., 20.

14. Thomas M. Gannon, S.J., and George W. Traub, S.J., *The Desert and the City: An Interpretation of the History of Christian Spirituality* (Chicago: Loyola University Press, 1969), 51-66.

15. Clebsch and Jaekle, 21.

16. Thomas C. Oden, *Care of Souls in the Classic Tradition* (Philadelphia: Fortress Press, 1984), 43-44.

17. Gregory the Great, *Pastoral Care*, trans. Henry Davis, Vol. 11, Ancient Christian Writers Series (Westminster, Md.: Newman, 1950).

18. Roberta Bondi, *To Love As God Loves* (Philadelphia: Fortress Press, 1987). See also her "The Abba and Amma in Early Monasticism: The First Pastoral Counselors?" *The Journal of Pastoral Care* 11 (December 1986): 311-20.

19. McNeill, 135.

20. Clebsch and Jaekle, 27.
21. Martin Luther, quoted in Clebsch and Jaekle, 211.
22. Theodore W. Jennings, Jr., *Beyond Theism: A Grammar of God-Language* (New York: Oxford University Press, 1985), 44.
23. For a brief but excellent discussion of the loss of the art of pastoral discipline in modern societies, see Don S. Browning's article "Discipline, Pastoral Care As (History)" in Rodney J. Hunter, ed., *The Dictionary of Pastoral Care and Counseling* (Nashville: Abingdon Press, 1990), 289-91.
24. Richard Baxter, *The Reformed Pastor*, ed. John T. Wilkinson (London: Epworth Press, 1939), 83, quoted in Seward Hiltner, *Preface to Pastoral Theology* (Nashville: Abingdon Press, 1958), 30.
25. Clebsch and Jaekle, 29.
26. Friedrich E. D. Schleiermacher, *On Religion, Speeches to the Cultured Despisers* (New York: Harper Torchbooks, 1958), 155-56, 175.
27. E. Brooks Holifield, *A History of Pastoral Care in America* (Nashville: Abingdon Press, 1983), 107-8.
28. Ibid., 153-54.
29. Ibid., 156.
30. Ibid., 167-72.
31. Ibid., 173.

2. Pastoral Care in the Twentieth Century

1. E. Brooks Holifield, *A History of Pastoral Care in America* (Nashville: Abingdon Press, 1983), 198.
2. William James, *The Varieties of Religious Experience* (New York: Random House, 1902).
3. James Leuba, *A Psychological Study of Religion* (New York: Macmillan, 1912); E. D. Starbuck, *The Psychology of Religion* (New York: Charles Scribner's Sons, 1899); George Albert Coe, *The Psychology of Religion* (Chicago: University of Chicago Press, 1916).
4. For a more detailed discussion of the Emmanuel movement, see Allison Stokes, *Ministry After Freud* (New York: The Pilgrim Press, 1985), 19-26; and Orlo Strunk, Jr., "Emmanuel Movement," in *Dictionary of Pastoral Care and Counseling*, ed. Rodney J. Hunter (Nashville: Abingdon Press, 1990).
5. See Strunk, "Emmanuel Movement," 911. A complete account of the correspondence between Freud and Pfister may be found in Oskar Pfister, *Psychoanalysis and Faith: The Letters of Sigmund Freud and Oskar Pfister* (New York: Basic Books, 1963).
6. Josiah Strong, *The New Era, or the Coming Kingdom* (New York: Baker and Taylor, 1893), x-xi, quoted in Charles H. Hopkins, *The Rise of the Social Gospel in American Protestantism: 1865-1915* (New Haven, Conn.: Yale University Press, 1940), 139.
7. Walter Rauschenbusch, quoted in Robert T. Handy, ed., *The Social Gospel in America, 1870–1920: Gladden, Ely, Rauschenbusch* (New York: Oxford University Press, 1966), 255-56.

8. Charles Sheldon, *In His Steps* (New York: H. M. Caldwell, 1897). For a description of Sheldon's writings and influence, see Hopkins, *The Rise of the Social Gospel*, 142-45.

9. E. Brooks Holifield, *A History of Pastoral Care in America* (Nashville: Abingdon Press, 1983), 210-11.

10. Karl Barth, *The Epistle to the Romans* (London: Oxford University Press, 1968). For a clear and helpful summary of neoorthodoxy and its implications for pastoral care, see Shirley C. Guthrie's article, "Neoorthodox Theology and Pastoral Care," in *Dictionary of Pastoral Care and Counseling*, ed. Rodney J. Hunter (Nashville: Abingdon Press, 1990), 780-81.

11. Anton T. Boisen, *The Exploration of the Inner World* (Chicago: Willett, Clark and Co., 1936).

12. Richard Cabot and Russell Dicks, *The Art of Ministering to the Sick* (New York: Macmillan, 1936).

13. Howard Clinebell, *Basic Types of Pastoral Care and Counseling* (Nashville: Abingdon Press, 1966; rev. and enl. ed., Abingdon Press, 1984).

14. Rollo May, *The Art of Counseling* (Nashville: Cokesbury Press, 1939).

15. Carl R. Rogers, *Counseling and Psychotherapy* (Boston: Houghton Mifflin Co., 1942).

16. Carl R. Rogers, *Client-Centered Therapy* (Boston: Houghton Mifflin Co., 1951).

17. It is perhaps worth noting here that the author's own introduction to clinical pastoral theory and methodology in 1945–1946 included the study of both Freud and Rogers. In my first unit of clinical pastoral training at Elgin State Hospital the basic psychological text was *Emotional Problems of Living*, by O. S. English and G. H. J. Pearson (New York: W. W. Norton, 1945), a Freudian primer of developmental and psychotherapeutic psychology. At the same time I was also introduced to Rogers' *Counseling and Psychotherapy* and encouraged to use nondirective counseling methods in my relationships with patients and parishioners. The discrepancies between these two theories in their fundamental presuppositions about the human psyche were, however, not explored in any significant depth.

18. Paul E. Johnson, *The Psychology of Religion* (Nashville: Abingdon Press, 1945).

19. Paul E. Johnson, *The Psychology of Pastoral Care* (Nashville: Abingdon Press, 1953). For Johnson's later theory, see his *Person and Counselor* (Nashville: Abingdon Press, 1967).

20. Seward Hiltner, *Pastoral Counseling* (Nashville: Abingdon Press, 1949), and *Preface to Pastoral Theology* (Nashville: Abingdon Press, 1958).

21. Carroll A. Wise, *Pastoral Counseling: Its Theory and Practice* (New York: Harper, 1951), and *The Meaning of Pastoral Care* (New York: Harper & Row, 1966).

22. Wise, *The Meaning of Pastoral Care*, 8.

23. Wayne E. Oates, *The Christian Pastor* (Philadelphia: Westminster Press, 1951), and *Protestant Pastoral Counseling* (Philadelphia: Westminster Press, 1962).

24. E. Brooks Holifield, "Oates, Wayne E.," in *Dictionary of Pastoral Care and Counseling*, ed. Rodney J. Hunter (Nashville: Abingdon Press, 1990), 795.

25. Eduard Thurneysen, *A Theology of Pastoral Care* (Atlanta: John Knox Press, 1962).

26. See Paul Tillich, *The Courage to Be* (New Haven, Conn.: Yale University Press, 1952), 164.

27. Thomas C. Oden, *Kerygma and Counseling* (Philadelphia: Westminster Press, 1966), and *The Structure of Awareness* (Nashville: Abingdon Press, 1969).

28. Clinebell, *Basic Types of Pastoral Care and Counseling*.

29. For a particularly illuminating report of such a study, see Roger A. Johnson, *Congregations As Nurturing Communities: A Study of Nine Congregations of the Lutheran Church in America* (Division for Parish Services, Lutheran Church in America, 1979). See also R. H. Sunderland, "Congregation, Pastoral Care of," in *Dictionary of Pastoral Care and Counseling*, ed. Rodney J. Hunter (Nashville: Abingdon Press, 1990), 213-15.

30. See, for example, James F. Hopewell, *Congregation: Stories and Structures* (Philadelphia: Fortress Press, 1987).

31. Don S. Browning, *The Moral Context of Pastoral Care* (Philadelphia: Westminster Press, 1976).

32. See Bonnie J. Miller-McLemore, *Also a Mother: Work and Family As Theological Dilemma* (Nashville: Abingdon Press, 1994), 104-5.

33. See, for example, David W. Augsburger, *Pastoral Counseling Across Cultures* (Philadelphia: Westminster Press, 1986). See also Peggy Way, "Cultural and Ethnic Factors in Pastoral Care," in *Dictionary of Pastoral Care and Counseling*, ed. Rodney J. Hunter (Nashville: Abingdon Press, 1990), 253-54.

34. Charles V. Gerkin, *Prophetic Pastoral Practice: A Christian Vision of Life Together* (Nashville: Abingdon Press, 1991), p. 19.

3. New Directions in Pastoral Care

1. For a concise statement concerning pastoral care in the Old Testament, see Gene M. Tucker, "Old Testament and Apocrypha, Traditions and Theology of Care in," in *Dictionary of Pastoral Care and Counseling*, ed. Rodney J. Hunter (Nashville: Abingdon Press, 1990), 799-807.

2. For a fuller description of the teachings and actions of Jesus that model the shepherding perspective, see A. L. Malherbe, "New Testament, Traditions and Theology of Care in," in *Dictionary of Pastoral Care and Counseling*, ed. Rodney J. Hunter (Nashville: Abingdon Press, 1990), 787-89.

3. Ibid., 789-92.

4. Roberta Bondi, "The Abba and Amma in Early Monasticism: The First Pastoral Counselors?" *The Journal of Pastoral Care* 40 (December 1986): 311-20.

5. For a brief but excellent description of basic principles of moral guidance in contemporary pastoral care, see James N. Lapsley, "Moral Dilemmas in Pastoral Perspective," in *Dictionary of Pastoral Care and Counseling*, ed. Rodney J. Hunter (Nashville: Abingdon Press, 1990), 752-55.

6. Alan Richardson and John Bowden, eds., *The Westminster Dictionary of Christian Theology* (Philadelphia: Westminster Press, 1983), 388.

7. For a fuller explication of the complex concept of grace and its relationship to pastoral care, see Rodney J. Hunter, "Grace and Pastoral Care" in *Dictionary of Pastoral Care and Counseling*, ed. Rodney J. Hunter (Nashville: Abingdon Press, 1990), 468-70. See also his "Law and Gospel in Pastoral Care," *Journal of Pastoral Care* 30 (1976): 146-58.

8. Martin Thornton, "Spiritual Direction, History and Tradition of," in *Dictionary of Pastoral Care and Counseling*, ed. Rodney J. Hunter (Nashville: Abingdon Press, 1990), 1210.

9. See, for example, two short articles in *Dictionary of Pastoral Care and Counseling*, ed. Rodney J. Hunter (Nashville: Abingdon Press, 1991): Charles V. Gerkin, "Psy-

choanalysis and Pastoral Care," 979-84; Richard R. Osmer, "Developmental Theory and Pastoral Care," 277-79.

10. Carroll A. Wise, *The Meaning of Pastoral Care* (New York: Harper & Row, 1966), 8.

11. H. Richard Niebuhr, *The Meaning of Revelation* (New York: Macmillan, 1941), 111. See also Charles V. Gerkin, *Widening the Horizons: Pastoral Responses to a Fragmented Society* (Philadelphia: Westminster Press, 1986), 56-57.

12. J. C. Wynn, *Family Therapy in Pastoral Ministry* (San Francisco: Harper & Row, 1991). See also Herbert Anderson, "Family, Pastoral Care and Counseling of," in *Dictionary of Pastoral Care and Counseling*, ed. Rodney J. Hunter (Nashville: Abingdon Press, 1990), 416-19.

13. E. Brooks Holifield, *A History of Pastoral Care in America* (Nashville: Abingdon Press, 1983), 260.

14. Walter Brueggemann, *The Prophetic Imagination* (Philadelphia: Fortress Press, 1978), 13. For a fuller explication of the implications of Brueggemann's ideas for pastoral care, see Charles V. Gerkin, *Prophetic Pastoral Practice* (Nashville: Abingdon Press, 1991), 70-71.

15. Ronald H. Sunderland, "Congregation, Pastoral Care of," in *Dictionary of Pastoral Care and Counseling*, ed. Rodney J. Hunter (Nashville: Abingdon Press, 1990), 213-14.

16. Ibid., 214.

17. Compare, for example, the approaches taken by the comparative ethnographer James F. Hopewell in *Congregation: Stories and Structures* (Philadelphia: Fortress Press, 1987); the church organization theorist Carl S. Dudley and his associates in *Building Effective Ministry: Theory and Practice in the Local Church* (San Francisco: Harper & Row, 1983); the theological ethicist Stanley Hauerwas in *A Community of Character: Toward a Constructive Christian Social Ethic* (Notre Dame: University of Notre Dame Press, 1981); the church development consultant Loren Mead in *New Hope for the Congregations* (New York: Seabury Press, 1972); and the Jewish family studies theorist Edwin H. Friedman in *Generation to Generation: Family Process in Church and Synagogue* (New York: Guilford Press, 1985).

18. Hopewell, *Congregation: Stories and Structures.* See also a somewhat abbreviated study led by Roger Johnson, *Congregations As Nurturing Communities: A Study of Nine Congregations of the Lutheran Church in America* (Division for Parish Services, Lutheran Church in America, 1979).

4. The Stories of Our Lives and the Christian Story

1. The use of the term *grammar* here follows the use of that term in cultural-linguistic approaches to relating theology to human experience. For elaboration of that use in theology, see George A. Lindbeck, *The Nature of Doctrine: Religion and Theology in a Postliberal Age* (Philadelphia: Westminster Press, 1984), esp. 18. See also Theodore W. Jennings, Jr., *Beyond Theism: A Grammar of God Language* (New York: Oxford University Press, 1985), 140-41.

2. For a cogent discussion of the task of consensus formation as it relates to the teaching ministry of the church, see Richard R. Osmer, *A Teachable Spirit: Recovering the Teaching Office of the Church* (Louisville: Westminster/John Knox Press, 1990), chap. 8.

NOTES

3. See Marshall McLuhan, *The Global Village: Transformation in World Life and Media* (New York: Oxford University Press, 1989).

4. This last is, of course, not to say that everyone who becomes a victim of HIV suffers from personal meaning fragmentation. It is to say, however, that the level of sexual promiscuity that so greatly contributes to the AIDS epidemic represents an apparent breakdown of the traditional sexual norms that have governed sexual relationships in the West for generations. The current controversy over whether young people should have access to condoms and be taught about "safe sex" or should simply be taught to abstain from overt sexual activity prior to marriage illustrates the fragmentation of meanings and values with regard to sexuality abroad in society. For a thoughtful discussion of issues related to AIDS in the ministries of the church, see Earl E. Shelp and Ronald Sunderland, *AIDS and the Church* (Philadelphia: Westminster Press, 1987).

5. See, for example, Heinz Kohut, *The Restoration of the Self* (New York: International Universities Press, 1977).

6. The concept of "good enough" was made common in psychological circles through the work of the British pediatrician and psychoanalyst D. W. Winnicott. For elaboration of Winnicott's phrase, see D. W. Winnicott, *Playing and Reality* (London and New York: Routledge, 1971), esp. 10.

7. For a more detailed discussion of meaning fragmentation in Western society, see my *Prophetic Pastoral Practice: A Christian Vision of Life Together* (Nashville: Abingdon Press, 1991).

8. Anton T. Boisen, "Theology in the Light of Psychiatric Experience," in *Vision From a Little Known Country: A Boisen Reader*, ed. Glenn H. Asquith, Jr. (Atlanta: Journal of Pastoral Care Publications, 1992), esp. 57.

9. For a brief but informative description of new emphasis on pastoral theology within Roman Catholicism, see R. L. Kinast, "Pastoral Theology, Roman Catholic," in *Dictionary of Pastoral Care and Counseling*, ed. Rodney J. Hunter (Nashville: Abingdon Press, 1990), 873-74.

10. See Thomas C. Oden, *After Modernity—What? Agenda for Theology* (Grand Rapids, Mich.: Academic Books), 1990.

11. Lindbeck, *The Nature of Doctrine*, esp. chaps. 1 and 2.

12. Ibid., 16.

13. Eduard Thurneysen, *A Theology of Pastoral Care* (Atlanta: John Knox Press, 1962).

14. Edward Thornton, *Theology and Pastoral Counseling* (Englewood Cliffs, N.J.: Prentice-Hall, 1964).

15. Lindbeck, *The Nature of Doctrine*, 16.

16. Ibid., 31.

17. Ibid., 22.

18. Ibid.

19. Ibid., 32.

20. Ibid., 33.

21. For a detailed discussion of the problems of theism in modern thought, see Jennings, *Beyond Theism*.

22. Lindbeck, *The Nature of Doctrine*, 40.

23. Ibid., 35.

24. For a more detailed discussion of the structuring of life through religious narratives, see my *Widening the Horizons: Pastoral Responses to a Fragmented Society* (Philadelphia: Westminster Press, 1986), esp. chap. 2.

25. See, for example, David K. Switzer, *The Dynamics of Grief* (Nashville: Abingdon Press, 1970); Lawrence E. Holst, *Hospital Ministry* (New York: Crossroad, 1985); and J. C. Wynn, *Family Therapy in Pastoral Ministry* (San Francisco: HarperSan Francisco, 1991).

26. For additional discussion of the image of the pastor as interpretive guide, see my *Widening the Horizons*, chap. 5.

II. Caring for the Community of the Christian Story

1. Recent pastoral theological discussion has involved significant conflict between the "functionalism" first proposed by William A. Clebsch and Charles R. Jaekle in *Pastoral Care in Historical Perspective* (Englewood Cliffs, N.J.: Prentice-Hall, 1964), and the "perspectivalism" set forth by Seward Hiltner in his groundbreaking *Preface to Pastoral Theology* (Nashville: Abingdon Press, 1958). Clebsch and Jaekle trace through the history of pastoral care four functions, each of which became dominant in a particular period of history: healing, guiding, sustaining, and reconciling. Hiltner grounded his pastoral theology in what he called the actual "operations" of parish ministry. He asserted that all that the pastor does may be viewed from three perspectives that must be integrated, though, as is the case with Clebsch and Jaekle, one perspective may be dominant in a given situation. Each act of ministry may be assessed from the perspectives of organizing the fellowship, communicating the gospel, and shepherding persons. What I propose in this book builds on both these earlier models, although the interpretive guidance model may well be seen primarily as a revised extension of Hiltner's pastoral theology.

5. Pastoral Care As Interpretive Leadership

1. See figure 2, chapter 1.

2. For a detailed discussion of the manner in which life is ordered through the medium of stories and the pastoral problem related to the altering of life stories, see my *Living Human Document* (Nashville: Abingdon Press, 1984), chaps. 4, 5, 6.

3. For a full and cogent explication of this theological presupposition regarding the church, see Jürgen Moltmann, *The Church in the Power of the Spirit* (New York: Harper & Row, 1977). "With his proclamation and through his embodiment of the kingdom of God, Christ made the church at the same time possible and impossible. He made it possible to the extent that the people of God gathers together in proximity to the kingdom of God. He made it impossible because this people presses beyond itself to this all-fulfilling kingdom" (24).

4. The term *local theology* is borrowed from Robert J. Schreiter as that term is developed in his *Constructing Local Theologies* (Maryknoll, N.Y.: Orbis Books, 1983). Schreiter's purpose is to explicate the ways in which the history of theology can be seen as a series of local theologies over time and to explicate the significance of a multicultural perspective for the ministry of the church.

5. In this section I am drawing primarily on the work of James M. Gustafson in his book *Treasure in Earthen Vessels* (New York: Harper & Row, 1961).

6. See Gustafson, *Treasure in Earthen Vessels*, 50.

7. David Tracy, *The Analogical Imagination: Christian Theology and the Culture of Pluralism* (New York: Crossroad, 1986), chap. 3.

8. Gustafson, *Treasure in Earthen Vessels*, 74.

9. Rodney J. Hunter, ed., *Dictionary of Pastoral Care and Counseling* (Nashville: Abingdon Press, 1990), 213.

10. H. Richard Niebuhr, *The Purpose of the Church and Its Ministry* (New York: Harper and Bros., 1956), 30.

11. Dieter T. Hessel, *Social Ministry*, rev. ed. (Louisville: Westminster/John Knox Press, 1992), 8.

12. Viewing this situation as an occasion *possibly* calling for discipline suggests something about how the problem of disciplining parishioners is presented to the contemporary pastor in quite a different way than it was in the first century, or even in the eighteenth century. The pastor at St. Matthew's approaches the problem of discipline with regard to the structures of marriage and family life primarily by means of the use of persuasion and influence, with few guidelines as to what is proper pastoral procedure, whereas in earlier times the expectations of both pastor and parishioner were much more clearly defined.

6. The Christian Community in a World of Many Communities

1. The meaning of the term *faith* as I am using it here is similar to the meaning first proposed by James W. Fowler in his seminal work on faith development, although I am not as convinced as Fowler that the formation of faith takes place in structured stages. For a brief description of the elements of faith, see James W. Fowler, *Weaving the New Creation* (San Francisco: HarperSanFrancisco, 1991), 100-102.

2. Chapter 1, p. 35.

3. Larry Kent Graham, *Care of Persons, Care of Worlds* (Nashville: Abingdon Press, 1992), 96.

4. Chapter 4, p. 111.

5. For a brief but classic explication of the narrative construction of ways of life, see Stephen Crites, "The Narrative Quality of Experience," *Journal of the American Academy of Religion* 39 (1971): 291–311.

6. Kenneth J. Gergen, *The Saturated Self* (New York: Basic Books, 1991), 15-16.

7. For an extended, albeit now somewhat dated social-psychological/theological analysis of intergenerational conflict, see my *Crisis Experience in Modern Life* (Nashville: Abingdon Press, 1979), chap. 8.

8. While writing *Crisis Experience in Modern Life*, I found the report of a longitudinal study done at the Menninger Foundation in Topeka, Kansas, which followed closely the differing styles of adaptation to contextual cultural standards, values, and ways of life of a group of children from birth to late adolescence, to be quite helpful: Alice E. Moriarty and Paul Toussieng, *Adolescent Coping* (New York: Grune and Stratton, 1976). These researchers at first categorized the children as either "censors" or "sensors." Further study, however led the researchers to create four subgroups: "obedient traditionalists," "ideological conservatives," "cautious modifiers," and "passionate renewers." Even within those categories they uncovered

evidence for ways of adapting to changing culture that were highly idiosyncratic for particular individuals.

9. Carl Rogers, *Client-Centered Therapy* (Boston: Houghton Mifflin Co., 1951).

10. Edwin H. Friedman, *Generation to Generation: Family Process in Church and Synagogue* (New York: Guilford Press, 1985).

11. For a careful theological/ethical critique of some of the psychological theories of the recent past, see Don S. Browning, *Religious Thought and the Modern Psychologies* (Philadelphia: Fortress Press, 1987).

12. Although numerous resources could be named for my thought in relation to the schema of figure 4, I am particularly indebted to the work of James M. Gustafson in his book *Treasure in Earthen Vessels* (New York: Harper and Row, 1961).

III. The Christian Story and the Stories of Individual and Family Life

1. Erik H. Erikson, *Ego Development and Social Change—Clinical Notes in The Psychoanalytic Study of the Child*, vol. 2. (New York: International Universities Press, 1946), 359-396. See also Erik H. Erikson, *Childhood and Society* (New York: W. W. Norton, 1950).

2. See, for example, Donald Capps, *Life Cycle Theory and Pastoral Care*. (Philadelphia: Fortress Press, 1983).

7. Care for the Stories of Life's Beginning

1. Erik Erikson, *Childhood and Society*, 2nd ed. (New York: W. W. Norton, 1963). For another, similar perspective on the psychological dynamics of early childhood, see also the writings of Donald W. Winnicott, especially his *The Maturational Processes and the Facilitating Environment* (London: Hogarth Press, 1965).

2. Both the experience I have had with role plays and that of many colleagues with whom I have discussed the matter seems to support the notion that, often even if specific requests are made as to in what way players portray a particular kind of character, the participants will fulfill their roles in a manner characteristic of their own personhood. Open-ended directions such as I gave in this case tend to enhance the degree to which this is the case.

3. The helpful phrase "not yet" is taken from the theologian Jürgen Moltmann in his work *The Trinity and the Kingdom* (San Francisco: HarperSanFrancisco, 1981), 39. See also my *The Living Human Document* (Nashville: Abingdon Press, 1984), 66-68; and *Widening the Horizons* (Philadelphia: Westminster Press, 1986), 54-55.

4. It is interesting and instructive for persons of the middle and upper classes to note that in the so-called lower classes in America, both black and white, the pattern of two-income families had been going on long before the 1950s. Poverty made that essential if the family was to avoid going on welfare.

5. David A. Hamburg, "The American Family Transformed," *Transaction: Social Science and Modern Society* 30, no. 2 (January/February 1993): 61.

6. Ibid., 65.

7. The rapid increase in the number of single-parent families headed by women has in recent years been widely discussed in the American popular press. See, for example, the extensive series of articles in *Newsweek*, 26 July 1993, 2 August 1993, and 30 August 1993. For a more detailed international sociological study of this phenomenon, see Ailsa Burns and Cath Scott, *Mother-Headed Families and Why They Have Increased* (Hillsdale, N.J.: Lawrence Erlbaum Associates, 1994). Burns and Scott briefly summarize their findings on the topic in the United States on page xiii of the introduction of the book: "The highest current prevalence [of single parent families headed by women] is found in . . . the United States. The number of U.S. children living with a single parent increased from about 9% in 1960 to 24% in 1986. Although in Sweden women of almost every kind of background are equally likely to be lone parents, this is not the case in the United States. U.S. lone mothers are younger than married mothers, are less-educated, and are likely to be African American. More than 50% of African-American families are mother-headed. U.S. writers accordingly stress the importance of African-American culture, the destructive effects of poverty on family life, and the shortage of young African-American men due to high mortality and other causes."

8. Valerie Polakow, *Lives on the Edge: Single Mothers and Their Children in the Other America* (Chicago: University of Chicago Press, 1993), 22.

9. See, for example, Kris Kissman and Jo Ann Allen, *Single-Parent Families* (Newbury Park, Calif.: Sage Publications, 1993), 5.

10 Polakow, *Lives on the Edge*, 46.

11. Estimates of the amount of child abuse to be found in America vary considerably, depending upon the source of the statistics. Lee Ann Hoff, whose book *People in Crisis*, 3rd ed. (Redwood City, Calif.: Addison-Wesley, 1989), has been widely used by educators in the crisis intervention field, says, "No one knows exactly how many children are abused each year since many cases are not reported. Besides the estimated 2,000,000 to 4,000,000 abused and neglected children, 2,000 to 5,000 deaths occur annually at the hands of parents and caretakers. . . . A tragedy related to child abuse is that of runaway children; 35% of these children leave because of incest and 53% because of physical neglect. The majority of runaway children are never reported missing by their parents; 80% are from white middle class families; 150,000 disappear each year, many dying of disease, exploitation, and malnutrition" (251).

12. James Newton Poling, *The Abuse of Power: A Theological Problem* (Nashville: Abingdon Press, 1991).

13. Philip Greven, *Spare the Child: The Religious Roots of Punishment and the Psychological Impact of Physical Abuse* (New York: Alfred A. Knopf, 1991), 48. See also his *Protestant Temperament: Patterns of Child-Rearing, Religious Experience, and the Self in Early America* (New York: Alfred A. Knopf, 1977).

14. Greven, *Spare the Child*, 10.

15. Poling, *The Abuse of Power*, 11. For a listing of the sources of his date, see his footnote on p. 193.

16. Ibid., 183-91.

8. Growing Up, Letting Go, and Forming Covenantal Bonds

1. The story of Cedric and Charles came to my attention through an autobiographical paper prepared by Cedric for an advanced studies seminar. Its inclusion

here is with the full knowledge and consent of my former student. His identity, however, for the purposes of confidentiality, must remain anonymous. Names and other identifying data have accordingly been slightly altered.

2. Don S. Browning, "Children, Mothers, and Fathers in the Postmodern Family," in Pamela D. Couture and Rodney J. Hunter, eds., *Pastoral Care and Social Conflict: Essays in Honor of Charles V. Gerkin* (Nashville, Abingdon Press, 1995). See also the essay by Pamela D. Couture, "Single Parents and Poverty: A Challenge to Pastoral Theological Method," in the same volume.

3. See, for example, Cornel West, *Race Matters* (New York: Vintage, 1994). See also Guy Corneau, *Absent Fathers, Lost Sons* (London: Shambhala, 1991).

4. Robert Woliver and Gail Muranaka Woliver, "Gifted Adolescents in the Emerging Minorities: Asians and Pacific Islanders," in Marlene Bireley and Judy Genshaft, eds., *Understanding the Gifted Adolescent: Educational, Developmental, and Multicultural Issues* (New York: Teachers College Press, 1991).

5. Beta Copley, *The World of Adolescence: Literature, Society and Psychoanalytic Psychotherapy* (London: Free Association Books, 1993), 83. See also Janice M. Irvine, ed., *Sexual Cultures and the Construction of Adolescent Identities* (Philadelphia: Temple University Press, 1994).

6. Merry White, *The Material Child: Coming of Age in Japan and America* (New York: The Free Press, 1993), chap. 7.

7. Gilbert Herdt and Andrew Boxer, *Children of Horizons: How Gay and Lesbian Teens Are Leading a New Way Out of the Closet* (Boston: Beacon Press, 1993).

8. Erik Erikson, *Young Man Luther: A Study in Psychoanalysis and History* (New York: W. W. Norton, 1958).

9. Quentin J. Schultze, project coordinator, and Roy M. Anker, project editor, *Dancing in the Dark: Youth, Popular Culture, and the Electronic Media* (Grand Rapids, Mich.: William B. Eerdmans, 1991), 255.

10. Cedric goes on to cite Cornel West, *Race Matters*, 56: "Presently, black communities are in shambles, black families are in decline, and black men and women are in conflict (and sometimes combat). In this way, the new class divisions produced by black inclusion (and exclusion) from the economic boom and the consumer of hedonism promoted by mass culture have resulted in new kinds of personal turmoil and existential meaninglessness in black America. There are few, if any communal resources to help black people cope with this situation."

11. Charles R. Foster, *Educating Congregations: The Future of Christian Education* (Nashville, Abingdon Press, 1994), 22.

12. Ibid., 31. See also Carol Markstrom-Adams, Greta Hofstra, and Kirk Dougher, "The Ego Virtue of Fidelity: A Case Study of Religion and Identity Formation in Adolescence," *Journal of Youth and Adolescence* 23, no. 4 (1994): 453-69.

13. Charles V. Gerkin, *Prophetic Pastoral Practice: A Christian Vision of Life Together* (Nashville: Abingdon Press, 1991), 124-25.

14. Roy SteinhoffSmith, "The Politics of Pastoral Care: An Alternative Politics of Care," in Pamela D. Couture and Rodney J. Hunter, eds., *Pastoral Care and Social Conflict: Essays in Honor of Charles V. Gerkin* (Nashville: Abingdon Press, 1995), 146. See also in that volume Charles W. Taylor, "Race, Ethnicity, and the Struggle for an Inclusive Church and Society," 152-64.

15. James F. Hopewell, *Congregation: Stories and Structures*. Philadelphia: Fortress Press, 1987.

16. Ibid., chap. 3.

17. Although there are resources too numerous to list that are useful to pastors in undertaking these tasks, I have found Stanley Hauerwas's *A Community of Character: Toward a Constructive Christian Social Ethic* (Notre Dame: University of Notre Dame Press, 1981) efficacious in delineating the goals of pastoral leadership of church communities to enable them to progress in their capacity to cope with the issues discussed in this chapter. I am not, however, as sectarian in my loyalty to a particular version of the Christian communal story as is Hauerwas.

18. By using the term "folk religion" in this context I mean to speak of that enormous group of persons for whom being religious has a very simplistic meaning, such as, for example, "getting saved" or "God told me what I should do." In most congregations pastors will find people like this as well as people who have given long and deep thought to the meaning of biblical texts, traditional church teachings, and searching prayer. For the latter group, both the wisdom of the tradition and the situation in the present world embody great mysteries that can only be considered, but never fully understood.

19. Richard R. Osmer, *A Teachable Spirit: Recovering the Teaching Office in the Church* (Louisville, Ky.: Westminster/John Knox Press, 1990), 17.

20. See Gerkin, *Prophetic Pastoral Practice,* 70-71.

21. See Dieter T. Hessel, *Social Ministry,* rev. ed. (Louisville, Ky.: Westminster/John Knox Press, 1992), 45.

22. See Charles V. Gerkin, *Widening the Horizons* and *Prophetic Pastoral Practice.*

23. Charles V. Gerkin, *Crisis Experience in Modern Life: Theory and Theology for Pastoral Care* (Nashville: Abingdon Press, 1979), 269.

9. Stories of the Adult Years

1. Erik H. Erikson, *Insight and Responsibility* (New York: W. W. Norton, 1964), 152.

2. Ibid., 131.

3. See, for example, Erikson's *Young Man Luther* (New York: W. W. Norton, 1958).

4. *The Christian Century* 19 (October 1994): 948-49 reports a particularly sad and tragic situation that occurred in a mainline Protestant church that the magazine had once designated one of the great churches of America. It seems that the rumors began that the pastor was gay. He had, however, been a very successful and well-loved leader of the congregation for some years. The resulting conflict resulted not only in the pastor's resignation, but a period of great turmoil in the church that took years of work by the congregation and an interim pastor to overcome.

5. Along with mutual support groups for gays and lesbians, there are now in most larger metropolitan centers support groups for adults who, after years of unhappy conformity to the standards of their biological sex, are undergoing the long and arduous process of sex change.

6. See Lillian B. Rubin, *Intimate Strangers: Men and Women Together* (New York: Harper & Row, 1983).

7. See James Dittes, *When the People Say No: Conflict and the Call to Ministry* (New York: Harper & Row, 1979).

8. See John Patton, *Pastoral Counseling: A Ministry of the Church* (Nashville: Abingdon Press, 1983).

9. In this regard I am reminded of a recent conversation with a pastor acquaintance who was involved in the painful process of assisting a young bride who had learned of her husband's homosexuality only on the wedding night when he was unable—but determined—to perform his "masculine role." It had become evident during and after the wedding night that in his shame-filled struggle with his gay orientation, he had attempted to overcome the realities of his life by way of an attempt at heterosexuality. The unhappy result was further pain and humiliation for both himself and his bride.

10. For an excellent discussion from a feminist perspective of the dilemmas faced by the mother who by choice or necessity decides to work outside the home, see Bonnie J. Miller-McLemore, *Also a Mother: Work and Family As Theological Dilemma* (Nashville: Abingdon Press, 1994). Miller-McLemore not only reveals her own experience with working motherhood, she opens to her readers a wide range of feminist theological resources for consideration of the problem.

11. In *No Man's Land: Men's Changing Commitments to Family and Work* (New York: Basic Books, 1993), Kathleen Gerson writes, "Men as a group may possess disproportionate power and privilege, but many individual men do not feel powerful. To some extent, this perception is akin to the proverbial fish which does not notice the water in which it swims. Most members of dominant groups take their privileges for granted—unless they are taken away. Nevertheless, even dominant groups are not entirely free. Just as subordinate groups often find ways to create power and opportunity, so powerful groups rarely control completely" (13).

12. *Time* (Elizabeth Gleick. "Should This Marriage Be Saved?" *Time* 145, no. 8 [Feb. 27, 1995]: 48-56.) recently devoted a large section of a weekly issue to the question, "Should This Marriage Be Saved?" In the article, Judith Wallerstein, a California clinical psychologist, is quoted as saying that after a study of 131 children of divorce over a span of fifteen years, she found there to be a higher risk for depression, poor grades, substance abuse and intimacy problems. "We started to report this," she says, "and people got angry. They said, 'Impossible! If it's good for the parents, it's good for the children.' They wanted to believe that divorce and women's lib would take care of everything." The Lassiters struggled with just this question for years as their children grew, but now had to find another basis for keeping their marriage alive.

13. Gerson, *No Man's Land*, 286.

14. John Snarey, *How Fathers Care for the Next Generation: A Four-Decade Study* (Cambridge, Mass.: Harvard University Press, 1993), 357.

15. Evelyn Eaton Whitehead and James D. Whitehead, *Christian Life Patterns: The Psychological Challenges and Religious Invitations of Adult Life* (Garden City, N.Y.: Doubleday, 1979), 136.

16. Don S. Browning, "Children, Mothers, and Fathers in the Postmodern Family," in Pamela D. Couture and Rodney J. Hunter, eds., *Pastoral Care and Social Conflict: Essays in Honor of Charles V. Gerkin* (Nashville: Abingdon Press, 1995), 75.

17. Ibid.

18. Richard Sennett, *Authority* (New York: Alfred A. Knopf, 1980), 95, as quoted in Donald Capps, *The Depleted Self: Sin in a Narcissistic Age* (Minneapolis: Fortress Press, 1993), 138.

10. Final Chapters in Life Stories

1. Arthur H. Becker, *Ministry with Older Persons: A Guide for Clergy and Congregations* (Minneapolis: Augsburg Press, 1986), 36.
2. For a brief but helpful discussion of the physical and neurological effects of aging, see James N. Lapsley, *Renewal in Late Life through Pastoral Counseling* (Mahwah, N.J.: Paulist Press, 1992), chap. 3, "The Elderly As Human Beings."
3. Jay Sokolovsky, ed., *The Cultural Context of Aging: Worldwide Perspectives* (New York: Bergin and Garvey, 1990), 118.
4. Marilyn Washburn, M.D., "Seeing Jesus at Grady Hospital," *Hospitality* 14, no. 8 (August 1995): 1-2.
5. Jay Sokolovsky and Carl Cohen, "Uncle Ed, Super Runner, and the Fry Cook: Old Men on the Street in the 1980's," in *The Cultural Context of Aging.*
6. Suzanne K. Steinmetz, *Duty Bound: Elder Abuse and Family Care* (Newbury Park, Calif.: Sage Publications, 1988).
7. Arthur H. Becker, *Ministry with Older Persons: A Guide for Clergy and Congregations* (Minneapolis: Augsburg Press, 1986), 73.
8. Ibid., 82.
9. Erik H. Erikson, Joan M. Erikson, and Helen Q. Kivnick, *Vital Involvement in Old Age: The Experience of Old Age in Our Time* (New York: W. W. Norton, 1986), 294.
10. For a different but related discussion of the time of aging and approaching death, see my earlier *Crisis Experience in Modern Life: Theory and Theology for Pastoral Care* (Nashville: Abingdon Press, 1979), chap. 3.
11. Freda A. Gardner, "Another Look at the Elderly," in Brian H. Childs and David W. Waanders, eds., *The Treasures of Earthen Vessels: Explorations in Theological Anthropology* (Louisville: Westminster/John Knox Press, 1994), 178.
12. Evelyn Eaton Whitehead and James D. Whitehead, *Christian Life Patterns: The Psychological Challenges and Religious Invitations of Adult Life* (New York: Crossroad, 1992), 177.
13. For a cogent discussion of possible techniques for pastoral counseling with the aging, see James N. Lapsley, *Renewal in Late Life through Pastoral Counseling* (New York: Paulist Press, 1992), chap. 9.
14. Christie W. Kiefera, "The Elderly in Modern Japan: Elite, Victims, or Plural Players?" in Jay Sokolovsky, ed., *The Cultural Context of Aging,* 191.
15. Mark Jury and Dan Jury, *Gramp. A Man Ages and Dies: The Extraordinary Record of One Family's Encounter with the Reality of Dying* (New York: Grossman, 1976).
16. Carole Cox, *The Frail Elderly: Problems, Needs, and Community Responses* (Westport, Conn.: Auburn House, 1993), 114.

11. Pastoral Care and the Fragility of Life

1. For an extended discussion of the ministry of the pastor in crisis, see my *Crisis Experience in Modern Life: Theory and Theology for Pastoral Care* (Nashville: Abingdon Press, 1979).
2. H. Richard Niebuhr, *Christ and Culture* (New York: Harper and Bros., 1951). I have not found any single book that compares with Niebuhr's classic study. I have,

however, found two books, one by a systematic theologian and one by a biblical scholar and philosopher of religion, that are extremely helpful with the issues contained in *Christ and Culture,* updated for the present period of history of Christ as related to contemporary culture. The first is William C. Placher, *Narratives of a Vulnerable God: Christ, Theology, and Scripture* (Louisville, Ky.: Westminster/John Knox Press, 1994); the second is James E. Will, *The Universal God: Justice, Love, and Peace in the Global Village* (Louisville, Ky.: Westminster/John Knox Press, 1994). Both are very different from Niebuhr's effort, yet both look deeply into the contemporary cultural situation.

3. The daily newspapers recently carried a story of a bright young man who had just graduated from a major university with honors. Much to everyone's surprise, instead of moving into a professional career, as he had been preparing to do during his college years, he gave his $25,000 savings to charity, abandoned his family, his future, and even his name, referring to himself as "Alexander Supertramp." Taking as his heroes Jack London and Henry David Thoreau, he set off by himself to live a life free of attachments. After months of apparently aimless wandering, his body was discovered in the wilds of Alaska. By his body was a note half-filled with apology for any pain he might have caused, but declaring that he had enjoyed the freedom of his abandonment of convention (the Atlanta *Journal Constitution,* 29 January 1996. See also John Krakauer, *Into the Wild* [New York: Villard Books, 1996]).

4. Robert Wuthnow, *Christianity in the Twenty-first Century: Reflections on the Challenges Ahead* (New York: Oxford University Press, 1993), 44.

5. Ibid., 45.

6. Ibid., 51.

7. Robert Wuthnow, *Small Groups—Key to Spiritual Renewal? A National Symposium and an Exploratory Survey* (Princeton, N.J.: George H. Gallup International Institute, 1990).

8. Donald Capps, *The Depleted Self: Sin in a Narcissistic Age* (Minneapolis: Fortress Press, 1993).

9. Christopher Lasch, *The Culture of Narcissism: American Life in an Age of Diminishing Expectations* (New York: Warner Books, 1979).

10. Elaine Scarry, *The Body in Pain: The Making and Unmaking of the World* (New York: Oxford University Press, 1985), 3.

11. Robert Wuthnow, *Christianity in the Twenty-first Century,* 21.

12. Michael Norman, "Living Too Long" *New York Times Magazine,* 14 January 1996, 36-38.

13. Dieter T. Hessel, *Social Ministry,* rev. ed. (Louisville, Ky.: Westminster/John Knox Press, 1992), xvi.

14. See Paul Tillich, *Systematic Theology,* vol. 3 (Chicago: University of Chicago Press, 1963), 276. See also my *Living Human Document* (Nashville: Abingdon Press, 1984), 64, 65.

BIBLIOGRAPHY

Augsburger, David W. *Pastoral Counseling Across Cultures*. Philadelphia: Westminster Press, 1986.

Becker, Arthur H. *Ministry with Older Persons: A Guide for Clergy and Congregations*. Minneapolis: Augsburg, 1986.

Bianchi, Eugene. *Aging As a Spiritual Journey*. New York: Crossroad, 1989.

Bireley, Marlene, and Judy Genshaft, eds. *Understanding the Gifted Adolescent: Educational, Developmental, and Multicultural Issues*. New York: Teachers College Press, 1991.

Burns, Ailsa, and Cath Scott. *Mother-Headed Families and Why They Have Increased*. Hillsdale, N.J.: Lawrence Erlbaum Associates, 1994.

Browning, Don S. *The Moral Context of Pastoral Care*. Philadelphia: Westminster Press, 1976.

Capps, Donald. *Life Cycle Theory and Pastoral Care*. Philadelphia: Fortress Press, 1983.

———. *The Depleted Self: Sin in a Narcissistic Age*. Minneapolis: Fortress Press, 1993.

Clarke, Rita-Lou. *Pastoral Care of Battered Women*. Philadelphia: Westminster Press, 1986.

Clebsch, William A., and Charles R. Jaekle. *Pastoral Care in Historical Perspective*. Englewood Cliffs, N.J.: Prentice-Hall, 1964.

Couture, Pamela D. *Blessed Are the Poor: Women's Poverty, Family Policy, and Practical Theology*. Nashville: Abingdon Press, 1991.

Couture, Pamela D., and Rodney J. Hunter, eds. *Pastoral Care and Social Conflict: Essays in Honor of Charles V. Gerkin*. Nashville: Abingdon Press, 1995.

Cox, Carole. *The Frail Elderly: Problems, Needs, and Community Responses*. Westport, Conn.: Auburn House, 1993.

Culbertson, Philip. *New Adam: The Future of Male Spirituality*. Minneapolis: Fortress Press, 1992.

Erikson, Erik H., *Insight and Responsibility*. New York: W. W. Norton, 1964.

———. *Childhood and Society*. New York: W. W. Norton, 1950 (rev. ed., 1963).

Farley, Edward. *Theologia*. Philadelphia: Fortress Press, 1983.

Gallagher, Sally K. *Older People Giving Care: Helping Family and Community*. Westport, Conn.: Auburn House, 1994.

Gerkin, Charles V. *Crisis Experience in Modern Life: Theory and Theology for Pastoral Care*. Nashville: Abingdon Press, 1979.

———. *The Living Human Document: Revisioning Pastoral Counseling in a Hermeneutical Mode*. Nashville: Abingdon Press, 1984.

———. "Pastoral Care and Models of Aging," in Barbara Payne and Earl D. C. Brewer, eds. *Gerontology in Theological Education: Local Program Development*. New York: The Haworth Press, 1989.

BIBLIOGRAPHY

———. *Prophetic Pastoral Practice: A Christian Vision of Life Together*. Nashville: Abingdon Press, 1991.

———. *Widening the Horizons: Pastoral Responses to a Fragmented Society*. Philadelphia: Westminster Press, 1986.

Gerson, Kathleen. *No Man's Land: Men's Changing Commitments to Family and Work*. New York: Basic Books, 1993.

Greven, Philip. *Spare the Child: The Religious Roots of Punishment and the Psychological Impact of Physical Abuse*. New York: Alfred A. Knopf, 1991.

Gustafson, James M. *Treasure in Earthen Vessels: The Church As a Human Community*. New York: Harper and Row, 1961.

———. *The Church As Moral Decision Maker*. Philadelphia: Pilgrim Press, 1970.

Hagan, Kay L., ed. *Women Respond to the Men's Movement*. San Francisco: HarperSan Francisco, 1992.

Herdt, Gilbert, and Andrew Boxer. *Children of Horizons: How Gay and Lesbian Teens Are Leading a New Way Out of the Closet*. Boston: Beacon Press, 1993.

Hiltner, Seward. *Preface to Pastoral Theology*. Nashville: Abingdon Press, 1958.

———. *The Christian Shepherd: Some Aspects of Pastoral Care*. Nashville: Abingdon Press, 1959.

Hodgson, Peter C. *Revisioning the Church: Ecclesial Freedom in the New Paradigm*. Philadelphia: Fortress Press, 1988.

Holifield, E. Brooks. *A History of Pastoral Care in America*. Nashville: Abingdon Press, 1983.

Hopewell, James F. *Congregation: Stories and Structures*. Philadelphia: Fortress Press, 1987.

Hunter, Rodney J., ed. *Dictionary of Pastoral Care and Counseling*. Nashville: Abingdon Press, 1990.

Irvine, Janice M. *Sexual Cultures and the Construction of Adolescent Identities*. Philadelphia: Temple University Press, 1994.

Kissman, Kris, and Jo Ann Allen. *Single-Parent Families*. Newbury Park, Calif.: Sage Publications, 1993.

Lapsley, James N. *Renewal in Late Life through Pastoral Counseling*. Mahwah, N.J.: Paulist Press, 1992.

Lasch, Christopher. *The Culture of Narcissism: American Life in an Age of Diminishing Expectations*. New York: Warner Books, 1979.

Lindbeck, George A. *The Nature of Doctrine: Religion and Theology in a Postliberal Age*. Philadelphia: Westminster Press, 1984.

Lyon, Brynolf. *Toward a Practical Theology of Aging*. Philadelphia: Fortress Press, 1985.

MacIntyre, Alasdair. *After Virtue: A Study of Moral Theory*. Notre Dame: Notre Dame University Press, 1981.

McNeill, John T. *A History of the Cure of Souls*. New York: Harper and Bros., 1951.

Moltmann, Jürgen. *The Church in the Power of the Spirit*. New York: Harper & Row, 1977.

———. *Creating a Just Future: The Politics of Peace and the Ethics of Creation in a Threatened World*. Philadelphia: Trinity Press International, 1989.

———. *The Future of Creation*. Philadelphia: Fortress Press, 1979.

———. *God in Creation: A New Theology of Creation and the Spirit of God*. San Franscico: HarperSanFrancisco, 1985.

———. *On Human Dignity: Political Theology and Ethics*. Philadelphia: Fortress Press, 1984.

BIBLIOGRAPHY

Moltmann-Wendel, Elisabeth, and Jürgen Moltmann. *Humanity in God*. New York: The Pilgrim Press, 1983.

Moseley, Romney. *Becoming a Self Before God: Critical Transformations*. Nashville: Abingdon Press, 1991.

Oden, Thomas C. *Pastoral Theology*. New York: Harper & Row, 1982.

———. *Care of Souls in the Classic Tradition*. Philadelphia: Fortress Press, 1984.

———. *Becoming a Minister*. New York: Crossroad, 1987.

Placher, William C. *Narratives of a Vulnerable God: Christ, Theology, and Scripture*. Louisville, Ky.: Westminster/John Knox Press, 1994.

Polakow, Valerie. *Lives on the Edge: Single Mothers and Their Children in the Other America*. Chicago: University of Chicago Press, 1993.

Poling, James Newton. *The Abuse of Power: A Theological Problem*. Nashville: Abingdon Press, 1991.

Rowatt, G. Wade, Jr. *Pastoral Care with Adolescents in Crisis*. Louisville, Ky.: Westminster/John Knox Press, 1989.

Sands, Kathleen M. *Escape from Paradise*. Philadelphia: Fortress Press, 1994.

Scarry, Elaine. *The Body in Pain: The Making and Unmaking of the World*. New York: Oxford University Press, 1985.

Schultze, Quentin J., and Roy M. Anker, project directors. *Dancing in the Dark: Youth, Popular Culture, and the Electronic Media*. Grand Rapids, Mich.: William B. Eerdmans, 1991.

Sennett, Richard. *Authority*. New York: Alfred A. Knopf, 1980.

Shelton, Charles M. *Morality and the Adolescent: A Pastoral Psychology Approach*. New York: Crossroad, 1989.

Snarey, John. *How Fathers Care for the Next Generation: A Four-Decade Study*. Cambridge: Harvard University Press, 1993.

Sokolovsky, Jay, ed. *The Cultural Context of Aging: Worldwide Perspectives*. New York: Bergin and Garvey, 1990.

Steinmetz, Suzanne K. *Duty Bound: Elder Abuse and Family Care*. Newbury Park, Calif.: Sage Pubications, 1988.

White, Merry. *The Material Child: Coming of Age in Japan and America*. New York: The Free Press, 1993.

Whitehead, Evelyn Eaton, and James D. Whitehead. *Christian Life Patterns: The Psychological Challenges and Religious Invitations of Adult Life*. New York: Crossroad, 1992.

Will, James E.. *The Universal God: Justice, Love, and Peace in the Global Village*. Louisville, Ky.: Westminster/John Knox Press, 1994.

INDEX

INDEX